MW01251006

PLANNING & SCHEDULING

USING

PRIMAVERA® 5.0

FOR ENGINEERING & CONSTRUCTION

Planning and Progressing a Single Project

Schedule With and Without Resources

In An

Established Project Environment

BY

PAUL EASTWOOD HARRIS

DISCLAIMER
The information contained in this book is to the best of the author's knowledge true and correct. The author has made every effort to ensure accuracy of this publication, but may not be held responsible for any loss or damage arising from any information in this book.

AUTHOR AND PUBLISHER
Paul E Harris
Eastwood Harris Pty Ltd
PO Box 4032
Doncaster Heights 3109
Victoria, Australia

Email: harrispe@eh.com.au
Web: http://www.eh.com.au
Tel: +61 (0)4 1118 7701
Fax: +61 (0)3 9846 7700

Please send any comments on this publication to the author.

ISBN 1-921059-09-5   A4   Paperback
ISBN 1-921059-10-9   A4   Spiral Bound

20 December 2005

INTRODUCTION

This book is an upgrade of the "Project Planning & Scheduling Using Primavera Version 4.1 for Engineering & Construction and Maintenance & Turnover" book and has been written to enable new users to learn the planning and scheduling functions of Primavera Version 5.0 in a single project environment.

Many users will have prior experience of SureTrak, P3 or Microsoft Project and the author explained where there are difference in the products functionality.

The author would appreciate any constructive comments on how this book may be improved.

SUMMARY

The book was written so it may be used as:
- ➢ A training manual for a two-day training course, or
- ➢ A self teach book, or
- ➢ A reference manual.

The screen shots for the book are taken from Primavera Version 5.0 but this book may be used to learn Primavera Version 3.5, 4.1 or 5.0.

The book has been written to be used as the basis for a two-day training course and includes exercises for the students to complete at the end of each chapter. After the course book may then be used by the students as a reference book.

This publication is ideal for people who would like to quickly gain an understanding of how the software operates and explains how the software differs from Primavera P3, SureTrak and Microsoft Project, thus making it ideal for people who wish to convert from these products.

The book may also be used as a reference manual, but with the understanding that it mainly covers the planning and scheduling aspects of the product.

CUSTOMIZATION FOR TRAINING COURSES

Training organizations or companies that wish to conduct their own training may have this book tailored to suit their requirements. This may be achieved removing, reordering or adding content to the book and by writing their own exercises. Please contact the author to discuss this service.

AUTHOR'S COMMENT

As a project controls consultant I have used a number of planning and scheduling software packages for the management of a range of project types and sizes. The first books I published were user guides/training manuals for Primavera SureTrak, P3 and Microsoft Project users. These were well received by professional project managers and schedulers, so I decided to turn my attention to Primavera Enterprise. This book follows the same proven layout of my previous books. I trust this book will assist you in understanding how to use Primavera Enterprise on your projects.

APPRECIATION

I would like thank my wife Susan Harris and my daughter Samantha Harris Susan Aaron for their assistance in the production of this publication.

CURRENT BOOKS PUBLISHED BY EASTWOOD HARRIS

Planning Using Primavera Project Planner P3® Version 3.1
ISBN 0-9577783-7-6 A4 Paperback   ISBN 0-9577783-8-4 A4 Spiral Bound
First Published March 2000

Planning Using Primavera SureTrak Project Manager® Version 3.0
ISBN 0-9577783-9-2 A4 Paperback   ISBN 0-9751503-0-8 A4 Spiral Bound
First Published June 2000

Planning and Scheduling Using Microsoft® Project 2002
ISBN 0-9751503-1-6 B5 Paperback   ISBN 0-9751503-2-4 A4 Spiral Bound
First Published January 2002

Planning and Scheduling Using Microsoft® Project 2003
ISBN 0-9751503-3-2 B5 Paperback   ISBN 0-9751503-4-0 A4 Spiral Bound
First Published June 2004

Project Planning and Scheduling Using Primavera® Version 4,1
For Engineering & Construction and Maintenance & Turnaround
ISBN 1-921059-00-1 A4 Paperback   ISBN 1-921059-01-X A4 Spiral Bound
First Published January 05

Project Planning and Scheduling Using Primavera® Version 4.1
For IT Project Office and New Product Development
ISBN 1-921059-02-8 A4 Paperback   ISBN 1-921059-03-6 A4 Spiral Bound
First Published March 05

Project Planning and Scheduling Using Primavera ®Contractor Version 4.1
For the Construction Industry
ISBN 1-921059-04-4 A4 Paperback   ISBN 1-921059-05-2 A4 Spiral Bound
First Published January 05

PRINCE2 ™ Planning & Control Using Microsoft® Project
ISBN 1 921059 06 0 B5 Paperback   ISBN 1-921059-06-0 A4 Spiral Bound
First Published May 2005

Planning and Control Using Microsoft® Project and PMBOK® Guide Third Edition
ISBN 1-921059-08-7 B5 Paperback   ISBN 1-921059-07-9 A4 Spiral Bound
First Published June 2005

Planning and Scheduling Using Primavera® Version 5.0 For Engineering & Construction
ISBN 1-921059-09-5 A4 Paperback   ISBN 1-921059-10-9 A4 Spiral Bound
First Published December 05

Planning and Scheduling Using Primavera® Version 5.0 For IT Project Office
ISBN 1-921059-11-7 A4 Paperback   ISBN 1-921059-12-5 A4 Spiral Bound
First Published December 05

1 INTRODUCTION

1.1 Purpose

The purpose of this book is to provide a method for planning, scheduling and controlling projects using Primavera Version 5.0 within an established Enterprise Project database or a blank database up to an intermediate level.

The screen shots in this book were captured using Primavera Version 5.0 and Windows XP. Users with other operating systems will have slightly different formatted dialog boxes/forms.

This book covers the following topics:

- Understand the steps required to create a project plan and monitor a project's progress.
- Understand the Primavera Enterprise environment
- Create a project and set up the preferences
- Define calendars
- Add activities
- Organize activities
- Format the display
- Add logic and constraints
- Use Tables, Views and Filters
- Print reports
- Record and track progress
- Customize the project options
- Create and assign resources
- Understand the impact of activity types and effort driven activities
- Status projects that contain resources
- Understand the different techniques for scheduling

The book is not intended to cover every aspect of Primavera Version 5.0, but it does cover the main features required to create and status a project schedule. It should provide you with a solid grounding, which will enable you to learn the other features of Primavera Version 5.0 by experimenting with the software, using the help files and reviewing other literature.

This book has been written to minimize superfluous text, allowing the user to locate and understand the information contained in the book as quickly as possible. It does NOT cover functions of little value to common project scheduling requirements. If at any time you are unable to understand a topic in this book, it is suggested that you use the Primavera Version 5.0 Help menu to gain a further understanding of the subject.

1.2   Required Background Knowledge

This book does not teach you how to use computers or to manage projects. The book is intended to teach you how to use Primavera Version 5.0 in a project environment. Therefore, to be able to follow this book you should have the following background knowledge:

- The ability to use a personal computer and understand the fundamentals of the operating system.

- Experience using application software such as Microsoft Office which would have given you exposure to Windows menu systems and typical Windows functions such as copy and paste.

- An understanding of how projects are managed, such as the phases and processes that take place over the lifetime of a project.

1.3   Purpose of Planning

The ultimate purpose of planning is to build a model that allows you to predict which activities and resources are critical to the timely completion of the project. Strategies may then be implemented to ensure that these activities and resources are managed properly, thus ensuring that the project will be delivered both **On Time** and **Within Budget**.

Planning aims to:

- Optimize time
- Evaluate different methods
- Optimize the use of resources
- Provide an early warning of potential problems
- Enable you to take proactive and not reactive action
- Identify risks
- Set priorities

Planning helps to avoid the delayed or untimely completion of a project and thus prevent:

- Increased project costs or reduction in scope and/or quality
- Additional change over and/or operation costs
- Extensions of time claims
- Loss of your client's revenue
- Contractual disputes and associated resolution costs
- The loss of reputation of those involved in a project
- Loss of a facility or asset in the event of a total project failure

1.4   Project Planning Metrics

There are three main components that may be measured and controled using planning and scheduling software:

- Time
- Cost
- Effort (resources)

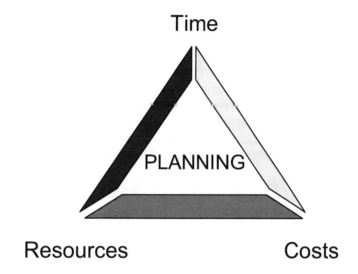

A change in any one of these components normally results in a change in one or both of the other two.

Other project management functions that are not traditionally managed with planning and scheduling software but may have components reflected in the schedule include:

- Document management and control,
- Quality Management,
- Contract Management,
- Issue Management,
- Risk Management,
- Industrial Relations, and
- Accounting.

The development of Enterprise Project Management systems has resulted in the inclusion of many of these functions in project planning and scheduling software and Primavera Version 5.0 includes modules for:

- Issue Management,
- Risk Management, and
- Document Management.

1.5 Planning Cycle

The planning cycle is an integral part of managing a project. A software package such as Primavera Version 5.0 makes this activity much easier.

When the original plan is agreed to, the **Baseline** or **Target** is set. The **Baseline** is a copy of the original plan. Each project may have up to 50 baselines but the number of Baselines that may be saved is set in the **Admin**, **Admin Preferences...** form.

After project planning has ended and project execution has begun, the actual progress is monitored, recorded and compared to the **Baseline** dates.

The progress is then reported and evaluated.

The plan may be changed by adding or deleting activities and adjusting Remaining Durations or Resources. A revised plan is then published as progress continues.

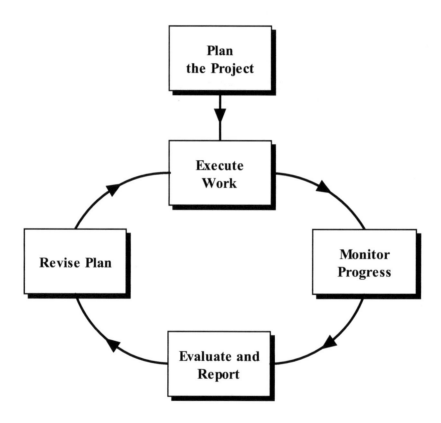

Progressing a Schedule assist in the management of a project by recording:

- Progress and the impact of project scope changes as the project progresses
- Historical data that may be used to support extension of time claims,
- The revised completion date and final forecast of costs for the project,
- Historical data that may be used in future projects of a similar nature and
- A history of progress that may be used in the event of litigation.

2   CREATING A PROJECT PLAN

The aim of this chapter is to give you an understanding of what a plan is and some practical guidance on how your schedule may be created and statused during the life of a project.

2.1   Understanding Planning and Scheduling Software

A project is essentially a set of unique operations or activities to be completed in a logical order to achieve a defined outcome by a definitive end time. A schedule is an attempt to model these activities, their durations and their relationships with other activities. These activities take time to accomplish and may employ resources such as people, materials, equipment and money that may have limited availability.

Planning and scheduling software allows the user to:

- Break down the project into products or deliverables under a Work Breakdown Structure (WBS).
- Break the project down into activities that are entered into the software under the WBS.
- Assign to activities their durations, predecessors, successors and constraints and then calculate the start and finish dates of all the activities.
- Assign roles and or resources to the activities and calculate the planned project resource requirements and costs.
- Monitor the actual progress of activities against the original plan and revise the plan when required.
- Monitor the consumption of resources and re-estimate the resources required to finish the project.
- Provide the cost to date, cost to complete and other cost performance data as required including Earned Value reports.

There are four modes or levels in which planning and scheduling software may be used.

	Planning	Tracking
Without Resources	**LEVEL 1** Planning without resources	**LEVEL 2** Tracking progress without resources
With Resources	**LEVEL 3** Planning with resources	**LEVEL 4** Tracking progress with resources

As the level increases, the amount of information required to maintain the schedule will increase. More importantly, your skill and knowledge in using the software will also need to increase. This book is designed to take you from Level 1 through to Level 4.

2.2   Enterprise Project Management

Primavera Version 5.0 is an Enterprise Project Management software package that allows many projects to be managed in one database. These projects may be summarized under a hierarchical structure titled the Enterprise Project Structure (EPS). This function is similar to summarizing activities of a project under a Work Breakdown Structure (WBS).

An EPS is used for the following purposes:

- To manage user access to projects within the database.
- To manage activities over multiple projects which have a common interest such as a critical resource.
- Top-down budgeting of projects and resources that may at a later date be compared to the bottom-up or detailed project estimates.
- To allow standardized reporting of all projects in the database.

Individual projects must be created within an EPS database. Primavera Version 5.0 has not been designed as a single project planning and scheduling software package and there is an administrative overhead in managing projects in an EPS database.

Primavera Version 5.0 has a function titled Portfolios that allows a limited number of projects to be viewed at a time. For example, this would allow you to view projects in a physical area or of a specific type or client.

2.3   Understanding Your Project

Before you start the process of creating a project plan, it is important to have an understanding of the project and how it will be executed. On large, complex projects, this information is usually available from the following types of documents:

- Project scope
- Functional specification
- Requirements baseline
- Contract documentation
- Plans and drawings
- Project execution plan
- Contracting and purchasing plan
- Equipment lists
- Installation plan
- Testing plan

It is important to gain a good understanding of the project process before starting to plan your project. You should also understand what level of reporting is required. Providing too little or too much detail will often lead to the schedule being discarded or not being used.

There are three processes required to create or maintain a plan at each of the four levels:

- Collecting the relevant project data.
- Entering and manipulating the data in software.
- Distributing the plan, reviewing and revising it.

The ability of the scheduler to collect the data is as important as the ability to enter and manipulate the information using the software. On larger projects, it may be necessary to write policies and procedures to ensure accurate collection of data from the various people, departments, stakeholders/companies, and sites.

2.4   Level 1 – Planning Without Resources

This is the simplest mode of planning.

2.4.1   Creating Projects

To create a project in Primavera Version 5.0, you will require the following information:

- Project ID (a code assigned to the project) and the Project Name.
- The Project Start Date (and perhaps the Finish Date).
- Responsible Manager.
- The Rate Type. Primavera Version 5.0 allows up to five rates per resource; this option allows you to select a rate as the default resources rate.

It would also be useful to know other information such as:

- Client name, and
- Other project information such as location, project number and stakeholders.

2.4.2   Defining the Calendars

Before you start entering activities into your schedule it is advisable to set up the calendars. These are used to model the working time for each activity in the project. For example, a six-day calendar is created for those activities that will be worked for six days a week. The calendar should include any public holidays and any other exceptions to available working days, such as planned days off.

Primavera Version 5.0 allows three types of calendars:

- **Global** – may be assigned to activities and resources in any project,
- **Project** – these are project specific calendars assigned to activities, and
- **Resource** – that are assigned to resources.

Project and Resource calendars may be linked to Global calendars enabling any change made to a Global calendar to be inherited by linked Project and Resource calendars.

2.4.3   Defining the Project Breakdown Structures

A project breakdown structure (PBS) is a way of categorizing the activities of a project into numerous codes that relate to the project. The codes act as tags or attributes of each activity.

During or after the activities are added to the schedule, they are assigned their PBSs so that they may be grouped, summarized, and filtered in or out of the display.

Primavera Version 5.0 has two principal methods of assigning PBSs to your project:

- The Work Breakdown Structure (WBS) function. The WBS function is similar to the P3 and SureTrak WBS function.
- The Activity Code function that operates in a similar way as P3 and SureTrak.

Before creating a project, you should design your PBSs by asking the following questions:

- Which phases are involved in the project (e.g., Design, Procure, Install and Test)?
- Which disciplines are participating (e.g., Civil, Mechanical and Electrical)?
- Which departments are involved in the project (e.g., Sales, Procurement and Installation)?

- What work is expected to be contracted out and which contractors are to be used?
- How many sites or areas are there in the project?

Use the responses to these and other similar questions to create the PBSs.

2.4.4   Adding Activities

Activities must be defined before they are entered into the schedule. It is important that you consider the following factors carefully:

- What is the scope of the activity? (What is included and excluded?)
- How long the activity is going to take?
- Who is going to perform it?
- What are the deliverables or output for each activity?

The project estimate is usually a good place to start looking for a breakdown of the project into activities, resources and costs. It may even provide an indication of how long the work will take.

Activities may have variable durations depending on the number of resources assigned. You may find that one activity that takes 4 days using 4 workers may take 2 days using 8 workers or 8 days using 2 workers.

Usually project reports are issued on a regular basis such as every week or every month. It is recommended that, if possible, an activity should not span more than two reporting periods. That way the activities should only be **In-Progress** for one report. Of course, it is not practical to do this on long duration activities, such as procurement and delivery activities that may span many reporting periods.

It is also recommended that you have a measurable finish point for each group of activities. These may be identified in the schedule by **Milestones** and are designated with zero duration. You may issue documentation to officially highlight the end of one activity and the start of another, thereby adding clarity to the schedule. Examples of typical documents that may be issued for clarity are:

- Issue of a drawing package
- Completion of a specification
- Placing of an order
- Receipt of materials (delivery logs or tickets or dockets)
- Completed testing certificates for equipment or systems

2.4.5 Adding the Logic Links

The logic is added to the schedule to provide the order in which the activities must be undertaken. The logic is designated by indicating the predecessors to or the successors from each activity.

The software will calculate the start and finish dates for each activity and the end date of the project based on the start date of the project, the logic among the activities, and durations of the activities.

It is good practice to create a **Closed Network** with the logic. In a **Closed Network,** all activities have one or more predecessors and one or more successors except:

- The project start milestone or first activity, which has no predecessors, and
- The finish milestone or finish activity, which has no successors.

The project's logic must not loop back on itself. Looping would occur if the logic were stated that A preceded B, B preceded C, and C preceded A. That's not a logical project situation and will cause an error comment to be generated by the software during network calculations.

Thus, when the logic is correctly applied, a delay to an activity will delay all its successor activities and delay the project end date when there is insufficient spare slippage time to accommodate the delay. This spare time is normally called **Float** but note that Microsoft Project uses the term **Slack**.

2.4.6 Constraints

To correctly model the impact of events outside the logical sequence, you may use constraints. A constraint would be imposed to specific dates such as the availability of a facility to allow work to commence. Constraints should be cross-referenced to the supporting documentation such as contract documentation Milestone Dates.

2.4.7 Scheduling the Project

The software calculates the shortest time in which the project may be completed, Activities will be moved forward in time until they meet a Relationship or Constraint. Unstatused activities without logic or constraints will be scheduled to start at the Project Start Date.

Scheduling the project will also identify the **Critical Path(s)**. The Critical Path is the chain(s) of activities that takes the longest time to accomplish and where a delay to any activity in the chain will delay the end date of the project. This chain defines the Earliest Finish date of the project. The calculated completion date depends on the critical activities starting and finishing on time. If any of them are delayed, the whole project will be delayed.

Activities that may be delayed without affecting the project end date have **Float**.

Total Float is the amount of time an activity may be delayed without delaying the project end date. The delay of an activity with a positive Total Float value may delay other activities with positive Total Float, however will not delay the end date of the project unless the delay is greater than the float. The delay of any activity with a zero Total Float value (and is, therefore, on the **Critical Path)** will delay other subsequent activities with zero Total Float and extend the end date of the project.

Free Float is the amount of time an activity may be delayed without delaying the start date of any of its immediate successor activities.

Activity ID	Activity Name	Orig Dur	Total Float	Free Float	February 2005				
					24	31	07	14	21
A1000	Project Sart Milestone	0d	0d	0d					
A1010	First Critical Activity	5d	0d	0d					
A1020	Second Critical Activity	5d	0d	0d					
A1030	Third Critical Activity	5d	0d	0d					
A1040	Activity with Total Float and No Free Float	5d	5d	0d					
A1050	Activity with Total Float and Free Float	5d	5d	5d					
A1060	Finish Milestone	0d	0d	0d					

2.4.8   Formatting the Display – Layouts and Filters

There are tools to manipulate and display the activities to suit the project reporting requirements. These functions are covered in the **LAYOUTS** and the **FILTERS** chapters.

2.4.9   Printing and Reports

There are software features that allow you to present the information in a clear and concise manner to communicate the requirements to all project members. These functions are covered in the **PRINTING AND REPORTS** chapter.

2.4.10   Issuing the Plan

All members of the project team should review the project plan in an attempt to:
- Optimize the process and methods employed, and
- Gain consensus among team members as to the project's logic, durations, and PBS.

Team members should communicate frequently with each other about their expectations of the project while providing each with the opportunity to contribute to the schedule and further improve the outcome.

2.5   Level 2 – Monitoring Progress Without Resources

2.5.1   Setting the Baseline

The optimized and agreed-to plan is used as a baseline for measuring progress and monitoring change. The software may record the baseline dates of each activity for comparison against actual progress during the life of the project. These planned dates are stored in a **Baseline**.

2.5.2   Tracking Progress

The schedule should be **Statused** (updated or progressed) on a regular basis and progress recorded at a point in time.

Whatever the frequency chosen for statusing, you will have to collect the following activity information in order to status a schedule:

- Actual Start Dates of activities that have begun, whether they were planned to start or not,
- Percentage Complete and Remaining Duration or Expected Finish date for started, but incomplete activities,
- Actual Finish Dates for completed activities, and
- Revisions to activities that have not started.
- Additions or deletions of activities that correspond to project scope changes

The schedule may be statused after this information has been collected, and then the recorded progress is compared to the **Baseline Dates**.

At this point, it may be necessary to further optimize the schedule to meet the required end date by discussing the schedule with the appropriate project team members. The date as of when progress is reported is commonly known as the **Data Date** or **Status Date** or **Update Date**. The data date is **NOT** the date that the report is printed but rather the date that reflects when the status information was gathered.

2.6   Level 3 – Scheduling With Resources, Roles & Budgets

2.6.1   Creating and Using Resources

First, one would usually establish a resource pool by entering all the project resources required on the project into a hierarchical table in the software. The required quantity of each resource is assigned to the activities. In an Enterprise environment these Resources may already be defined for you.

Entering a cost rate for each resource enables you to conduct a resource cost analysis, such as comparing the cost of supplementing overloaded resources against the cost of extending the project deadline.

Estimates and time-phased cash flows may then be produced from this resource/cost data.

2.6.2   Creating and Using Roles

Primavera Version 5.0 has an additional function titled **Roles** which is used for planning and managing resources.

- A Role is a skill or trade or job description and may be used as an alternative to resources during the planning period of a project.
- Roles are defined in a hierarchical structure and hold a **Proficiency Level**.
- Roles may be assigned to activities in a similar way to resources and be replaced by resources at a later date once it has been decided who is to be assigned the work.
- In Primavera version 5.0 a Role may now be assigned a rate.

2.6.3   The Relationship Between Resources and Roles

Primavera Version 5.0 has the ability to define roles and associate them with resources. A role is a job title, trade or skill and may have many resources. A multi-skilled resource may have multiple roles. For example, a role may be a Clerical Assistant and there may be five clerical assistants in a company who would be assigned the Clerical Assistant Role. If one clerical assistant were also a data entry person, then this resource would be assigned two roles: Clerical Assistant and Data Entry.

2.6.4   Activity Type and Duration Type

Activities may be assigned an **Activity Type** and **Duration Type**, which affect how resources are calculated. There are additional software features that enable the user to more accurately model real-life situations. These features are covered in the **ASSIGNING RESOURCES ROLES AND EXPENSES** chapters.

2.6.5   Budgets

The Budget function enables Top-Down Budgeting at a summary level against each EPS node in an accounting style. Budgets may be compared to the detailed estimates calculated after resources have been assigned to Activities. This function is not covered in detail in this book.

2.7   Level 4 – Monitoring Progress of a Resourced Schedule

2.7.1   Statusing Projects with Resources

When you status a project with resources, you will need to collect some additional information:

- The quantities and/or costs spent to-date per activity for each resource, and
- The quantities and/or costs required per resource to complete each activity.

You may then status a resourced schedule with this data.

2.7.2   Tools and Techniques for Scheduling

At this point, the book covers some additional software functions, making creating and editing schedules simpler.

2.8   The Balance Between the Number of Activities and Resources

On large or complex schedules, you need to maintain a balance between the number of activities and the number of resources that are planned and tracked. Generally, the more activities a schedule has, the fewer resources should be created and assigned to activities.

When you have a schedule with a large number of activities and a large number of resources assigned to each activity, you may end up in a situation where you and members of the project team are unable to understand the schedule and you are unable to maintain it.

Instead of assigning individual resources such as people by name, consider using the Role function and assign Skills or Trades to Activities. On very large projects you may consider using Crews or Teams.

This technique is not so important when you are using a schedule for estimating the direct cost of a project (by assigning costs to the resources) or if you will not be using the schedule to track a project's progress (such as a schedule that is used to support written proposals).

In large schedules it is more important to minimize the number of resources that will be updated regularly, since updating every resource assigned to each activity at each schedule update is very time consuming. You would be acting as a timekeeper updating resources and not a scheduler looking after the future of the project. When electronic timesheets are employed this is less of an issue, but there is still a substantial overhead in maintaining a large number of resources against a large number of activities.

3   STARTING UP AND NAVIGATION

After clicking on the icon or menu item on your desktop to start Primavera Version 5.0, you will be presented with the **Login** form.

3.1   Logging In

Clicking on the ☐ icon under **Database** will open the **Edit Database Connections** form where you may select an alternative database to open:

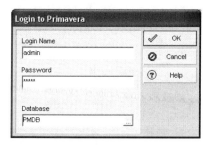 

- Select the required database,
- Click the ⟨ Select ⟩ icon,
- Enter your Login Name and Password, which are case sensitive, and then
- Click ⟨ OK ⟩ to open the selected database.

To specify how you wish the software to start up, after the software has started go to **Edit**, **User Preferences…**, click on the **Application** tab.

3.2   Welcome Form

You may then be presented with the Welcome form.

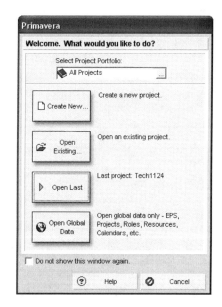

- Select **Project Portfolio** which will display only those projects assigned to the selected portfolio; this is in effect a filter that operates on projects.

- ⟨ Create New… ⟩ takes you to the **Create a New Project** wizard; this topic is covered in the next chapter.

- ⟨ Open Existing… ⟩ will allow you to select a project from the selected portfolio.

- ⟨ Open Last ⟩ will take you to the last project you opened.

- ⟨ Open Global Data ⟩ will take you to the location specified in the **Application** tab specified in **Application Starts Up** in the **Edit**, **User Preferences…** form.

- Click on **Do not show this window again** and the next time you login you will be taken directly to the location nominated in the **User Preferences…**, **Application** tab.

3.3   The Home Workspace

To open the **Home Workspace** click on the 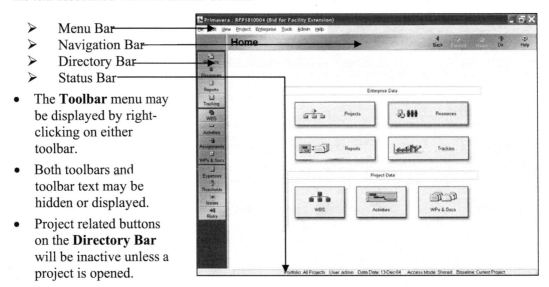 button on the Navigation toolbar; a screen will appear titled **Home**.

Select **View**, **Toolbars** from the menu. The option to hide or display the **Navigation** and **Directory** toolbars and the **Status Bar** is available as well as the options to hide or display the text associated with the toolbar buttons.

> Menu Bar
> Navigation Bar
> Directory Bar
> Status Bar

- The **Toolbar** menu may be displayed by right-clicking on either toolbar.
- Both toolbars and toolbar text may be hidden or displayed.
- Project related buttons on the **Directory Bar** will be inactive unless a project is opened.

3.4   The Projects Workspace

The sample database supplied with Primavera Version 5.0 will be used to demonstrate how to navigate around the screens. Click on the **Projects icon** to open the **Projects Workspace**:

- The $+$ and $-$ icons, to the left of the EPS names, are used to display or hide levels of the EPS. The picture shows that the Apex Construction EPS has three projects.
  > Automated System,
  > Office Building Addition and
  > Conveyor System.
- Open the **Enterprise Project Structure (EPS)** form by

  selecting **Enterprise, Enterprise Project Structure...** from the menu. It is now clear which titles are EPS Nodes and which are Projects.

- Information an EPS node or project is available at the bottom of the screen by selecting the EPS node or Project and selecting the **General** tab in the lower half of the screen.

3.5 Opening a Project

Enterprise and Project data may be accessed in the **Projects** window. To access Project information, such as activities and relationships, a project must be opened. One or more projects may be opened at:

- Project Level, or
- Any level in the EPS, and information regarding one or more projects associated with the EPS level may be accessed.

Therefore opening the project at EPS level will open up all the projects associated with that EPS level. There are several methods of opening a project:

- Select one or more projects:
  - ➢ Select a single project by clicking on it, or
  - ➢ Hold down the **Ctrl** key and click multiple projects, or
  - ➢ Select the EPS level at which you wish to open a group of associated projects, then right-click and select Open Project from the menu or strike keys **Ctrl+O**, the project will then be opened in the **Activity Workspace**.
- Select **File**, **Open…** to open the **Open Project** form:
  - ➢ Select the required project/s from the list.
- Using the **Portfolio** function.
  - ➢ The **Open Project** form also allows the selection of a **Portfolio** which reduces the number of projects that are displayed in the **Open Project** form.
  - ➢ Once a **Portfolio** has been selected using **File**, **Select Project Portfolio…** only those projects in the Portfolio will be displayed in the **Projects Workspace**.

3.6 Navigating Around a Project

Once a project is open the **Activities** ion on the **Directory** bar needs to be clicked on to open the **Activities Workspace**.

After a project has been opened there are a total of four toolbars available:

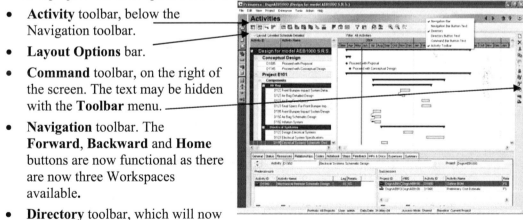

- **Activity** toolbar, below the Navigation toolbar.
- **Layout Options** bar.
- **Command** toolbar, on the right of the screen. The text may be hidden with the **Toolbar** menu.
- **Navigation** toolbar. The **Forward**, **Backward** and **Home** buttons are now functional as there are now three Workspaces available.
- **Directory** toolbar, which will now have all options active.

 Once you are familiar with the toolbars it would be preferable to hide the text which would release more area of screen to display project data.

3.6.1 Command Toolbar

The Command toolbar may have the text hidden but may not be hidden completely and is used to operate on activities such as adding, copying, deleting, cutting and pasting and assigning Roles, Resources, Activity Codes and Relationships.

3.6.2 Activities Toolbar

The Activities toolbar is displayed with the **Activities Workspace** and may be hidden as well as used to hide, display or format the information on the screen.

3.6.3 Navigation Toolbar

When a button on the **Navigation** toolbar is clicked an additional **Workspace** is opened. When a **Workspace** such as the **WBS** or **Activities** is opened, it remains active after the view is opened. The **Back** and **Forward** buttons on the **Navigation** toolbar are used to scroll through the open **Workspaces**.

3.6.4 Directory Toolbar

The **Directory** toolbar is used to select and open additional Workspaces. After a project has been opened and a Workspace such as the **Project**, **WBS**, **Activities**, **Resources** and **Resource Assignments** has been opened, the ⬛ and ⬛ on the **Navigation** toolbar are used to return to previously opened Workspaces. All the Workspaces associated with a project are closed when a project is closed.

3.6.5 Top and Bottom Panes of a Workspace

Workspaces such as the **Project**, **WBS**, **Activities**, **Resources** and **Resource Assignments** have Top and Bottom Panes, some of which may be formatted to meet your requirements. The Bottom pane may also be hidden from view in most Workspaces. The following commands will allow you to format the top and bottom panes.

- Selecting **View**, **Show on Top** and **Show on Bottom** will give you options of what to display when there are options available.

- Selecting **View**, **Show on Bottom**, **Activity Details** or right-clicking with the mouse and selecting **Activity Details** from the menu will hide or display the **Details** form at the bottom of the screen.

- Some **Details** forms may be formatted to display only the tabs that are of use to the scheduler. To format the display right click in the top of the details pane and select **Customize Activity Details…**, the arrows are used to hide and display tabs and reorder them.

3.7 Right-clicking with the Mouse

It is very important that you become used to using the right-click function of the mouse as this is often a quicker way of operating the software than using the menus. The right-click will normally display a menu, which is often different depending on the displayed **View** and selected Active Pane. It is advised that you experiment with each view to become familiar with the menus.

3.8 Application of options within Forms

Once a format or options have been selected within a form, click on:

- The [✓ OK] button to apply the format and closes the form, or
- The [🗗 Apply] button to apply the format and leaves the form open.

3.9 Closing Down

The closing down options are:

- Select **File**, **Close All** or **Ctrl+W** to close all **Projects** and **Workspaces** and return to the **Home Workspace**.
- Select **File**, **Exit** to shut down all projects and close Primavera Version 5.0.

3.10 Terminology Differences between E&C and IT Versions

There are two main differences between E&C and IT versions are:

- The Duration of an Activity is titled **Original Duration** in E&C and **Planned Duration** in IT.

- The **Budgeted Costs and Units** fields in E&C are titled **Planned Costs and Units** in IT.

These Terminology differences are displayed in all Activity fields.

IT – Originally TeamPlay in Primavera Version 3.5

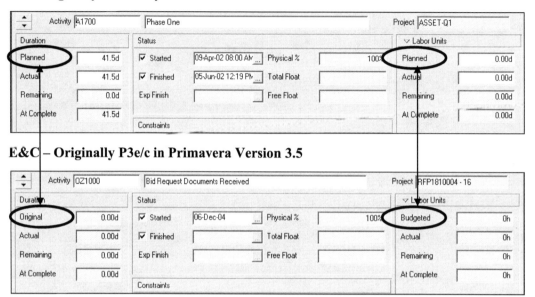

E&C – Originally P3e/c in Primavera Version 3.5

- **Progress Reporter** in P3e/c Version 3.5 was titled **TeamPlayer** in **TeamPlay** and was renamed Timesheets in Primavera Version 4.1.

WORKSHOP 1

Navigating Around the Workspaces

Background

To become familiar with Primavera Version 5.0 you will open a database and navigate around the Workspaces.

Your Workspace may be different from the one used to write this book.

Assignment

1. Open your database. If a project is open select **File, Close All** to close the project and/or if the **Home Workspace** is not displayed click on the ⬆ button to take you to the home page.
2. From the **Home Workspace** hide and display the **Navigation** and **Directory** toolbars by right-clicking and by using the **View, Toolbars** menu.
3. Hide and display the **Status Bar** by using the **View, Toolbars** menu.
4. Click on the **Projects** button to open the **Projects Workspace**.
5. Expand and close the EPS using the ⊞ and - buttons to the left of the project descriptions.
6. Select a project you have access to and open the **Project Workspace** by right-clicking on the project and selecting **Open Project**, then click on the 🔲 button to open the activities workspace.
7. Move back to the **Projects** and **Home Workspace** and then back to the **Activity Workspace** using the ◀, ▶ and ⬆ buttons.
8. Display the **Activity Details** form in the Bottom pane by selecting **View, Show on Bottom, Activity Details**.
9. Hide and display the bottom pane by clicking on the ▽ button on the **Activity** toolbar.
10. Open the **Activity Details** form, right-click and select **Customize Activity Details…** then hide and display some tabs.
11. Close the project by selecting **File, Close All** and return to the **Project Workspace**.

4   CREATING A NEW PROJECT

There are several methods for creating a new project:

- Add a New Project which does not have any activities, or
- Use the Project Architect wizard, or
- Import a project created from another Primavera Version 5.0 database or created with another software program such as P3, SureTrak or Microsoft Project, or
- Copy an existing project and edit it.

Before discussing creating a project file, we will discuss two topics:

- The file types that Primavera Version 5.0 will operate with, and
- The **Enterprise Project Structure (EPS)** to which projects are assigned when they are created:

4.1   File Types

Primavera Version 5.0 will run on Oracle, Microsoft SQL Server databases for multi user installations or Microsoft SQL Server Desktop Engine (MSDE) for stand alone. Primavera Version 4.1 used Interbase for stand-alone installations, where as Primavera Version 5.0 will only operate with the database format with which it has been installed and set up with.

Primavera Version 5.0 will import and export to the following file types using the wizards found under the menu commands **File**, **Import…** and **File**, **Export…**:

- **XER**. A Primavera proprietary format used to exchange **Projects** between Primavera Version 5.0 databases regardless of the database type in which it was created.
- **PLF**. A Primavera proprietary format used to exchange **Layouts** between Primavera Version 5.0 databases regardless of the database type in which it was created.
- **ANP**. A Primavera proprietary format used to save the position of activities in a Activity Network.
- **Project (*.mpp)**. This is the default file format that Microsoft Project 2000, 2002 and 2003 uses to create and save files.
- **Microsoft Project 98 (*.mpp)**. This is the format created by Microsoft Project 98.
- **MPX (*.mpx).** This is a text format data file created by Microsoft Project 98 and earlier versions. MPX is a format that may be imported and exported by many other project scheduling software packages.
- Microsoft Project formats such as **Project Database (*.mpd)**, **Microsoft Access Database (*.mdb)** and **(*.mpt)** can be imported, however **Microsoft Project** is required to be installed on the computer. This function was new to Version 4.1,
- **Primavera Project Planner P3** and **SureTrak** files saved in **P3** format. A SureTrak project in SureTrak format should be saved in Concentric (P3) format before importing.
- **XLS**. Primavera Version 5.0 has a new function allowing the import and export of data in Excel format.

 It is recommended that you read the notes carefully in the user manual before importing a schedule from a non- Primavera Version 5.0 format and even consider importing into a blank database to clearly understand how the data is imported.

4.2   Enterprise Project Structure (EPS)

It is likely that your organization has defined an EPS that is available for new projects to be assigned too, but:

- You may need to add an additional EPS node for your project, or
- If you are starting with a blank database and an EPS has not been defined, you will need to create at least one **EPS** node to assign your project to.

To add, delete or modify the EPS node structure:

- Select **Enterprise, Enterprise Project Structure...** to open the **Enterprise Project Structure (EPS)** form.
- The picture shows the EPS of a demonstration database supplied with Primavera Version 5.0.
- The [Add] button is used to create a new EPS node.
- The node is then assigned an:
  - ➢ **EPS ID**,
  - ➢ **EPS Name** and
  - ➢ **Responsible Manager**.

- The arrows under the [Paste] button are used to reorganize the EPS nodes.
- The remainder of the buttons are for modifying the structure, as you require.

4.3   Creating a Blank Project

You may create a new project at any point in time by selecting **File**, **New** from the menu. You will be guided through the **Create a New Project** wizard which will require the following information:

- The **EPS** node the project is to be assigned to.
- The **Project ID**, a code to represent the project (a maximum of 20 characters), and **Project Name**.
- A **Planned Start** date, which is the earliest date any unstarted activity will be scheduled to commence and an optional **Must Finish By** date. When a **Must Finish By** date is set the project float will be calculated to this date and not to the latest activity finish.
- The **Responsible Manager** is selected from the OBS structure. If the OBS has not been defined or the responsibility not assigned then Enterprise may be selected as the Responsible Manager.
- The **Resource Rate Type**. Each resource may have five different rates. This is where the default rates are selected but may be changed after a resource has been assigned to an activity.
- At this point you may either create the project and start working or run the **Project Architect**. The **Project Architect** will allow you to access a methodology or a predefined project template. **Project Architect** is not covered in detail in this book.

4.4　Project Architect Wizard and Methodology Manager

The Methodology Manager is a separate program for storing project methodologies that are represented by activities with WBS, OBS, Activity Codes, Roles, Resources, etc., which form the basis of a project template. The Methodology Manager has three types of Methodologies:

- **Base Methodologies** that may be used to create a total project.
- **Plug-in Methodologies** which are sets of activities that may be used to develop a project created from a **Base Methodology**.
- **Activity libraries** are smaller sets of activities that may be reused in any project.

Plug-in Methodologies and **Activity libraries** are similar but more powerful than the P3 **Fragnets**.

Methodology Manager also has the following important functions that may be used when creating a new project.

- **Estimating Factors**, allow high and low values to be assigned to each Activity Duration and Resource in a Methodology. When a Methodology is imported into a project using the **Project Architect,** a **Project Complexity** between the value of 0 and 100 is specified and the values for the Activity Durations and Resources are proportioned between the low value (when a **Project Complexity** of 0 is assigned) and the high value (when a **Project Complexity** of 100 is assigned).
- **Estimation Weights** may be assigned to Activities and WBS Nodes. After a Methodology has been imported into a project the **Estimation Weight** may be used to apportion the total estimated labor and nonlabor resource quantities to Activities in a process termed **Top-Down Estimating** using the **Tools, Top-Down Estimation** function.

4.5　Importing a Project

You may be required to import a project that has been created in another program supplied by someone from within or outside your organization. Primavera Version 5.0 is equipped with a set of tools for importing projects from other sources. Files may be imported from:

- Another Primavera Version 5.0 database, irrespective of the database it was created in, using the **XER** format file.
- Primavera Project Planner P3 and SureTrak in **P3** format.
- Microsoft Project **(*.mpp)**, **(*.mpd)**, **(*.mbd)** and **(*.mpt)** files when you have Microsoft Project installed on your computer.
- Other scheduling software using **(*.mpx)** file formats.
- Data in Excel format **(*.xls)**.

Select **File**, **Import…** to open a wizard that will guide you through the process of importing projects into your schedule. You may wish to consider importing a project into a blank database so it is clear what Resources, Calendars and Codes have been added to the database.

4.6 Copy an Existing Project

A project may be copied from the **Projects Workspace**:

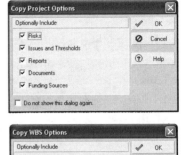

- Highlight the project you wish to copy and select **Edit**, **Copy** or **Ctrl+C**,

- Highlight the EPS Node that you wish to associate the new project with and select **Edit**, **Paste** or **Ctrl+V**,

- The **Copy Project Options** form will then be displayed, allowing you to choose which Project data items you wish to copy with the project; select ✓ OK ,

- The **Copy WBS Options** form will be displayed, allowing you to choose which WBS data items you wish to copy with the project; select ✓ OK ,

- The **Copy Activity Options** form will be displayed, allowing you to choose the Activity data items you wish to copy with the project; select ✓ OK ,

- Open and edit the new project.

4.7 Setting Up a New Project and EPS Nodes

To check or modify some of the basic Project or EPS information entered when a project was created, ensure that the **Project Details** form is displayed in the bottom of the screen:

- Highlight a project or EPS node,

- Select **View**, **Show on Bottom**, **Project Details** and click on the **General** tab:

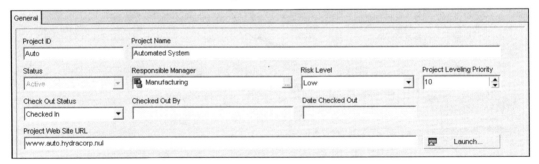

- The **Risk Level** may be used to sort and filter Projects and EPS nodes.

- The **Project Leveling Priority** is used when leveling a project to reduce peaks in resource requirements. Value of 1 is the highest and 100 the lowest.

- **Check Out Status** enables the user to determine if the project is checked or checked out. (New to Version 4.1) **Checked Out By** and **Date Checked Out** enables the user to track down the project if it is currently checked out.

4.8 Project Dates

At this point, a project would not have normally started and you would set the project start date sometime in the future using the **Planned Start** field in the **Projects** Workspace, **Details** form, **Dates** tab. To open this form:

- Highlight your new project,
- Select **View**, **Show on Bottom**, **Project Details** and click on the **Dates** tab:

- **Scheduled Dates**
  - ➤ The **Planned Start** is the date before which no activity will be scheduled to start.
  - ➤ The **Must Finish By** date is an optional date. When this date is entered it is used to calculate the **Late Finish** of activities, thus all **Total Float** will be calculated to this date. This topic is covered in the **ADDING ACTIVITY DEPENDENCIES** chapter.
  - ➤ The **Finish date** is a calculated date and is the date of the completion of all activities.
  - ➤ The **Data Date** is used when statusing a project. This topic is covered in the **TRACKING PROGRESS** chapter.
  - ➤ The **Actual Start** date is inherited from the first stated activity.
  - ➤ The **Actual Finish** date is inherited from the last completed activity when all activities are complete.

- **Anticipated Dates**
  - ➤ The **Anticipated Start** and **Anticipated Finish** dates would be assigned before a WBS structure and Activities have been created. The start and finish dates columns and bars at the EPS level adopt these dates when there are no activities. After Activities have been created, they may remain as a historical record only and are not displayed or inherited anywhere else.

4.9 Saving Additional Project and EPS Information - Notebook Topics

Often additional information about a Project or EPS node is required to be saved with the project such as location, client and type of project. This data may be saved in the **Projects Workspace**, **Details** form, **Notebook** tab.

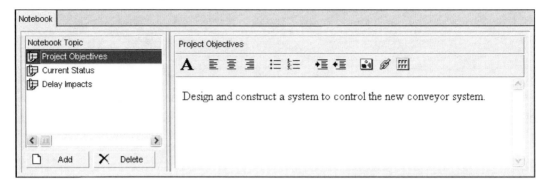

To add a **Note** to a Project:

- Click on $\boxed{\text{Add}}$ which will open the **Assign Notebook Topic** form.

- Select a **Topic** from the list by clicking on the **Notebook Topic** you wish to select and click on the 🖳 button to add the topic to the Notebook.

- Close the form by clicking on the 🖳 button.

- You may now add notes to the selected **Project Notebook Topic**.

- Notes may be added to **EPS** nodes in the same way as Projects.

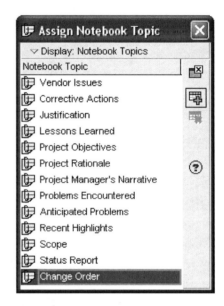

To create a new **Notebook Topic**:

- Select **Admin**, **Admin Categories...** to open the **Admin Categories** form and select the **Notebook Topics** tab.

- The check boxes make the Categories available to EPS nodes and/or Projects.

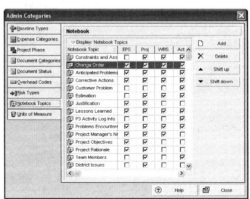

WORKSHOP 2

Creating Your Project

Background

You are an employee of OzBuild Pty Ltd and are responsible for planning the Bid preparation required to ensure that a response to an RFQ (Request For Quote) from Wilson Bedding is submitted on time.

While short-listed, you have been advised that the RFQ will not be available prior to 03 December 2007.

Note: The date format will be displayed according to the **User Preferences** settings set by selecting **Edit**, **User Preferences...** and selecting the **Dates** tab.

Assignment

1. Create a new OBS titled Bid Manager by selecting **Enterprise, OBS...**.
2. From the **Projects** Workspace create a new EPS node at the top of the list of Nodes by selecting **Enterprise, Enterprise Project Structure...**, with the following information:
   - EPS ID – BIDS
   - EPS Name – Bid Projects
   - Responsible Manager – Bid Manager.
3. Create a second level EPS node:
   - EPS ID – OzBuild
   - EPS Name – OzBuild Bid Projects
   - Responsible Manager – Bid Manager.
4. Create a new project with the following information by selecting **File**, **New...** to open the **Create a New Project** wizard:
   - EPS – OzBuild Bid Projects
   - Project ID – REF071203
   - Project Name – Bid for Facility Extension
   - Planned Start Date – Mon 03Dec07
   - Must Finish By – Leave Blank
   - Responsible Manager – Bid Manager
   - Rate Type – Price/Unit
   - Project Architect – Do not run
   - Click on **Finish** to create the project.

(Continued)

5. Add the following project information in the **Project Details** in the **Bottom Pane**:
    - Set the Status in the **Dates** tab to What-If
    - Dates tab
        - ➢ Anticipated Start 03 Dec 07
        - ➢ Anticipated Finish 25 Jan 08

        You should now see a bar in the Bar Chart above spanning these dates although there are no activities in the schedule.
    - Add a Notebook Topic using a suitable topic such as Vendor Issues stating, "RFQ will not be available prior to 03 December 2007."

6. Your project should look like this:

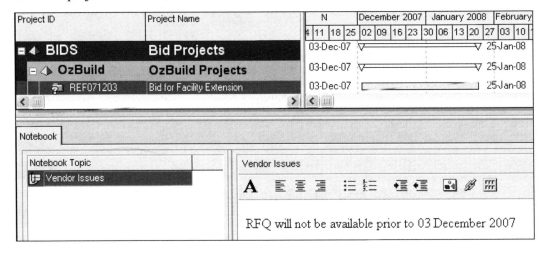

5 DEFINING CALENDARS

The finish date (and time) of an activity is calculated from the start date (and time) plus the duration over the calendar associated with the activity. Therefore, a five-day duration activity that starts at the start of the workday on a Wednesday, and is associated with a five-day workweek calendar (with Saturday and Sunday as non-work days) will finish at the end of the workday on the following Tuesday.

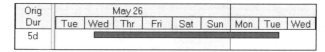

Primavera Version 5.0 has three categories for calendars:

- **Global** – These calendars are available to all Projects and Resources.
- **Project** – These calendars are only available to the projects they are created for and may only be created for a project when that project is open.
- **Resource** – A Resource calendar may be assigned to one or more Resources, which in turn may be assigned to an activity in any project. A Resource will be scheduled according to a Resource Calendar when the **Activity Type** is set to **Resource Dependent**, otherwise the activity is scheduled according to the Activity Calendar.

You may create a new or edit an existing Calendar to reflect your project requirements, such as adding holidays or additional workdays or adjusting work times. For example, some activities may have a 5-day per week calendar and some may have a 7-day per week calendar.

This chapter will cover the following topics:

Topic	Menu Command
• Assigning the **Default Activity / Project Calendar**.	This calendar is assigned to new activities. From the **Projects** Workspace, click on the **Defaults** tab in the **Details** form.
• Creating, Copying, Editing or Deleting Calendars	**Enterprise, Calendars...**, select the **Global**, **Project**, or **Resource** button then click [Add] (to create a new calendar by copying an existing calendar) or [Modify...], or [Delete].
• Renaming an existing calendar	**Enterprise, Calendars...**, select **Global**, **Project**, or **Resource**, click on description and then modify the description.

5.1 Accessing Global and Project Calendars

Calendars may be accessed from the **Calendars** form for copying, editing and deleting by selecting **Enterprise, Calendars…** from Workspaces such as **Home**, **Projects** and **Activities**. The following rules dictate when you are able to access the calendars:

- A **Global Calendar** may be accessed with or without any projects open.
- A **Project Calendar** may only be copied, edited and deleted when the project is active, e.g., the project has been opened.
- To list, create and edit more than one existing **Project Calendar** at the same time all the projects in question must be open. Open more than one project:
  - ➢ **Ctrl-click** the projects and select **File**, **Open**, or
  - ➢ Highlight a **WBS Node** and select **File**, **Open**, or
  - ➢ Open a **Portfolio** of projects.

5.2 Assigning the Project Default Project Calendar

A **Default Project Calendar** is assigned to each project from the **Global** or **Project** calendar list and all new activities are assigned the project **Default Project Calendar** when they are created.

To assign the **Default Activity Calendar** to a project:

- Open the **Projects Workspace** and highlight the project,
- Click on the **Defaults** tab in the **Details** form; you will see the current **Default Project Calendar** in the box **Calendar**.

To change the project **Default Project Calendar**:

- Click on the ⬜ button to the right of the heading Calendar to open the **Select Default Project Calendar** form:

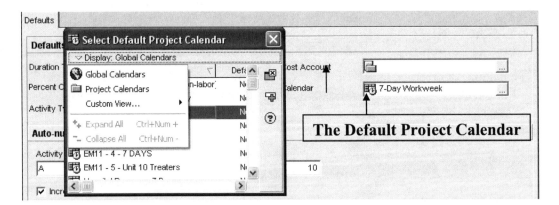

- Select either **Global Calendars** or **Project Calendars** menu item from the drop down box under the ⬚ ∨ Display: Project Calendars heading, and
- Select the calendar you wish to make the **Default Project Calendar**, then
- Click on the 🖼 button or **Double-Click** on the calendar to assign the new calendar.

5.3   Creating a New Calendar

A project must be active to create a **Project Calendar** for the project.

To create a new calendar:

- Select **Enterprise**, **Calendars…**,
- Select the **Global**, **Project**, or **Resource** button,
- Then click either the [▯ Add] button to create a new calendar, or
- Select an existing calendar to copy.

5.4   Copying Calendars

A **Project Calendar** may be copied as a **Global Calendar**:

- Open the project that the calendar currently resides in,
- Select **Enterprise**, **Calendars…**,
- Select the **Project** button and highlight the calendar to be copied, and
- Click on the [◉ To Global] button.

To copy a calendar from one project to another:

- Copy the **Project Calendar** as a **Global Calendar**, and
- Create a new **Project Calendar** by copying the **Global Calendar**.

5.5   Renaming a Calendar

To rename a calendar:

- Select **Enterprise**, **Calendars…**,
- Double click on the calendar description to edit in the same way as renaming a directory in Explorer.

5.6   Deleting a Calendar

To delete a calendar:

- Select **Enterprise**, **Calendars…**,
- Select the calendar and click on the [✕ Delete] button.

5.7   Resource Calendars

A **Resource** calendar may be assigned to one or more Resources. This is different to the philosophy of Microsoft Project, P3 and SureTrak, where each resource has its own calendar based on a project calendar and many resources are not able to share one calendar.

A Resource will be scheduled according to the assigned **Resource Calendar** when the **Activity Type** is set to **Resource Dependent**; otherwise the activity is scheduled according to the **Activity Calendar**.

5.8 Editing Calendar Working Days of an Existing Calendar

Prior to editing a calendar, particularly if it is a global calendar, click on the [🖵 Used By...] button to open the **Calendar Used By** form to determine which other Projects and Resources also use the calendar. To edit a calendar:

- Select **Enterprise**, **Calendars…**,
- Select the **Global**, **Project**, or **Resource** button,
- Then click [🖵 Modify...] to open the **Calendar** form to modify an existing calendar:

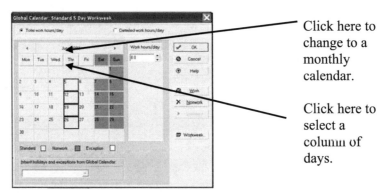

Click here to change to a monthly calendar.

Click here to select a column of days.

- Click in the month to change the calendar view to monthly. This makes it quicker to navigate around the calendar and works in the other calendar view:

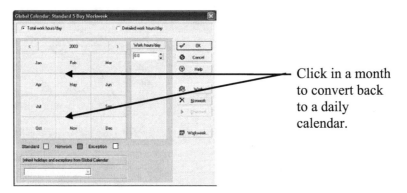

Click in a month to convert back to a daily calendar.

- To make **Nonwork Days** into **Work Days**, highlight the day(s) you want to edit by:
  - ➢ Click on an individual day, or
  - ➢ Ctrl-click to select multiple days, or
  - ➢ Click on a column or columns of days by clicking the day of the week box, which is located below the month and year. Ctrl-click will allow multiple columns to be selected.
  - ➢ Then click on the [✗ Nonwork] button to make these days nonworking.
- To make **Work Days** into **Nonwork Days**, highlight the day(s) you want to edit as described in the paragraph above and then click on the [🐾 Work] button to make these days working days.
- To return individual days to the default setting, select the day and click on the [▷ Standard] button.

5.9 Adjusting Working Hours

The working hours of a standard week are termed **Calendar Weekly Hours** and the working hours of selected individual days may be edited.

5.9.1 Editing Calendar Weekly Hours

To edit the hours of every weekday of a calendar:

- From the **Calendar** form select ⊞ Workweek... to open the **Calendar Weekly Hours** form:

- Adjust the hours for each day in this form and click ✓ OK to accept the changes.

5.9.2 Editing Selected Days Working Hours

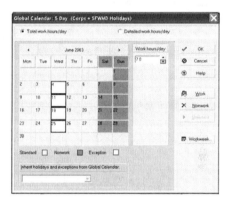

To edit the working hours of individual days:

- Select the days you wish to edit by Shift-clicking, Ctrl-clicking individual days or selecting one or more columns,

- Adjust the hours in the box below the title **Work hours/day**.

- The edited days will now adopt the color of **Exception** days.

5.9.3 Editing Detailed Work Hours/Day

To edit the detailed working hours of individual days:

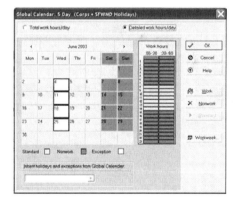

- Select the days you wish to edit by Shift-clicking, Ctrl-clicking individual days or selecting one or more columns,

- Click on the **Detailed work hours/day** button,

- Adjust the hours to the nearest half hour by double-clicking on the table below the title **Work hours** to change them from working to nonworking.

- The edited days will now adopt the color of **Exception** days.

When any calendar is changed or edited, the end date of all activities assigned with the calendar will be recalculated based on the new calendar. This may make a considerable difference to your project schedule dates.

When calendars have different start and end times then some activities will span one day more than the duration of the activity, because for example the last hour of the task will roll into the next day.

5.10 Inherit Holidays and Exceptions from a Global Calendar

When creating a new Project or Resource calendar a Global Calendar may be selected from the drop down box and this function will copy the calendar holidays from the selected Global Calendar into the displayed calendar.

The Global and the new Project or Resource calendars will remain linked (in the same way as a Global Calendar in SureTrak and P3) and a change to a Global calendar holiday will be reflected in a calendar with Inherited Holidays.

5.11 Calculation of Summary Durations

Primavera Enterprise effectively calculates in hours and the summary durations are calculated by the factors set up in the **Admin**, **Admin Preferences…**, **Time Periods** tab.

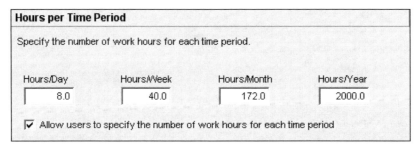

When **Allow users to specify the number of work hours for each time period** is checked then users may set their own time periods in the **Edit**, **User Preferences…**, **Time Units** tab.

IMPORTANT NOTE: This option needs to be understood as it affects how summary durations are displayed. Primavera Version 5.0 calculates in hours, but activity durations may be summarized and displayed in days or weeks or months. These options work fine when all calendars are based on the same number of work hours per day and days per week. When tasks are scheduled with calendars that do not conform to the **Edit**, **User Preferences…**, **Time Units** tab settings (e.g. when settings are set for 8 hours per day but there are tasks scheduled on a 24 hour/day calendar), the summary durations will be incorrect and the results often create confusion for new users.

See below how two with the same duration on different calendars are displayed:

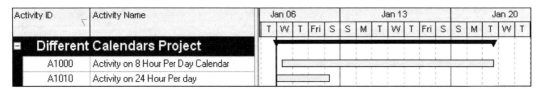

Other scheduling software also exhibit this summary duration conversion problem when using multi-calendars. This display can lead to a great deal of confusion. To avoid confusion when using multi-calendars, it is suggested that you only display durations in hours.

WORKSHOP 3

Maintaining the Calendars

Background

The normal working week at OzBuild Pty Ltd is Monday through Friday, 8 hours per day excluding public holidays. The installation staff works Monday through Saturday, 8 hours per day.

The company observes the following holidays:

	2006	2007	2008	2009
New Year's Day	2 January*	1 January	1 January	1 January
Good Friday	14 April	6 April	21 March	10 April
Easter	17 April	9 April	24 March	13 April
Christmas Day	25 December	25 December	25 December	25 December
Boxing Day	26 December	26 December	26 December	28 December*

* These holidays occur on a weekend and the dates in the table above have been moved to the next weekday.

Although we may be able to use a standard calendar we will create two new calendars for this project.

Assignment

1. Select **Enterprise, Calendars...** to open the **Calendars** form and click on the **Project** button.
2. Create a Project Calendar titled "OzBuild 5 Day per Week" by copying the most appropriate calendar and add the holidays above.
    - Use, if available, an existing Global 8 hour per day and 5 days per week calendar which preferably does not have any holidays.
    - Make any holidays not listed above into work-days.
    - Assign the holidays above.
3. Create a new calendar titled "OzBuild 6 Day per Week" for the 6-day week by copying the same Global calendar. (If the same calendar is not copied the work hours may be different.)
    - Click on the [Workweek...] button to open the **Calendar Weekly Hours** form and make all the Saturdays a workday by assigning 8 hours' work.
    - Make any holidays not listed above into work-days.
    - Assign the holidays above.

6   CREATING A PRIMAVERA PROJECT WBS

The **Project WBS** function is a function that is designed to record a hierarchical WBS that has been developed on a traditional basis as outlined in many project management documents. A well structured WBS should:

- Include all the project deliverables and
- Be set at the appropriate level for summarizing project activities and reporting project progress.

The **Project WBS** function is used to group and summarize activities under a hierarchical structure in the same way as the WBS function in P3 and SureTrak, and the Custom Outline Codes in Microsoft Project 2003. It is also similar to Outlining in all versions of Microsoft Project, however in Primavera Version 5.0 the Activities are assigned to a hierarchical WBS Node and are not demoted under a Parent task as with Outlining with Microsoft Project. The WBS structure is used to organize and summarize your project activities, including costs and resources during planning, scheduling and statusing of Projects.

The project should be granulated (broken down) into manageable areas by using a project breakdown structure based on attributes of the project such as the Phases or Stages, Systems and Subsystems, Processes, Disciplines or Trades, and Areas or Locations of work. These headings are normally the basis of the project breakdown structure, are used to create the Primavera Version 5.0 WBS structure, and should present the most useful view of your project.

Defining the project breakdown structure may be a major task for project managers. The establishment of a Primavera Version 5.0 Methodology, more commonly called project templates, makes this operation simpler because a standard breakdown is predefined and does not have to be created for each new project.

Primavera Version 5.0 also has an **Activity Code** function similar to the **Activity Code** function in Primavera P3 and SureTrak software and the Custom Outline Codes in Microsoft Project 2003. This feature allows the grouping of activities under headings other than the "WBS Structure." Unlike in Primavera P3 and SureTrak software, **Activity Codes** are not the primary method of organizing activities. They are covered in the **ACTIVITY CODES AND GROUPING ACTIVITIES** chapter.

Topic	Menu Command
• Creating and Deleting a WBS Node	The menu commands **Add**, **Delete**, **Copy**, **Cut** and **Paste** all work to create, delete, move and copy WBS Nodes.
• WBS Categories	WBS Categories are created using the **Admin**, **Admin Categories…**, **Project Phase** tab and are assigned to WBS Nodes by inserting the **Project Phase** column in the WBS Workspace.

A **WBS Node** is a term used by Primavera Version 5.0 that is often called a **WBS Code** and is a single point in the WBS structure that activities are assigned to. A Primavera Version 5.0 WBS Node may record more information than P3, SureTrak or Microsoft Project including the following data:

- **Anticipated Dates**, which are used by the system when there are no activities under the WBS Node,

- **Notes**, which are recorded under **Notebook Topics**,

- **Budget**, **Spending Plan** and **Budget Change Log**,

- **WBS Milestones** which may be used for calculating earned value,

- Links to documents, and

- The rules for calculating **Earned Value** for that WBS Node.

The start and finish dates of a WBS Node are adopted from the earliest start date and latest finish date of the detailed activities under that WBS Node and use the Anticipated Dates when there are no activities assigned to a WBS Node.

The duration of a WBS Node is calculated from the start and finish dates over the Project Calendar.

The aim of this chapter is to outline sufficient information to create a WBS structure to enable activities to be assigned to a WBS Node so a schedule may be created.

6.1   Opening and Navigating the WBS Workspace

To view, edit or create a **WBS** structure:

- The project must have been opened.

- The **WBS** Workspace is displayed by selecting **Project**, **WBS** or by clicking on the WBS icon in the **Directory** bar.

- The picture below is of the Apex project showing the WBS Nodes on the left hand side of the screen and the WBS bars on the right hand side of the screen.

- The buttons in the **WBS** toolbar allow different views of the WBS. Click on each button to see its purpose.

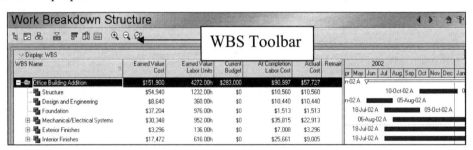

6.2 Creating and Deleting a WBS Node

Right-click to display the menu or select the **Edit** menu command. The commands **Add**, **Delete**, **Copy**, **Cut** and **Paste** all work to create, delete, move and copy WBS Nodes.

- **Add** will add a new WBS Node under the level that you are currently highlighting.

- **Delete** will delete the WBS Node. When a WBS Node has been assigned activities you will be given the option to either delete the activities or reassign the activities by selecting the **Merge Element(s)** option in the **Merge or Delete WBS Element(s)** form.

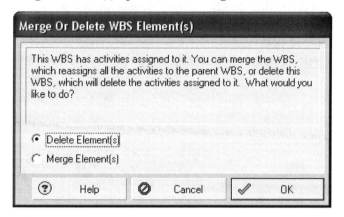

- **Copy** copies a WBS Node and the associated activities.

- **Cut** prepares to move a WBS Node and the associated activities to another location.

- **Paste** pastes a **Cut** or **Copied** WBS Node. After selecting **Paste**, the **Copy WBS Options** form is presented which allows you to select which data is pasted with the WBS Node.

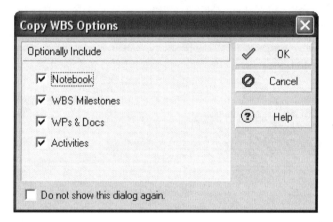

6.3 WBS Node Separator

The WBS Node separator is defined in the **Settings** tab of the **Project Details** form in the **Projects Workspace**.

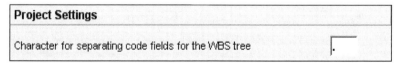

6.4 Work Breakdown Structure Lower Pane Details

The lower pane has eight Tabs:

- **General**, in this tab you may assign:
  - ➢ The **WBS Code** and **Description**,
  - ➢ The **Responsible Manager**,
  - ➢ **Anticipated Dates**, and
  - ➢ The **Status**, there are four Status types, Planned, Active, Inactive and What-If. The status of a WBS Node controls viewing and access to the Nodes and Activities assigned to the nodes by Primavera Timesheet users.

- **Notebook**, this is used in the same way as the activity Notebook and is used to record notes about the WBS Node.

- **Budget Summary**, **Budget Log** and **Spending Plan** are used together as a top-down method of assigning budgets and are independent of the costs assigned at activity level.

- **WBS Milestones** are created at **WBS Node** level and provide a summary method of assigning a Performance % Complete to activities assigned to that node. For this function to operate there must be at least one activity assigned to a **WBS Node**.

- **Earned Value** is where the rules for calculating the Estimate to Complete, ETC and other Earned Value parameters are set.

- **WPs & Docs** allows the assignment of documents to a WBS Node and operates in the same way as the activities **WPs & Docs** tab.

6.5 WBS Categories

WBS Nodes may be assigned categories, which allow WBS Nodes within an EPS to be grouped and sorted.

- WBS Categories are created using the **Admin**, **Admin Categories...**, **Project Phase** tab.

- WBS Categories are assigned to WBS Nodes by inserting the **Project Phase** column in the WBS Workspace.

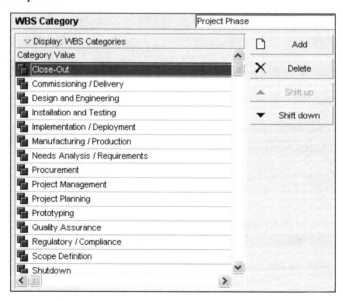

WORKSHOP 4

Maintaining the Work Breakdown Structure

Background

A review of the internal reporting requirements shows that you need to identify the Bid Work Phases:

- Research
- Estimate
- Proposal

Assignment

1. Click on the ⬚ button to open the **WBS** Workspace.
2. To ensure your view is displayed correctly select **View**, **Group and Sort...**, and click on the ⬚ Default button.
3. Right-click and select **Add** to add the WBS Node and continue to add the three WBS Nodes above.
4. Use the arrows on the command bar to put them in the correct order.
5. Your answer should be displayed like the picture below:

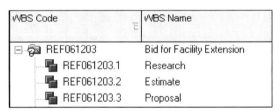

6. Return to the Activities View by clicking on the ⬚ or the Activities icon on the Director toolbar, you screen may look like this:

Activity ID	Activity Name	Original Duration	Remaining Duration	Schedule % Complete	Start	Finish
▬	**Bid for Facility Extension**	0	0	0%		
	Research	0	0	0%		
	Estimate	0	0	0%		
	Proposal	0	0	0%		

7. If it looks different, select **View**, **Layout**, **Open...**, select the **Classic WBS Layout** and click on the ⬚ Open button

---

7 ADDING ACTIVITIES & ORGANIZING UNDER THE WBS

Activities should be well-defined, measurable pieces of work with a measurable outcome. Activity descriptions containing only nouns such as "Bid Document" have confusing meanings. Does this mean read, write, review, submit or all of these?

Adequate activity descriptions always have a verb-noun structure to them. A more appropriate activity description would be "Write Bid Document" or "Review and Submit Bid Document." The limit for activity names is 120 characters, but try to keep activity descriptions meaningful yet short and concise so they are easier to print.

When activities are created, they may be organized under hierarchical WBS Codes. This process will be covered in the next chapter **ORGANIZING ACTIVITIES USING WBS CODES**.

The creation and sequencing of detailed and summary activities are discussed in the following chapters:

- Understanding **Activity Codes**,
- Creating **Detailed** activities (in this chapter),
- Adding the logic in the **ADDING THE DEPENDENCIES** chapter.

This chapter will cover the following topics:

Topic	Menu Command
• Setting **Auto-numbering Defaults** and other defaults for new Activities	Select the **Default** tab from the **Bottom** pane in the **Project Workspace**.
• **Adding New Activities**	Select a line in the schedule and strike the **Ins** (**Insert Key**) or right-click and select the **Add** menu item.
• **Activity Details** form	May be displayed in the bottom pane by selecting **View**, **Show on Bottom**, **Activity Details**.
• **Copying** activities in **Primavera Version 5.0**	Select the activities and copy & paste to the required location.
• **% Complete Type**	Use the **% Complete Type** drop down box in the **General** tab of the **Activity Details** form.
• **Milestones**	Use the **Activity Type** drop down box in the **General** tab of the **Activity Details** form.
• Assigning WBS Nodes to activities	• Create an activity in an existing WBS band, • Drag one or more activities into the desired band, • Display the WBS column and click on the WBS cell to display the **Select WBS** form, or • Open the **General** tab in the lower window.

7.1 New Activity Defaults

After creating a new project and before opening it to add new activities it is important to set the defaults that you wish activities to have, such as the Activity ID Numbers and Calendars. By setting them correctly before adding activities you will save a significant amount of time because you will not have to change a number of attributes against all activities at a later date. These defaults are set in the **Defaults** tab of the **Project Details** form:

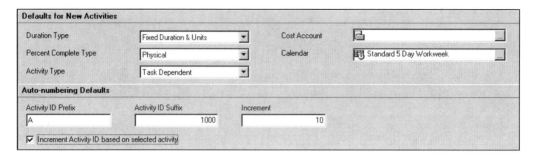

7.1.1 Duration Type

None of the **Duration Type** options affects how the schedule calculates until one or more resource is assigned to an Activity. The following options are available:

- **Fixed Units**
- **Fixed Duration and Units/Time**
- **Fixed Units/Time**
- **Fixed Duration & Units**

If you do not plan to add resources to Activities, then you do not need to assign a **Duration Type** and it may be left as the default.

This topic will be covered in detail in the **ASSIGNING RESOURCES AND COSTS TO ACTIVITIES** chapter.

7.1.2 Percent Complete Type

The **Percent Complete** type should be understood if it is intended to be used to update (status or progress) the schedule. This option sets the relationship between activities' Remaining Duration and their Percent Complete. In Primavera Version 5.0 this option may be set for each activity and the default set in the **Percent Complete Type** drop down box. The options are:

- **Physical**   The Percent Complete and Remaining Duration are Unlinked with this option and may be independently entered. This option is used for activities where the progress is not proportional to the duration of the activity. This is the same as Unlinking Remaining Duration and Schedule Percent Complete in P3 and SureTrak.

- **Duration**   With this option the Percent Complete and Remaining Duration are Linked and may NOT be independently entered. This is how Microsoft Project always calculates and is the same as Linking Remaining Duration and Schedule Percent Complete in P3 and SureTrak.

- **Units**   This option calculates the Percent Complete based on the Actual and Remaining Units when resources are assigned to activities.

In P3 and SureTrak these options are set for all activities at project level with the **Link Remaining Duration and Schedule Percent Complete**. In Microsoft Project there are no options and Task Percent Complete is always linked to the Remaining Duration. In Primavera Version 5.0 this option may be set for each activity, allowing more flexibility in how the schedule calculates.

7.1.3   Activity Types and Milestones

An Activity may be assigned the following Activity Types using the drop down box in the Project Defaults tab:

- **Task Dependent**
- **Resource Dependent**
- **Level of Effort**
- **Start Milestone**
- **Finish Milestone**
- **WBS Summary**

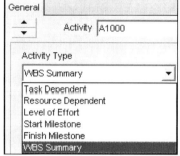

TASK TYPE	DESCRIPTION
• **Task Dependent**	These Activity Types have a duration and will only calculate the duration using the assigned calendar even when one or more resources are assigned to an activity.
• **Resource Dependent**	These Activity Types have a duration and will calculate the duration only using the assigned calendar when NO resources are assigned to the activity. These activities acknowledge resource calendars when resources are assigned. This is similar to an Independent Activity Type in P3 and SureTrak.
• **Level of Effort**	This Activity type is covered in the **ASSIGNING ROLES, RESOURCES AND EXPENSES** chapter, and are similar to P3 and SureTrak Hammock activities.
• **Start Milestone**	A Start Milestone has a start date and no finish date and is scheduled at the start of a timeperiod.
• **Finish Milestone**	A Finish Milestone has a finish dat, no start date and is scheduled at the end of a timeperiod. Changing a milestone from Strat to Finish would not affect a schedule when all the tasks are on one calendar but would move the milestone from the start of a day to the finish of the previovs day.
• **WBS Summary**	This Activity type is covered in the **ASSIGNING ROLES, RESOURCES AND EXPENSES** chapter, and calculate in the same way as P3 and SureTrak WBS activities.

A Milestone has zero duration and is used to mark the start or finish of a major event. Primavera Version 5.0 differentiates between **Start** and **Finish Milestones** in the same way as P3 and SureTrak, where a Start Milestone has a start date and no finish date and a Finish Milestone has a finish date and no start date. This is unlike Microsoft Project, which only has one type of Milestone. Later versions of Microsoft Project allow Milestones with durations.

7.1.4   Cost Account

This drop down box is used to select the default Cost Account for all new Resources and Expenses and is blank by default. Cost Accounts are covered in detail in the **ACTIVITY, PROJECT AND RESOURCES CODES** chapter.

7.1.5   Calendar

This topic was covered in detail in the **CALENDARS** chapter. This drop down box is used to select the default calendar for an activity. A **Default Project Calendar** is assigned to each project from the **Global** or **Project** calendar list.

All new activities are assigned the project **Default Project Calendar** when they are created however individual calendars may be assigned for each activity.

7.1.6   Auto-numbering Defaults

The **Auto-numbering Defaults** decide how new activities are numbered. The first activity added to a new project will be based on the defaults set in this form.

- The **Increment Activity ID based on selected activity** check box controls which of the **Auto-numbering Defaults** rules are acknowledged after the first activity is added:
  - ➢ When checked, new activities will inherit the number of the highlighted activity plus the **Increment** number, and
  - ➢ When unchecked, new activities will use the **Activity ID Prefix,** plus the **Activity ID Suffix** plus the Increment from the last activity.

 There are no Activity ID Codes such as found in P3 and SureTrak.

7.2   Adding New Activities

It is often quicker to create a schedule in a spread sheet and import the data into the scheduling software. Primavera Version 5.0 now offers a spreadsheet import function found under **File**, **Import…** which is very user friendly. This is covered in detail in **UTILITIES** chapter.

To add an Activity to a project you must first open the project, select the appropriate WBS Node and then:

- Select **Edit**, **Add**, or
- Press the **Insert** key on the keyboard.

7.3   Copying Activities in Primavera Version 5.0

Activities may also be copied from another project or copied from within the same project using the normal Windows commands, **Copy** and **Paste**, by using the menu commands **Edit, Copy** and **Edit, Paste** or **Ctrl+C** and **Ctrl+V**.

One or more activities may be selected to be copied by:

- **Ctrl**-clicking, or
- Holding the **shift** key and clicking on the first and last activity in a range.

With this operation be sure to select the whole activity or activities, not just a cell.

When pasting, you are presented with the **Copy Activity Option** form where you may select which data is to be copied and pasted:

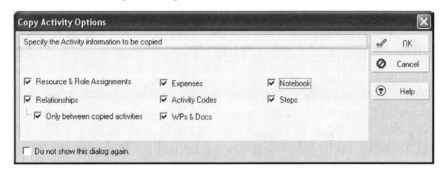

To copy an activity from one project to another, both projects must be open.

7.4   Copying Activities from other Programs

Activity data may NOT be copied from, or updated from other programs (such as Excel), by cutting and pasting.

7.5   Elapsed Durations

An activity may NOT be assigned an **Elapsed** duration, where the activity is scheduled 24hrs/day and 7 days per week, in the same way as in Microsoft Project.

7.6   Finding the Bars in the Gantt Chart

At times you will find there are no bars displayed in the Gantt Chart because the Timescale has scrolled too far into the past or future. Double-click in the Gantt Chart and the Timescale will scroll to display the activity bars. There are no rolling dates as in P3 or SureTrak.

7.7   Activity Information – Bottom Layout

The Bottom Layout has a number of tabs where information about the highlighted activity may be viewed and edited. (These are not in any specific order as the tabs may be reordered on the screen.)

• **General**	This form displays the: • **Activity ID** and **Activity Description** And two pieces of Project Data that may not be edited: • **Project** and **Responsible Manager** It also displays activity attributes including some which were set as defaults in the **Project Workspace**: • **Activity Type**, **Duration Type**, **% Complete Type**, **Activity Calendar**, **WBS**, **Responsible Manager** and **Primary Resource**.
• **Status**	This is where the following data is displayed/edited: • The **Durations**, • The **Status**, where Actual Dates and % Complete may be entered, • Where **Constraints** are entered and • By selecting from the drop down box the **Labor** and **Nonlabor Units** or **Costs** and **Material Costs** may be displayed.
• **Summary**	This form displays summary information about the activity. It has three buttons that select which data will be displayed: • **Units**, or **Costs**, or **Dates**
• **Resources**	**Resources** and **Roles** may be assigned to activities and assignment information displayed.
• **Expenses**	**Expenses** may be added and edited here. These are intended for on off costs that do not require a resource to be created.
• **Notebook**	Notes about activities may be made here by adding a **Notebook Topic** and then adding notes about the topic.
• **Steps**	This function enables an activity to be broken down into increments titled **Steps** that may be marked up as complete as work on the Activity progresses.
• **Feedback**	This is where comments made in the timesheet module may be viewed.
• **WP's & Docs**	This is where files that have been listed in the **Work Products and Documents** Workspace may be associated with activities and then opened from this form.
• **Codes**	Project Codes may be created and activities associated with these codes with this form. These codes are similar to P3 and SureTrak Activity Codes and activities may be organized in a similar way.
• **Relationships** **Predecessors** **Successors**	This is where the activity's predecessors and successors are added, edited and deleted. This is covered in the **ADDING THE DEPENDENCIES** chapter.

7.8   Assigning Calendars to Activities

Activities often require a different calendar from the **Project Calendar** that is assigned in the **Project Information** form. Primavera Version 5.0 allows each activity to be assigned a unique calendar. An **Activity Calendar** may be assigned by the **General** tab of the **Bottom Layout** or by displaying the **Calendar** column.

7.8.1   Assigning a Calendar Using General tab of the Bottom Layout Form

- Select one activity that you want to assign to a different calendar. Multiple activity selection may not be used,
- Open the **General** tab of the **Bottom Layout**,
- Click on the ▦ button in the **Activity Calendar** box to open the **Select Activity Calendar** form,
- Select either **Global** or **Project** from the dropdown list in the top left hand menu and
- Select an Activity calendar by clicking in the ⊞ button.

7.8.2   Assigning a Calendar Using a Column

You may also display the **Calendar** column and edit the activity calendar from this column. The process of displaying a column is covered in the **FORMATTING THE DISPLAY** chapter.

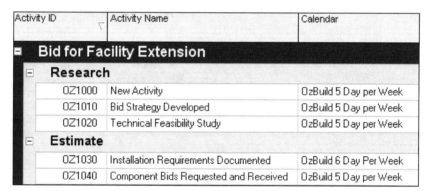

7.9   Undo

Primavera Version 5.0 has a new multiple **Undo** function that operates on Resources, Resource Assignments, and Activities windows, but no **Redo** function.

There are many functions that will erase the Undo memory such as scheduling, summarizing, importing, opening a project, opening Code forms, opening User and Admin Preferences and closing the application.

7.10 Assigning Activities to a WBS Node

Activities are assigned to a WBS Node from the Activities Workspace. They may be assigned using the following methods:

- A new activity will inherit the WBS Node that is highlighted when an activity is created.

- A new activity will inherit the WBS Node of a selected existing activity when the project is organized by WBS Nodes and an activity is created.

- Select the activity and click on the WBS box in the **General** tab in the lower window. This will open the **Select WBS** form where you may assign the WBS Node. The $+$ and the $-$ are used to expand or rollup the WBS structure. Click on the button to assign the node.

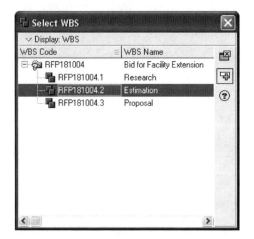

- Select one or more activities and move the mouse to the left of the activity description and the mouse will change into the shape displayed in the picture below. You may then drag the activities to another WBS Node.

Be sure the Mouse pointer changes to this shape before dragging.

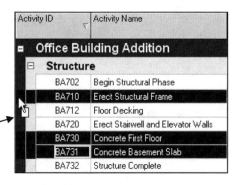

- Insert the WBS column by clicking on the button and selecting WBS from the **Columns** form under **General**. Clicking in the WBS column of an activity will open the **Select WBS form**.

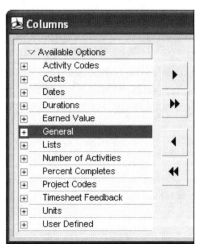

7.11 Reordering or Sorting Activities

You may not drag activities up or down the schedule in the same way as other products. There are two principal methods of ordering activities after they have been added:

- Using the **Sort** function. To open the **Sort** form:

  ➢ Select **View**, **Group and Sort...** and click on the ![Sort...] button, or

  ➢ Click on the 📖 **icon** and click on the ![Sort...] button to open the **Sort** form,

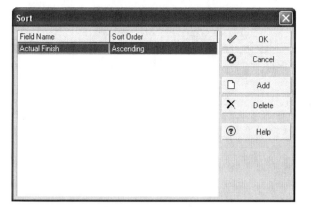

- Highlighting a column title and clicking. The activities within a band will be reordered within that band in the order indicated with an arrow in the right hand side of the column header. The order will be either Ascending or Descending:

The arrow indicating the direction of sort.

Activities ordered by Activity ID.

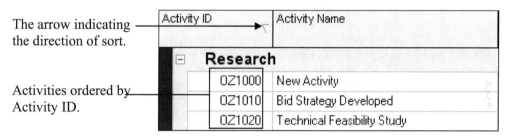

This function changes the settings made in the **Sort** form.

 The Activities ID's are not renumbered when they have been reordered as they are with Microsoft Project.

7.12 Summarizing Activities Using WBS

The WBS bands may be summarized in the same way as in other project planning and scheduling software. The picture below shows the activities displayed under the WBS Nodes:

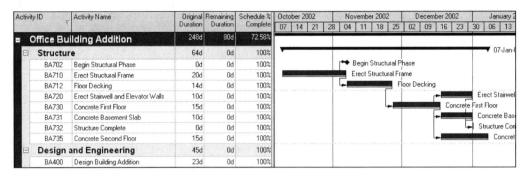

The picture below shows the activities summarized under the WBS Nodes:

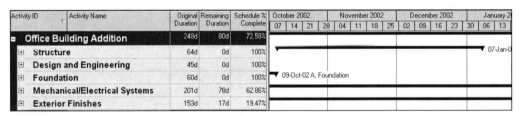

WBS Nodes may be summarized or expanded by:

- Double-click on any WBS band description. The band will either roll up when expanded or expand when rolled up.

- Select **View**, **Expand All** or **View**, **Collapse All** from the menu.

- Right-click and select **Expand All** or **Collapse All** from the menu.

- Click on the $\boxed{+}$ or the $\boxed{-}$ to the right of the WBS Node description to expand or collapse the WBS Node.

WBS Nodes may be reordered by clicking the arrow buttons in the Command Toolbar to the right hand side of the WBS Workspace.

WORKSHOP 5

Adding Activities

Background
We need to setup the defaults and add the activities to the schedule.

Assignment
1. Go to the **Projects Workspace**, highlight the required project and select the **Defaults** tab in the **Activity Details** pane. If required, adjust the following parameters.

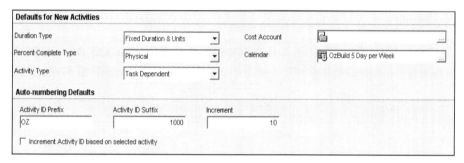

2. Open the **Activities Workspace** and add the following activities under the appropriate WBS. Click on the Activity ID column header if the activities become out of order.

Act ID	Activity Name	Original Duration	Activity Type	OzBuild Calendar
Research				
OZ1000	Bid Request Documents Received	0 d	Start Milestone	5 Day
OZ1010	Bid Strategy Developed	1 d	Task Dependent	5 Day
OZ1020	Technical Feasibility Study	8 d	Task Dependent	5 Day
Estimate				
OZ1030	Installation Requirements Documented	4 d	Task Dependent	**6 Day**
OZ1040	Component Bids Requested and Received	3 d	Task Dependent	5 Day
OZ1050	Project Schedule Developed	4 d	Task Dependent	**6 Day**
OZ1060	Technical Details Schedule Drafted	9 d	Task Dependent	5 Day
OZ1070	Costs from Component Bids Compiled	2 d	Task Dependent	5 Day
Proposal				
OZ1080	Bid Document Drafted	3 d	Task Dependent	5 Day
OZ1090	Draft Bid Document Reviewed	1 d	Task Dependent	5 Day
OZ1100	Design Validated	1 d	Task Dependent	5 Day
OZ1110	Proposal Draft Bid Document Revised	1 d	Task Dependent	5 Day
OZ1120	Component Work Packages Negotiated	6 d	Task Dependent	5 Day
OZ1130	Bid Document Finalized	1 d	Task Dependent	5 Day
OZ1140	Submit Bid	0 d	Finish Milestone	5 Day

3. Reschedule the project by pressing F9 and check that the Data Date is set at the 3 December 2007.
4. Your answer should look like the picture below:

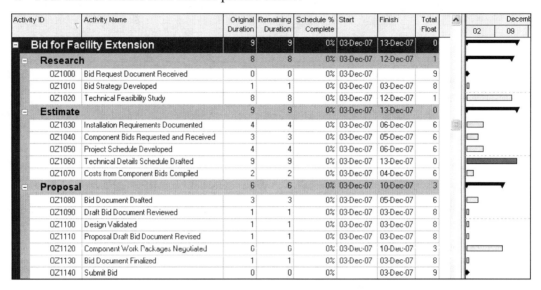

Note: Depending on the Layout that your software has loaded your data may be displayed in different columns and with different bar formatting. Layouts are covered in the **GROUP, SORT AND LAYOUTS** chapter. Should your layout not enable you to check your data entry try selecting a different layout using the command **View**, **Layouts**, **Open…** and select another layout from the list such as the Classic or Default WBS Layout.

8 FORMATTING THE DISPLAY

This chapter shows you how to set up the on-screen presentation so that the schedule will be easier to read and more consistent. This chapter covers the following display customizing topics:

Topic	Menu Command
• Formatting Columns	Open the **Column** form: • Select **View, Columns…**, or • Click on the ⊞ button.
• Formatting Activity Bars	Open the **Bar** form: • Select **View, Bars…**, or • Click on the ▦ button.
• Format Gridlines	**Bar Chart Gridlines** are formatted in the **View, Bar Chart Options…** form, **Sightlines** tab.
• Format Data Date	The **Data Date** is formatted in the **Bar Chart Options…** form, **Data Date** tab.
• Formatting Row Height	Open the **Table, Font and Row** form by: • Selecting **View, Table Font and Row….**
• Formatting Colors	There are limited options for formatting colors: • **Text** colors are formatted in the **Color** form accessed from the **Table, Font and Row** form which is opened by selecting **View, Table Font and Row…,** ⎡AaBbYyZz⎤ button. • **Bar Colors** are covered in the **Formatting the Bars** paragraph of this chapter. • **Band** colors are selected as part of the formatting of the layout by selecting **View, Group and Sort…** or clicking on the ▣ button.
• Formatting Fonts	There are limited options for formatting fonts: • **Text** fonts are formatted in the **Font** form accessed from the **Table, Font and Row** form which is opened by selecting **View, Table Font and Row…,** ⎡AaBbYyZz⎤ button. • **Notebook** entries may be edited when entered.
• Format Timescale	• Click on the ▦ button, or • Select **View, Timescale…**, or • Right-click in the Bar Chart area and select **Timescale….**

The formatting is applied to the current **Layout** and is automatically saved as part of the Layout when another Layout is selected. Views are covered in the **GROUP, SORT AND LAYOUTS** chapter.

8.1 Formatting in the Project Workspace

The formatting of the Project Workspace is very similar to the formatting of the Activity Workspace and will not be covered separately.

8.2 Formatting Columns

8.2.1 Selecting the Columns to be Displayed

The columns displayed on the screen are formatted through the **Columns** form which may be opened by the following:

- Select **View**, **Columns...**, or

- Click on the ⊞ button, or

- Right-click to open a menu and select **Columns...**:

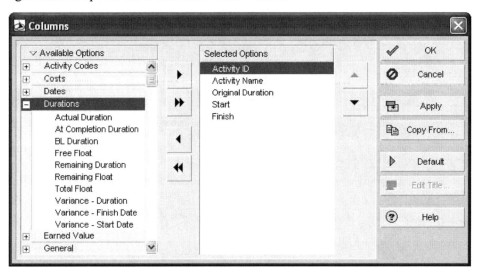

The **Column** form may be resized by dragging the edges.

- The available columns are displayed in the right hand window and may be listed under **Categories** or as a single **List**. To select how the column titles are displayed, click on the **Available Options** drop down box and then select **Group and Sort By** to choose either **List** or **Categories**.

- The columns to be displayed are listed in the right hand **Selected Options** window and are copied from the **Available Options** to and from **Selected Options** using the ▸ and ◂ buttons.

- The ▷ Default button sets the columns back to the default column display.

8.2.2 Setting the Order of the Columns from Left to Right on the Screen

The order of the columns on the screen, from left to right, is the same as the order in the **Columns** form **Selected Options** window from top to bottom. The order of the columns may be altered:

- Highlight the column in the **Columns** form **Selected Options** window and use the ▲ and ▼ buttons, or

- Right-click on the column title in a Workspace and drag the column.

8.2.3 Adjusting the Width of Columns

You may adjust the width of the column in two ways:

- By dragging the column title separator; move the mouse pointer to the nearest vertical line of the column. A ↔ icon will then appear and enable the column to be adjusted by Right-clicking & dragging.

- From the **Column** form select [Edit Title...] to open the **Edit Column Title** form and enter the width of the column in pixels.

8.2.4 Editing the Column Description and Alignment

The column description may be edited from the **Edit Column Title** form, which is displayed by opening the **Edit Column** form and selecting the [Edit Title...] button. The alignment of the title is also edited here.

8.3 Formatting the Bars

The bars in the Gantt Chart may be formatted to suit your requirements for display. Primavera Version 5.0 does not have the option to format individual bars but is able to assign a filter to a bar style so that a style is applied to activities that meet a filter definition.

8.3.1 Formatting Activity Bars

To format all the bars you must open the **Bar** form:

- Select **View, Bars…,** or
- Click on the 📋 button, or
- Right-click in the bars area and select **Bars…** from the menu.

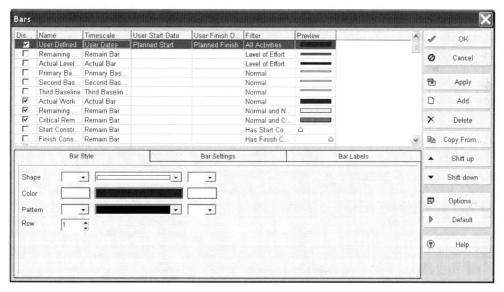

The following notes are the main points for using this function. Detailed information is available in the help facility by searching for "Bar styles dialog box."

- Each bar listed in the table may be displayed on the bar chart by checking the box in the **Display** column.

- New bars may be added by clicking on the [🗋 Add] button and deleted by clicking on the [✕ Delete] button.

- The bar at the top of the list is placed on the screen and then the one below drawn over the top of it, so it would be simple to hide one bar with a second. The [▲ Shift up] and [▼ Shift down] buttons are used to move the bars up or down the list and therefore determine which bar is drawn on top of the next.

- The **Name** is the title assigned to the bar and may be displayed in the printout legend.

- The **Timescale** option is similar to the **Show For … Tasks** option in the Microsoft Project **Bar Styles** form or the **Data Item** in the SureTrak **Format Bars** form, and allows the nomination of a predefined bar which is selected from the drop down box. Version 4.1 introduced **User Defined Dates** that may be used for formatting **User Defined Bars Styles**, see the first line on the bars form above.

- Double clicking on a cell in the **Filter column** opens the **Filters** form where you are able to select the filter/s which will determine which activities are displayed with the bar format. Filters will be covered in detail in the **FILTERS** chapter.

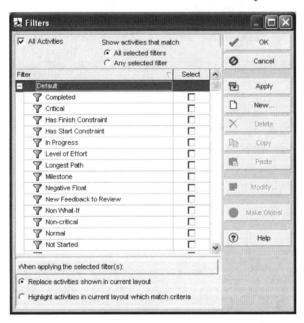

- **Negative Float** is displayed in a similar way as in Microsoft Project and requires another bar in addition to the **Positive Float** bar and both the **Timescale** and **Filter** selected as Negative Float.

- The **Float** bar shows **Total Float**; there is no **Free Float** bar available.

 It is often useful to create a bar that only displays the text. This bar may be displayed or not displayed as required, which is much simpler than reformatting a bar to show text.

8.3.2   Bar Style Tab

The appearance of each bar is edited in the lower half of the form. The bar's start, middle, and end points may have their color, shape, pattern, etc., formatted.

The bars may be placed on one of three rows numbered from 1 to 3, from top to bottom one bar above the other. If multiple bars are placed on the same row, the bar at the top of the list will be drawn first and the ones lower down the list will be drawn over the top.

8.3.3   Bar Settings Tab

Grouping Band Settings
- **Show bar when collapsed** option displays the detailed bars on a single line when the WBS Node has been summarized; see the two pictures below:
  - ➢   Before summarizing:

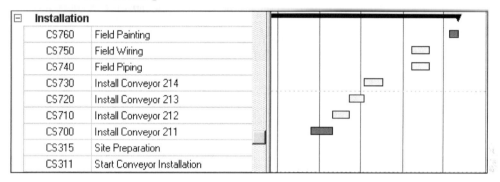

  - ➢   After summarizing:

This is similar to the Microsoft Project **<u>A</u>lways roll up Gantt bars** option in the **Layout** form.

Show bar for grouping bands
This shows a summarized bar all the time and hides the detailed bars below.

Grouping Band Settings
This sets the style for summary bars only, which are displayed when the WBS Node is both summarized and not summarized.

    When formatting the **Bar Style** for Milestones it is important to take note of the checked boxes and Filter format. If the box **Show bar for grouping bands** is checked, Milestones will appear at the ends of Summary Bars and not in line with the actual activities they belong too. The filter in this case will read **Summary** and not **Milestone**.

Bar Necking Settings

Bar Necking displays a thinner bar during times of inactivity such as weekends and holidays and applies only to Current Bar setting column in the **Bars** form.

Un-necked bars

Necked bars

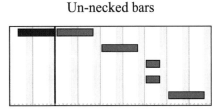 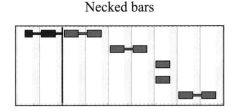

- **Calendar nonwork time** necks the bar based on the activity's calendar.

- **Activity nonwork intervals** necks the bar when Out of Sequence Progress options of Actual Dates or Retained Logic causes a break in the work. See the **Advanced Scheduling Options** paragraph.

8.3.4   Bar Labels Tab

This tab allows the placement of text with a bar, above, below, to the left and to the right. The pictures below show how the start and finish dates are formatted and displayed on the bar chart:

- Select the bar that you wish to add the label to.

- Click on the `Add` and the `X Delete` buttons at the bottom of the **Bars** form to add and delete a **Label** item.

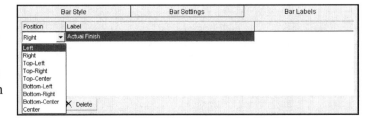

- Select the **Position** and **Label** from the drop down boxes in the **Bar Labels** tab.

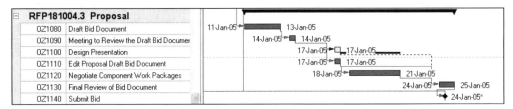

- The dates on the bar chart are adopted from the **User Preferences** and may not be formatted separately.

- Each **Notebook Topic** may be displayed on a bar one at a time by selecting the topic in the **Bar Labels** tab. After the box containing the label is displayed on the screen it may be adjusted in size by dragging.

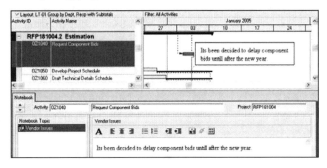

8.3.5 Bar Chart Options Form

The **Bar Chart Options** form is displayed by clicking on the [Options...] button from the **Bars** form or by selecting **View**, **Bar Chart Options…**.

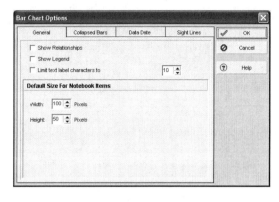

- The **General** tab has a variety of options for formatting the bar chart which are mainly self explanatory.

  ➢ **Show Relationships** has the same result as clicking on the ⤷ icon and displays the relationships.

  ➢ **Show Legend** Displays a legend on the bar chart in the Activities view, see below:

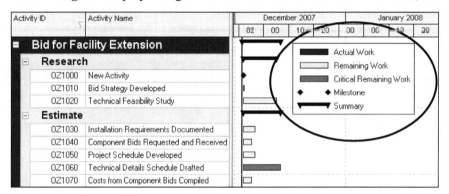

  ➢ The default size of the box displaying a **Notebook** topic may be set in the **Bar Chart Options** form, **General** tab, which is displayed by clicking on the [Options...] button from the **Bars** form.

- The **Collapsed Bar** tab is to format the bars when a WBS band has been collapsed and displays a summarized bar.

- The **Data Date** tab is for formatting the Data Date, its style, color and size

- Primavera Version 5.0 introduced a new **Sight Lines** tab bar which now allows the specification of both Major and Minor vertical and horizontal Sight Lines, which brings the functionality up to match P3, SureTrak and Microsoft Project:

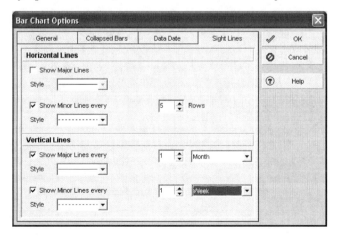

8.4 Row Height

Row heights may be adjusted to display text that would otherwise be truncated by a narrow column.

- The height of all rows may be formatted from the **Table**, **Font and Row** form by selecting **View**, **Table Font and Row…**. The options in this form are self-explanatory.

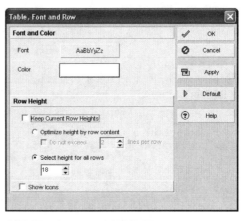

- The **Show Icons** option will display a different icon in front of the Activity and WBS.

- The height of a single row may be manually adjusted in a similar way to adjusting row heights in Excel, click on the row; the pointer will change to a double-headed arrow ⇳; then drag the row with the mouse. These manually adjusted rows are not saved with a Layout.

8.5 Format Fonts and Font Colors

The format font options are:

- The **Bar Chart** fonts are formatted in the **Table, Font and Row** form (displayed in the paragraph above) by selecting **View**, **Table Font and Row…**.

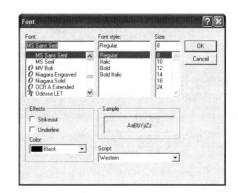

   - Clicking on the ⬚AaBbYyZz⬚, the **Font** button, will open the font form where normal Windows functions are available.
   - Clicking on the **Color** button will allow the selection of a color for the background of both the **Bar Chart** and the **Columns** area.

- The **Notebook Topics** may be formatted using the formatting features above where the Notebook items are entered in the lower pane.

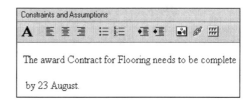

- Some forms may have the fonts for displaying data edited when there is a menu on the top left hand side with the **Table Font and Row…** menu item.

- The text in a **Text Box** that has been inserted onto the Bar Chart may be formatted when the box is created.

8.6 Format Colors

There are the main options for formatting colors:

- **Band** colors in layouts are formatted in the **Group and Sort** form by clicking on the 🔲 button or selecting **View**, **Group and Sort…**.

- **Text** colors were covered in the **Format Font and Colors** paragraph.

- **Bar Colors** were covered in the **Formatting the Bars** paragraph.

- **Timescale** and **Column Headers** see the **Format Timescale Command** paragraph.

- **Gridline** colors may not be formatted.

- The **Data Date** is formatted in the **Bar Options** form, **Data Date** tab.

- The **Relationship Lines**, also known as **Dependencies**, **Logic**, or **Links**, may not be formatted and are displayed with the following characteristics:

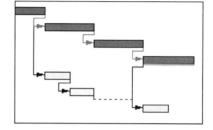

  - ➢ Solid Red for Critical,
  - ➢ Solid Black for Driving, and
  - ➢ Dotted Black for Non-driving.

  Constraints will be covered in more detail in the **ADDING RELATIONSHIPS** chapter.

8.7 Format Timescale

8.7.1 Moving and Rescaling the Timescale

To display hidden parts of the schedule the timescale may be grabbed and moved by placing the cursor in the top half of the Timescale, the cursor will turn into a 🖑, right-click and drag left or right.

The timescale may be rescaled, therefore increasing or decreasing the length of the bars and displaying more or less of the schedule by placing the cursor in the bottom half of the Timescale, the cursor will turn into a 🔍, right-click, and drag left to make the bars shorter and right to make the bars longer.

When there are no bars in view when you are viewing a time ahead or behind the activity dates you may double-click in the **Gantt Chart** area to bring them back into view.

8.7.2 Format Timescale Command

The **Timescale** form provides a number of options for the display of the timescale, which is located above the Bar Chart. To open the **Timescale** form:

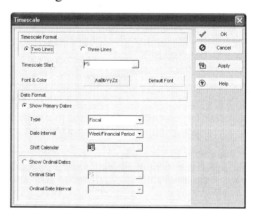

- Click on the 🔳 button, or

- Select **View**, **Timescale…**, or

- Right-click in the Bar Chart area and select **Timescale…**

The options available in the **Timescale** form are:

- **Timescale Format in Primavera Version 5.0 now** allows in the timescale
  - ➤ Two Lines, or
  - ➤ Three lines

	2008		
January	February	March
30	06	13	20	27	03	10	17	24	02	09	16	23

January 2008	February 2008	March 2008
30	06	13	20	27	03	10	17	24	02	09	16	23

- **Font & Color**
  - ➤ The 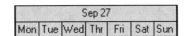 button opens the **Edit Font and Color** form which enables the timescale and column headers font and color to be changed.
  - ➤ By clicking on the [Default Font] button all changes will be reversed.

- **Date Interval** sets the timescale and has the options in the picture to the right:

  | Year/Quarter |
  | Year/Month |
  | Quarter/Month |
  | Month/Week |
  | Week/Day 1 |
  | Week/Day 2 |
  | Day/Shift |
  | Day/Hour |

  - ➤ The **Week/Day 1** displays the Days like this:

Sep 27	Oct 04
M	T	W	T	F	S	S	M	T	W	T	F	S	S

  - ➤ The **Week/Day 2** displays the Days like this:

Sep 27						
Mon	Tue	Wed	Thr	Fri	Sat	Sun

  - ➤ The **Date Interval** may also be adjusted by clicking on the 🔍 or the 🔍 which moves the timescale setting up and down the list shown above.

- **Shift Calendar** breaks the day into time intervals to suit the shift intervals when the **Day/Shift** option has been selected.

- **Date Format**
  - ➤ **Calendar** displays a normal calendar.
  - ➤ **Fiscal Year** displays the fiscal year in the year line. The Fiscal Year Start Month is set in the **Settings** tab of the **Project Details** form in the **Projects Workspace**.
  - ➤ **Week of the Year** displays the week of the year starting from "1" for the first week in January and is often termed **Manufacturing Week**.

➢ **Ordinal Dates** displays the timescale to be counted by the unit selected in the **Date Interval**. This is useful for displaying a schedule when the start of the project is unknown. Ordinal dates display the time scale by counting in the selected units starting from a user definable start date. This option works in a similar way to the P3 function where the Ordinal start date may be selected. When 3 lines are displayed the ordinal dates and calendar dates may displayed

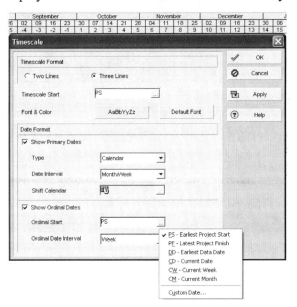

 Fiscal Year: When the scale was set to Month/Week on the author's system the Fiscal Year did not display in accordance with date formatting settings. When the scale was set to Week and Days, the Date were displayed in US format (MM/DD/YYYY) which is not correct for countries that use the DD/MM/YYYY format.

8.8   Inserting Attachments - Text Boxes and Curtain

A text box may be inserted in a bar chart area:

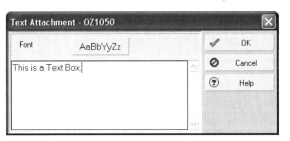

- Select the Activity the Text Box is to be associated with,
- Right-click in the Bar Chart to open the menu,
- Select **View, Attachments**, **Text** and
- Type in the text and format the font by clicking on the AaBbYyZz button.

- A **Text Box** may be repositioned by clicking on the text and using the curser to drag the corners and sides.

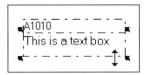

A **Curtain**, used to highlight periods of time over part of the bar chart, may be displayed in a similar way to P3 and SureTrak:

- Right-click in the Bar Chart to open the menu,
- Select **Attachments**, **Curtain**,
- Check the **Display curtain attachment** box to hide or display the Curtain.
- The start and finish dates of the Curtain may be set by:
  - ➢ Using the **Start Date** and **Finish Date** boxes, or
  - ➢ Grabbing the left or right edge of the Curtain in the Bar Chart (the cursor will change to a 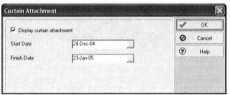) and dragging the start or finish date, or
  - ➢ Grabbing the Curtain in the center (the cursor will change to a 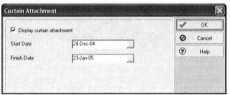) and dragging the whole Curtain.

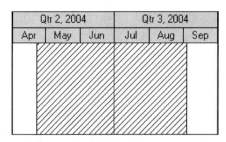

8.9 Gantt Chart Curtains

Primavera Version 5.0 introduced a function allowing the placing of multiple curtains on the Gantt Chart which may be all hidden or displayed.

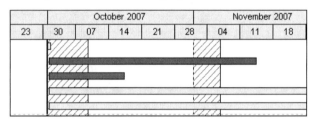

Select <u>V</u>iew, <u>A</u>ttachments to display the **Curtain** menu:

- **A**dd Curtain opens the **Curtain Attachment** form used to create a curtain:

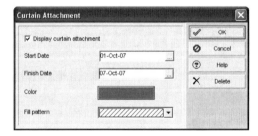

- <u>S</u>how All shows all the curtains,
- **H**ide All hides all the curtains and
- Clicking on a curtain in the Gantt Chart also opens the **Curtain Attachment** form where individual curtains may be deleted or hidden.

WORKSHOP 6

Formatting the Bar Chart

Background
Management has received your draft report and requests that some changes be made to the presentation.

Assignment
Format your schedule as follows:

1. Depending on the default settings your Gantt Chart view may differ from that shown, e.g., there may be no summary bars for example.
2. Add a Calendar and Activity Type column to the right of the Activity Name.
3. Adjust the column widths by dragging the column headers divider lines.
4. Press the **F9** key and click on the ⬛ Schedule button which will schedule the project and calculate the float.
5. Now hide and display the **Float Bar** (Total Float bar) then leave the bar displayed.
6. Create a bar titled 'Activity Name' which does not display a bar and shows the Activity Name to the left and display it
7. Change the Row Height to 30 points by selecting **View, Table Font and Row…**.
8. Now check the **Optimize height by row content box**, not exceeding 1 line per row.
9. Now change the setting back to its original format of 18 point height for all rows.
10. Format Timescale to Year and Month, then Week and Day 1, then Month and Week.
11. Format the Vertical lines with a solid Major line every month and a Minor line every week by selecting **View, Bar Chart Otpions…** and select the **Sight Lines** tab.
12. Expand and contract the timescale and adjust it so that all the descriptions and bars are visible.

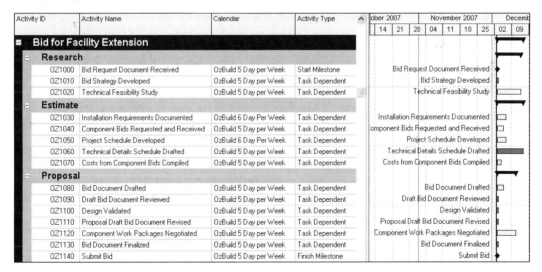

---

9   ADDING RELATIONSHIPS

The next phase of a schedule is to add logic to the activities. There are two types of logic:

- **Relationships** (**Dependencies** or **Logic** or **Links** between activities), and
- Imposed **Constraints** to activity start or finish dates. These are covered in the **CONSTRAINTS** chapter.

Primavera Version 5.0's Help file and other text use the terms **Relationships** and **Logic** for **Relationships** but does not use the terms **Dependencies** or **Links**.

We will look at the following techniques in this chapter:

Topic	Notes for creating a SF Relationship
• Graphically in the Bar Chart.	Drag the ⤵ mouse pointer from one activity to another to create a dependency.
• By opening the **Activity Details** form.	Predecessor and Successors may be added and deleted from the **Relationships** tab.
• By editing or deleting a dependency using the **Edit Relationship** form.	Double-click on an activity link in the **Bar Chart** or **PERT** view.
• Opening the **Assign Predecessor** form or the **Assign Successor** form from the menu.	• Select **Edit, Assign, Predecessors…**, or • Select **Edit, Assign, Successors…**.
• By displaying the **Predecessor** and/or **Successor** columns.	Double clicking in the Predecessor or Successor cells will open the **Assign Predecessor** form and the **Assign Successor** form.
• Chain Linking or Automatically Linking activities with a start to finish relationship.	Select the activities in the order they are to be linked, right click and select **Link Activities**.

Relationships

There are two types of dependencies that are discussed in scheduling:

- **Hard Logic**, also referred to as **Primary Logic**, are dependencies that may not be avoided: for example, a footing excavation has to be prepared before concrete may be poured into it.
- **Soft Logic**, also referred to as **Sequencing Logic**, **Preferred Logic** or **Secondary Logic** may often be changed at a later date to reflect planning changes: for example, determining in which order the footing holes may be dug.

There is no simple method of documenting which is hard logic and which is soft logic as notes may not be attached to relationships. A schedule with a large amount of soft logic has the potential of becoming very difficult to maintain when the plan is changed. As a project progresses, soft logic converts to hard logic due to commitments and commencing activities.

Constraints

Constraints are applied to Activities when relationships do not provide the required result. Typical applications of a constraint are:

- The availability of a site to commence work.
- The supply of information by a client.
- The required finish date of a project.

Constraints are often entered to represent contract dates and may be directly related to contract items using Notebook Topics.

Constraints are covered in detail in the **CONSTRAINTS** chapter.

9.1 Understanding Relationships

There are four types of dependencies available in Primavera Version 5.0:

- Finish-to-Start (**FS**) (also known as conventional)
- Start-to-Start (**SS**)
- Start-to-Finish (**SF**)
- Finish-to-Finish (**FF**)

Two other terms you must understand are:

- **Predecessor**, an activity that controls the start or finish of another immediate subsequent activity.
- **Successor**, an activity whose start or finish depends on the start or finish of another immediately preceding activity.

The following pictures show how the dependencies appear graphically in the **Bar Chart** and **PERT** (also known as PERT and Relationship Diagram views).

The **FS** (or conventional) dependency looks like this:

While the **SS** dependency is like this:

The **SF** dependency looks like:

The **FF** dependency would be:

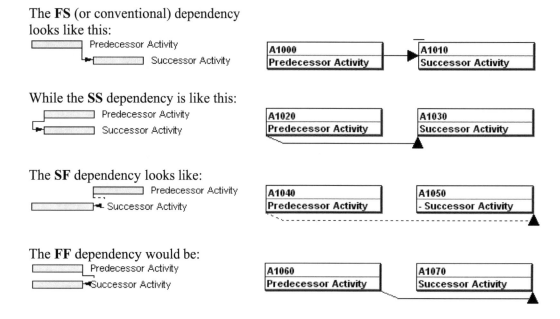

9.2 Understanding Lags and Leads

A **Lag** is a duration that is applied to a dependency to make the successor start or finish earlier or later.

- A successor activity will start later when a positive **Lag** is assigned. Therefore, an activity requiring a 3-day delay between the finish of one activity and start of another will require a positive lag of 3 days.

- Conversely, a lag may be negative (also called a **Lead)** when a new activity may be started before the predecessor activity is finished.

- **Leads** and **Lags** may be applied to any relationship type, including Summary Activity relationships.

An example of a **FS** with positive lag

An example of a **FS** with negative lag:

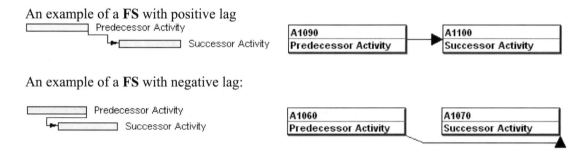

Here are some important points to understand about Lags:

- Lags are by default calculated by Primavera Version 5.0 using the **Successors Calendar**. (Primavera P3 and SureTrak software only uses the predecessor's calendar. Microsoft Project uses the Project Calendar or may have an Elapsed Duration Lag.)

- Lags for the project being calculated may be assigned one of four calendars from the **Calendar for Scheduling Relationship lag** drop down box in the **General Schedule Options** form. This form is opened by selecting **Tools**, **Schedule…** and clicking on the ▷ Advanced… tab. The four Lag Calendar options are:
  - ➢ Predecessor Activity Calendar,
  - ➢ Successor Activity Calendar,
  - ➢ 24 Hour Calendar, and
  - ➢ Project Default Calendar.

 You must be careful when using a lag to allow for delays such as curing concrete when the Lag Calendar is not a seven-day calendar. Since this type of activity lapses nonwork days, the activity could finish before Primavera Version 5.0's calculated finish date.

9.3 Displaying the Relationships on the Bar Chart

The relationships may be displayed or hidden by clicking on the button on the **Activity Toolbar** or by checking and un-checking the **Show Relationships** box in the **Bar Chart Options** form, **General** tab.

The color of the dependency lines:

- Critical – Solid Red
- Non-critical Driving – Solid Black
- Non-driving – Dotted Black
- Blue – a selected relationship.

The **Relationship Lines** may NOT be formatted.

9.4 Adding and Removing Relationships

9.4.1 Graphically Adding a Relationship

To add relationships you can click on the end of the predecessor activity bar, which will change the mouse arrow to a ⌐. Then simply hold down the left mouse, drag to the start of the successor activity and release the mouse button.

To create other relationships such as **Start to Start**, drag from the beginning of the predecessor to the beginning of the successor bar.

To confirm or edit the link or add lag after a link has been added, the **Edit Relationship** form may be opened:

- Select the relationship line on the Gantt Chart; it will turn to blue and an arrow, ↑ , will appear, then
- Double-click to open the **Edit Relationship** form:

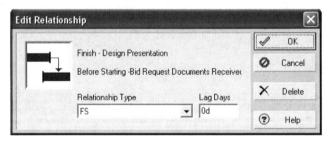

9.4.2   Adding and Deleting Relationships with the Activity Details Form

The **Activity Details** form in the lower pane may be used for adding and deleting relationships.

- Select either the **Predecessor, Successor** or the **Relationship**s tab (they all operate in a similar way). The **Successor** tab is displayed below:

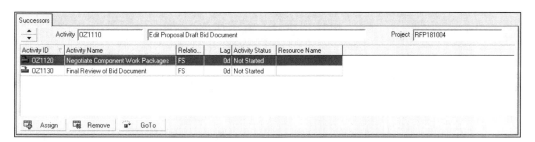

- The **Predecessor** and **Successor** tabs may both be formatted and the columns you require may be displayed:
  - ➤ Right-click in the **Predecessor** or **Successor** tabs and
  - ➤ Select ⌐ Customize Successor Columns... ⌐ to open the **Predecessor** or **Successor Columns** form.
  - ➤ The picture below displays the fields that are available:

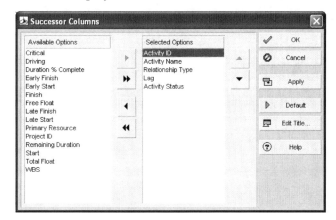

  - ➤ The data fields you require are added, deleted and reordered using the arrows. The title may also be edited using the **Edit Column Titles** form by clicking on the ⌐ Edit Title... ⌐ button.

- **Add** a predecessor or successor:
  - ➤ Click on the ⊞ Assign button, or
  - ➤ Double-click in the Predecessor or Successor column of an activity to open the **Assign Predecessor** or **Successor** form, then select the relationship from the list:

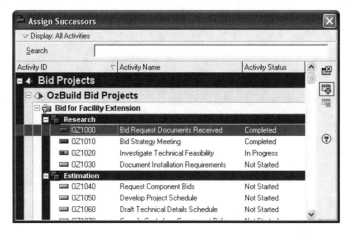

  - ➤ You may use the **Search** function and type in the first characters of either the Activity ID or the Description to narrow down your search.
  - ➤ Double-click on the Activity or click on the ⊞ icon to assign the predecessor or successor.
- Enter the Relationship Type from the **Relationship Type** drop-down list and the lag, if required, from the **Lag** drop-down list.
- To enter another relationship click on the next activity line. The **Assign Predecessor** or **Successor** form will remain open.
- **Delete** a relationship by selecting a relationship and clicking on the ⊞ Remove button.
- It is possible to follow the network path by jumping to an activity highlighted in the **Predecessor** or **Successor** form by clicking on the ⊡ GoTo button.
- Move up and down the list of activities by clicking on the ▲▼ buttons in the top left hand side of the **Predecessor** or **Successor** tabs. This button exists in every lower pane tab.

9.4.3 Chain Linking

Activities may also be linked by selecting two or more activities in the order you wish them to be linked, right click and select **Link Activities:**

- This option will only form Start to Finish relationships.
- This option does not enable the user to Chain Unlink.

9.5 Using the Command Toolbar Buttons to Assign Relationships

The **Assign Predecessors** button, ⊞, may be used to open the **Assign Predecessors** form and the **Assign Successors** button, ⊞, may be used to open the **Assign Successors** form.

9.6 Dissolving Activities

When an activity is deleted then a chain of logical activities may be broken. The **Edit, Dissolve** command and the **right click Dissolve** command will delete an activity but join the predecessors and successors with a Finish to Start relationship.

9.7 Circular Relationships

A **Circular Relationship** is created when a loop is created in the logic. The relationship will be blue and when you reschedule you will be presented with the **Circular Relationships** form, which identifies the loop.

9.8 Scheduling the Project

Once you have your activities and the logic in place, Primavera Version 5.0 calculates the activities' dates/times. More specifically, Primavera Version 5.0 **Schedules** the project to calculate the **Early Dates**, **Late Dates**, **Free Float** and the **Total Float**. This will allow you to review the **Critical Path** of the project. (Microsoft Project uses the term **Slack** instead of the term **Float**.) To schedule a project:

- Select **Tools**, **Schedule…,** or

- Strike the **F9** button to open the **Schedule** form:

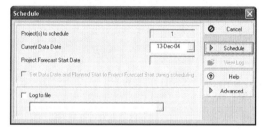

> Check the **Current Data Date**, which before a schedule is progressed should be the start date of the project.

- Click on the ▷ Schedule button.

Sometimes it is preferable to have the software recalculate the schedule each time an edit is made to an activity which affects any activity dates. To turn on automatic calculation, select **Tools, Schedule…,** ▷ Advanced… button. Select **Schedule automatically when a change affects dates**.

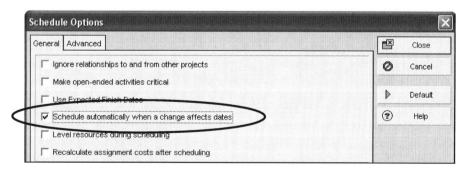

The default calculation setting for Microsoft Project and SureTrak is Automatic Calculation and Manual for P3 and Primavera Version 5.0.

9.9 Critical Activities Definition

Critical Activities Definition criteria is defined in the **Settings** tab of the **Project Details** in the **Projects Workspace.**

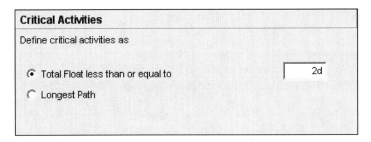

Defining critical activities affects how the activities are displayed.

- **Total Float less then or equal to** allows float to be set at any value. It is useful to set this at 2 days when multiple calendars are used, say a 5 day/week and a 7 day/week. This is because when there is a relationship from a 7 day/week predecessor to a 5 day/week successor over a weekend then float will be generated on the first activity although this is the driving relationship, the activity will have two days float.

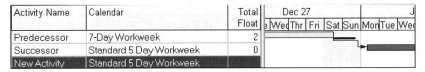

- **Longest Path** compensates for multiple calendars and selects the longest path through the schedule normally displaying a single chain of activities.

WORKSHOP 7

Adding the Relationships

Background

You have determined the logical sequence of activities, so you may now create the relationships.

Assignment

1. Input the logic below using several of the methods detailed in this chapter:

Activity ID	Activity Name	Original Duration	Predecessors
Bid for Facility Extension Workshop ...		33	
Research		9	
OZ1000	Bid Request Document Received	0	
OZ1010	Bid Strategy Developed	1	OZ1000
OZ1020	Technical Feasibility Study	8	OZ1010
Estimate		11	
OZ1030	Installation Requirements Documented	4	OZ1020
OZ1040	Component Bids Requested and Received	3	OZ1030
OZ1050	Project Schedule Developed	4	OZ1030
OZ1060	Technical Details Schedule Drafted	9	OZ1020
OZ1070	Costs from Component Bids Compiled	2	OZ1040
Proposal		33	
OZ1080	Bid Document Drafted	3	OZ1050, OZ1060, OZ1070
OZ1090	Draft Bid Document Reviewed	1	OZ1080
OZ1100	Design Validated	1	OZ1090
OZ1110	Proposal Draft Bid Document Revised	1	OZ1090
OZ1120	Component Work Packages Negotiated	6	OZ1100
OZ1130	Bid Document Finalized	1	OZ1120, OZ1110
OZ1140	Submit Bid	0	OZ1130

2. Hide the **Activity Name** bar.

3. Display the Logic Links using the **Bar** form. (If your links are displayed by default, then hide and then display them again).

4. Add the necessary bars to display Milestones, Normal bars and Critical Bars. Note: The bar formatting on the next page was created by resetting the bars to **Default** and removing text from the columns.

5. Add the Total Float Column.

6. Reschedule the project and check your results against the diagram on the next page.

ANSWER TO WORKSHOP 7

Activity ID	Activity Name	Original Duration	Predecessors	Start	Finish	Total Float
Bid for Facility Extension Workshop ...		33		03-Dec-07	16-Jan-08	0
Research		9		03-Dec-07	13-Dec-07	0
OZ1000	Bid Request Document Received	0		03-Dec-07		0
OZ1010	Bid Strategy Developed	1	OZ1000	03-Dec-07	03-Dec-07	0
OZ1020	Technical Feasibility Study	8	OZ1010	04-Dec-07	13-Dec-07	0
Estimate		11		14-Dec-07	28-Dec-07	0
OZ1030	Installation Requirements Documented	4	OZ1020	14-Dec-07	18-Dec-07	1
OZ1040	Component Bids Requested and Received	3	OZ1030	19-Dec-07	21-Dec-07	1
OZ1050	Project Schedule Developed	4	OZ1030	19-Dec-07	22-Dec-07	4
OZ1060	Technical Details Schedule Drafted	9	OZ1020	14-Dec-07	28-Dec-07	0
OZ1070	Costs from Component Bids Compiled	2	OZ1040	24-Dec-07	27-Dec-07	1
Proposal		13		31-Dec-07	16-Jan-08	0
OZ1080	Bid Document Drafted	3	OZ1050, OZ1060, OZ1070	31-Dec-07	03-Jan-08	0
OZ1090	Draft Bid Document Reviewed	1	OZ1080	04-Jan-08	04-Jan-08	0
OZ1100	Design Validated	1	OZ1090	07-Jan-08	07-Jan-08	0
OZ1110	Proposal Draft Bid Document Revised	1	OZ1090	07-Jan-08	07-Jan-08	6
OZ1120	Component Work Packages Negotiated	6	OZ1100	08-Jan-08	15-Jan-08	0
OZ1130	Bid Document Finalized	1	OZ1120, OZ1110	16-Jan-08	16-Jan-08	0
OZ1140	Submit Bid	0	OZ1130		16-Jan-08	0

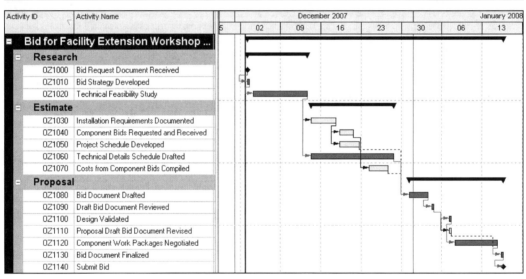

10 ACTIVITY NETWORK VIEW

The **Activity Network**, also known as the **PERT View**, displays activities as boxes connected by the relationship lines. See below:

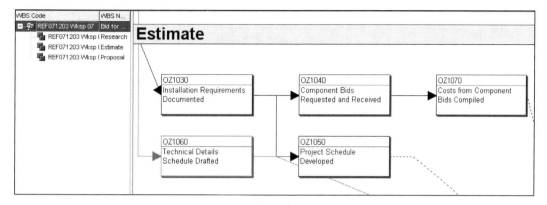

This chapter will not cover this subject in detail but will introduce the main features.

Many features available in the **Gantt Chart View** are also available in the **Activity Network** View, including:

Topic	Menu Command
• Viewing a Project Using the **Activity Network View**	• Select **View, Layout, Open…**, and select an Activity Network layout, or • Click on the **Layout Options** bar, just below the **Activities** toolbar on the left hand side of the screen, and select **Layout, Open…**, or • Select **View, Show on Top, Activity Network**, or • Click on the ⊞ button on the **Activities** toolbar.
• Adding and Deleting Activities in the **Activity Network** View	• Use the **Add** and **Delete** keys, or • Use the menu commands **Edit, Add** and **Delete**.
• Adding, Editing and Deleting Relationships	• Graphically drag from one activity to another, or • Use the **Predecessor** and **Successor** tabs in the **Activity Details** form.
• Formatting the Activity Boxes	• Select **View, Activity Network, Activity Network Options…**, or • Right-click in the **Activity Network** area and select **Activity Network Options…**.

10.1 Viewing a Project Using the Activity Network View

To view your project in the Networking View, **Open Layout** form:

- Select **View**, **Layout**, **Open...**, or

- Click on the **Layout Options** bar, just below the **Activities** toolbar on the left hand side of the screen and select **Layout**, **Open...**.

- Then select an Activity Network Layout, for example the **02 PERT Predecessor/Successor**, from the drop down list.

10.2 Adding, Deleting and Dissolving Activities in the Activity Network View

A **New Activity** may be created without a relationship by:

- Using the **Insert** key, or
- Selecting **Edit**, **Add**.

Activities may be deleted by:

- Using the **Delete** key, or
- Selecting **Edit**, **Delete**.

Activities may be **Dissolved**, which deletes the activity but maintains the logic with its predecessors and successors connected with FS relationships. Select **Edit**, **Dissolve**.

10.3 Adding, Editing and Deleting Relationships

Relationships may be added, deleted or edited using the following methods:

10.3.1 Graphically Adding a Relationship.

- To create a FS relationship, move the mouse to the right hand side of the predecessor activity box (the pointer will change to a ↴) and drag to the left hand side of the successor activity. Selecting the left or right hand side of the predecessor and successor activity bar will determine the type of relationship that is created.

- To edit the relationship, select the relationship (it will change to blue), double-click to open the **Edit Relationship** form and edit the relationship.

10.3.2 Using the Activity Details Form

Open the **Relationships** tab in the **Activity Details** form:

- When the **Activity Details** form is not displayed, select **View**, **Show on Bottom**, **Activity Details**.

- Add, edit and delete activities in the same way as with the Bar Chart.

10.4 Formatting the Activity Boxes

Activity Boxes may be formatted from the **Activity Network Options** form, which is displayed when an Activity Network view is displayed:

- Select **View**, **Activity Network**, **Activity Network Options…**, or
- Right-click in the PERT area and select **Activity Network Options…**:

  - ➢ A selection of box templates are available from the drop down box under the Activity Box Template title. These templates display different data in the box.
  - ➢ Click on 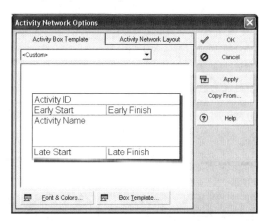 to format the text font and colors,
  - ➢ Click on Box Template… to edit the template or add and remove data items from the activity boxes.

- Click on the **Activity Network Layout** tab to display further options which are self-explanatory:

  - ➢ **Show progress** will place a diagonal line through an in-progress activity and a cross through a completed activity.
  - ➢ The **spacing factors** are a percentage of the box sizes.

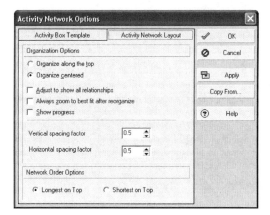

10.5 Reorganizing the Activity Network

Activities in the **Activity Network** view may be repositioned by dragging. There are 2 functions available when right clicking in the **Activity Network** view:

- **Reorganize** will reposition activities that have not been manually positioned and
- **Reorganize All** will reposition all activities including those that have been manually positioned.

10.6 Saving and Opening Activity network Positions

When activities are manually dragged into new positions on the screen for presentation purposes, it is possible to save and reload these positions at a later date:

- **View**, **Activity Network**, **Save Network Positions…** will create a *.anp file and
- **View**, **Activity Network**, **Open Network Positions…** will allow a *.anp file to be located and loaded which will reposition the activities as they were saved.

10.7 Early Date, Late Date and Float Calculations

To help understand the calculation of late and early dates, float and critical path, we will now manually work through an example. The boxes below represent activities.

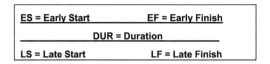

- The forward pass calculates the early dates: EF = ES + DUR – 1

Start the calculation from the first activity and work forward in time.

- The backward pass calculates the late dates: LS = LF – DUR + 1

Start the calculation at the last activity and work backwards in time.

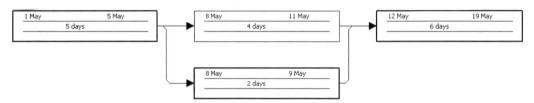

The **Critical Path** is the path where any delay causes a delay in the project and runs through the top row of activities.

Total Float is the difference between either the **Late Finish** and the **Early Finish** or the difference between the **Late Start** and the **Early Start** of an activity. The lower 2 days' activity has float of 9 – 7 = 2 days. None of the other activities have float.

Free Float is the difference between the Predecessor Early Finish and the Successor Early Start.

 An activity may not be on the Critical Path and may have more than one predecessor. A **Driving Relationship** is the predecessor that determines the Activity Early Start.

WORKSHOP 8

Scheduling Calculations

Background

We want to practice calculating early and late dates with a simple manual exercise.

Assignment

1. Calculate the early and late dates for the following activities, assuming a Monday-to-Friday working week and the first activity starting on 01 Oct 07.

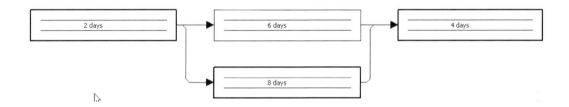

<	October 2007					>
Sun	Mon	Tue	Wed	Thr	Fri	Sat
	1	2	3	4	5	6
7	8	9	10	11	12	13
14	15	16	17	18	19	20
21	22	23	24	25	26	27

2. Apply the Activity Network View of your OzBuild schedule by clicking on the ⊞ icon.
3. Click on each node of the WBS and notice how only activities assigned to each node are displayed.

4. Click on the three Zoom icons 🔍 🔍 🔍 and notice their effect of the schedule.

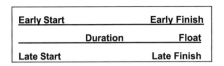

Forward Pass $EF = ES + DUR - 1$

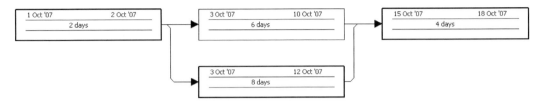

Backward Pass $LS = LF - DUR + 1$

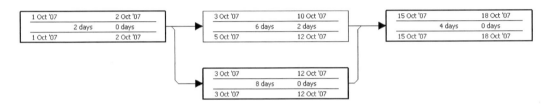

Below is how your schedule may look like when just the Research node is selected.

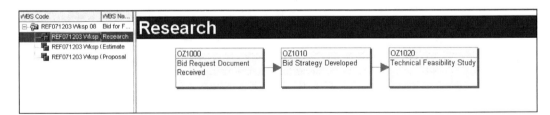

11 CONSTRAINTS

Constraints are used to impose logic on activities that may not be realistically scheduled with logic links. This chapter will deal with the following constraints in detail:

- **Start On or After**
- **Finish On or Before**

These are the minimum number of constraints that are required to effectively schedule a project.

Start On or After (also known as an "Early Start" or "Start No Earlier Than" constraint) is used when the start date of an activity is known and does not have a predecessor. Primavera Version 5.0 will not calculate the activity early start date prior to this date.

Finish On or Before (also known as "Late Finish" or "Finish No Later Than" constraint) is used when the latest finish date is stipulated. Primavera Version 5.0 will not calculate the activity's late finish date after this date.

The following table summarizes the methods used to assign Constraints to Activities or how to add notes to activities:

Topic	Notes for Creating a Constraint
• Setting a **Primary** and **Secondary** constraint with the **Activity Details** form.	Open the **Status** tab on the **Activity Details** form.
• Setting Constraints using columns.	The following columns may be displayed and the constraints assigned or edited: • Primary Constraint • Primary Constraint Date • Secondary Constraint • Secondary Constraint Date
• Adding Notes, these could be about constraints or other activity information.	The **Activity Details** form has a **Notebook** tab, which enables Notes to be assigned to **Notebook Topics**.

Primavera Version 5.0 will permit two constraints against a given activity. P3 and SureTrak also allow two constraints but Microsoft Project only permits one except when a Deadline constraint is applied.

A full list of **constraints** available in Primavera Version 5.0 are:

- **<None>**   This is the default for a new activity. An activity is scheduled to occur **As Soon As Possible** and does not have a Constraint Date.

- **Start On**   Also known as **Must Start On** and sets a date on which the activity will start. Therefore, the activity has no float. The early start and the late start dates are set to be the same as the Constraint Date.

- **Start On or Before**   Also known as **Start No Later Than** or **Late Start**, this constraint sets a date after which the activity will not start.

- **Start On or After**   Also known as **Start No Earlier Than** or **Early Start**, this constraint sets a date before which the activity will not start.

- **Finish On**   Also known as **Must Finish On**, this constraint sets a date on which the activity will finish and therefore has no float. The early finish and the late finish dates are set to be the same as the Constraint Date.

- **Finish On or Before**   Also known as **Finish No Later Than** or **Late Finish**, this sets a date after which the activity will not finish.

- **Finish On or After**   Also known as **Finish No Earlier Than** or **Early Finish**, this sets a date before which the activity will not finish.

- **As Late As Possible**   Also known as **Zero Free Float**. An activity will be scheduled to occur as late as possible and does not have any particular Constraint Date. The Early and Late dates have the same date.

- **Mandatory Start**   This relationship prevents float being calculated through this activity and effectively breaks a schedule into two parts.

- **Mandatory Finish**   This relationship prevents float being calculated through this activity and effectively breaks a schedule into two parts.

Earlier Than constraints operate on the **Early Dates**, and **Later Than** constraints operate on **Late Dates**. The picture below demonstrates how constraints calculate Total Float of activities (without predecessors or successors) against the first activity of 10 days' duration:

An activity assigned with an **As Late as Possible** constraint in Primavera Enterprise, Primavera Version 5.0, Primavera P3 and SureTrak software will schedule the activity so it absorbs only **Free Float** and will not delay the start of successor activities. In Microsoft Project, an activity assigned with an **As Late as Possible** constraint will be delayed to absorb the Total Float and delay all its successor activities, not just the activity with the constraint.

11.1 Assigning Constraints

11.1.1   Number of Constraints per Activity

Two constraints are permitted against each activity. They are titled Primary and Secondary Constraint. After the Primary has been set, a Secondary may be set when the combination is logical and therefore a reduced list of constraints is available from the Secondary Constraint list after the Primary has been set.

11.1.2   Setting a Primary Constraint Using the Activity Details Form

To assign a constraint using the **Activity Details** form:

- Select the activity requiring a constraint,
- Open the **Status** tab on the **Activity Details** form,
- Select the **Primary Constraint** type from the **Date** drop down list under **Primary**:

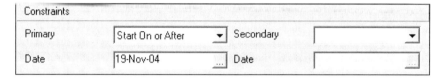

11.1.3   Setting a Secondary Constraint Using the Activity Details Form

To assign a constraint using the **Activity Details** form:

- Select the activity requiring a constraint,
- Open the **Status** tab on the **Activity Details** form,
- Select the **Secondary Constraint** type from the **Date** drop down list under **Secondary**:

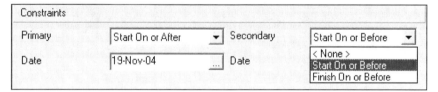

The picture above shows that after a **Primary Start On or After** constraint is set there are only two Secondary Constraints available. Once a constraint is set the date will have an asterisk "*" next to it.

> ➤ An Early Constraint, e.g., a Start On or After, will have the "*" next to the Early Start Date, and
> ➤ A Late Constraint, e.g., a Start On or After, will have the "*" next to the Late Start Date.

The author found when setting constraints that sometimes the constraint time was incompatible with either the Activity Calendar or Constraint Type. Therefore when setting constraints you may consider displaying the time by selecting **Edit**, **User Preferences…**, **Dates** tab to ensure the constraint time is compatible with the activity calendar.

11.1.4 Setting Constraints Using Columns

The following constraint columns may be displayed and the Constraints edited or assigned using these columns:

- Primary Constraint
- Primary Constraint Date
- Secondary Constraint
- Secondary Constraint Date

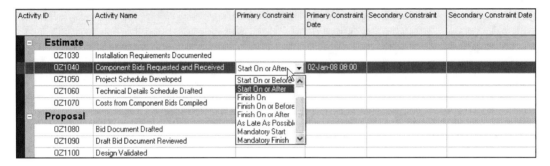

11.1.5 Typing in a Start Date

A **Start On or After** constraint may be assigned from the **Activity Information** form or the **Start Date** column by typing a date into the **Start** field:

- A **Start On or After** constraint is assigned by overtyping the Start date, and the **Confirmation** form will confirm this action.

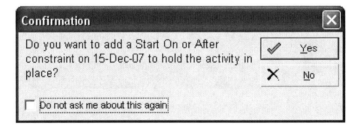

A date typed into the finish date will not assign a Finish Date constraint but will adjust the duration of the activity.

In Microsoft Project, a date typed into either the Start or Finish field will set a constraint; Primavera Version 5.0 does not operate in this way.

11.2 Project Must Finish By Date

It is also possible to impose an absolute finish date on the project using the **Project Workspace**, **Dates** tab:

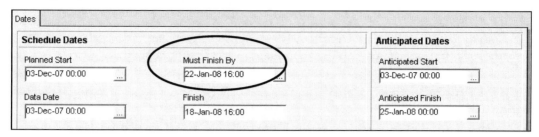

Imposing a **Must Finish By** date makes Primavera Version 5.0 calculate the late dates from the **Must finish by** date rather than the calculated early finish date. This will introduce positive float to activities when the calculated **Early finish** date is prior to the **Must Finish By** date.

This will also create negative float when the activity's calculated early finish date is after to the must finish by date, but it is not obvious where the negative float is being driven from as there are no constraints assigned to activities.

This function is similar to the P3 and SureTrak function but very different to the way Microsoft Project "Project Information, Finish Date" operates. After a Finish Date is set in Microsoft Project all new Tasks are set with an As Late As Possible constraint and the Start Date is calculated. Primavera Version 5.0 does not set As Late As Possible constraints after a **Must Finish by** date is set and the Project Start Date is still editable.

 It is not obvious where the float is being generated once a **Must finish by** date is imposed on a project. This is often confusing to people new to scheduling and it is recommended that you do not use a **Must finish by** date. Instead tie all activities to a **Finish milestone** which has a **Late finish** constraint.

11.3 Activity Notebook

It is often important to note why constraints have been set. Primavera Version 5.0 has functions that enable you to note information associated with an activity, including the reasons associated for establishing a constraint.

The **Activity Details** form has a **Notebook** tab, which enables Notes to be assigned to **Notebook Topics** and has some word processing-type formatting functions.

11.3.1   Creating Notebook Topics

Notebook Topics are created by selecting **Admin**, **Admin Categories...** and then selecting the **Notebook Topics** tab. After a topic has been created this topic may be made available to the following data fields by checking the appropriate box:

- EPS
- Project
- WBS, and
- Activities

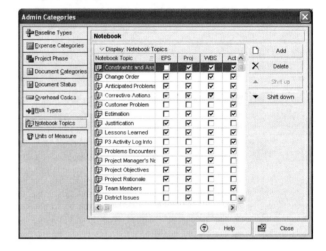

11.3.2   Adding Notes

To add a note to an activity:

- Select the **Notebook** tab in the **Activity Details** form,
- Add a **Topic**, and
- Type in the note.

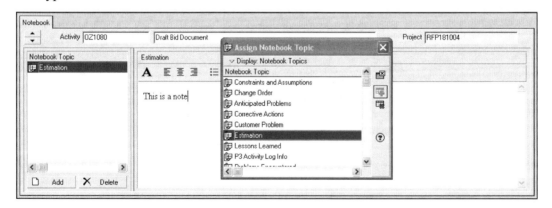

WORKSHOP 9

Constraints

Background
Management has provided further input to your schedule as the client has said that they require the submission on 22 Jan 08.

Assignment

1. Observe the calculated finish date and the critical path of the project before applying any constraints.

2. Display the **Date** and **Time** in the columns by selecting **Edit, User Preferences…,** **Dates** tab to ensure the constraint time is compatible with the activity calendar.

3. Display the **Total Float** column, **Total** and **Negative Float** bar for all activities.

4. The client has said that they require the submission on 22 Jan 08. Apply a **Finish On or Before** constraint and assign a constraint date of 22 Jan 08 to the **Submit Bid** activity and review float. Reschedule and there should be no change in the Total Float. Ensure you check the time of the constraint is the same as the start time of the activities.

5. Now return to the **Project Workspace**, **Dates** tab and assign a **Project Must Finish By** constraint of 22 Jan 08, return to the **Activity Workspace** and reschedule. All activities now have their float calculated to this date and have positive float.

6. Remove **Project Must Finish By** constraint of 22 Jan 08 and reschedule.

7. Due to the proximity to Christmas, management has requested that you delay the **Component Bids Requested and Received** until first thing in the New Year (02 Jan 08). Consensus is that a better response and sharper prices will be obtained after the Christmas rush. Record this in the activity notes.

   ➤ To achieve this, set a **Start On or After** constraint and a constraint date of 02 Jan 08 on the **Component Bids Requested and Received** activity.

   ➤ Now reschedule. Observe the impact on the critical path and end dates.

   You will notice that the Finish Constraint on the **Submit Bid** activity has created some negative float, which is displayed in the **Total float** column and the **Negative Float** bar, but not with the **Total Float** bar.

8. Add a Notebook Topic against the **Component Bids Requested and Received** activity indicating why there is a constraint of 2 Jan 08.

9. Open the **Bars** form and display the **Negative Float** bar.

10. After review, it is agreed that two days may be deducted from **Component Work Packages Negotiated** activity. Change the duration of this activity to four days and reschedule.

11. Remove the time by selecting **Edit, User Preferences…,** **Dates** tab.

Note: Depending on the calendar you initially copied your times may be different to the examples over the page.

ANSWER TO WORKSHOP 9

After applying a **Project Must Finish By** constraint and before delaying the **Request Component Bids** until 22 Jan 08:

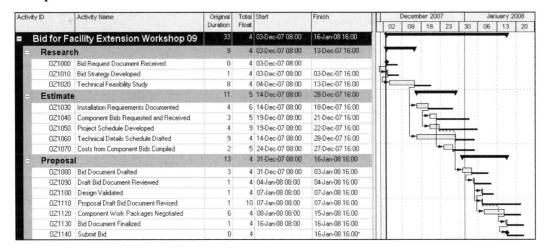

After delaying the **Request Component Bids** until 02 Jan 08 and displaying the Negative Float bar:

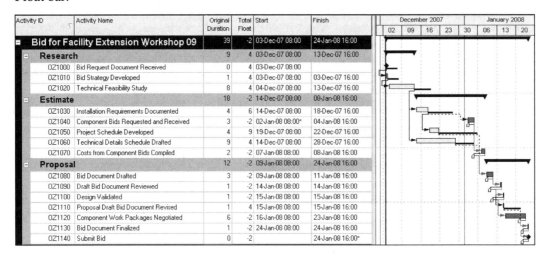

After trimming one day from **Negotiate Component Work Packages**:

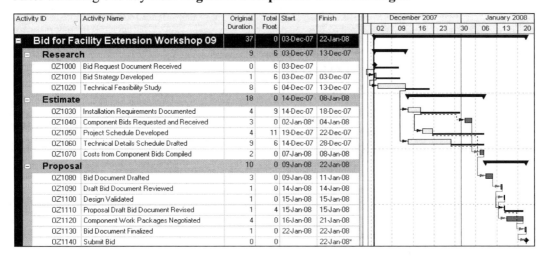

12 FILTERS

This chapter covers the ability of Primavera Version 5.0 to control which activities are displayed, both on the screen and in printouts, by using **Filters**.

12.1 Understanding Filters

Primavera Version 5.0 has an ability to display activities that meet specific criteria. You may want to see only the incomplete Activities, or the work scheduled for the next couple of months, or the Activities that are in progress.

Primavera Version 5.0 defaults to displaying all activities. There are a number of pre-defined filters available that you may use or edit. You may also create one or more of your own.

A filter may be applied to display or to highlight only those activities that meet a criteria.

There are three types of filters:

- **Default** filters which are supplied with the system and may not be edited or deleted but may be copied and then edited or modified.
- **Global** filters which are made available to anyone working in the database, and
- **User-Defined** filters which are defined by a user and available only to that user unless it is made into a **Global** filter.

Drop down or Auto filters as in Excel and Microsoft Project are not available.

Topic	Menu Command
• To apply, edit, create or delete a filter open the **Filters** form.	• Click on the 🖾 button, or • Select **View**, **Filters...**, or • Right-click in the columns area and select **Filters....**

12.2 Applying a Filter

12.2.1 Filters Form

Filters are applied from the **Filters** form which may be opened by:

- Clicking on the 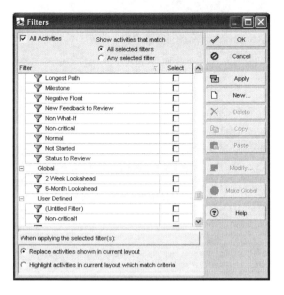 button, or
- Selecting **View**, **Filters…**, or
- Right-clicking in the columns area and selecting **Filters…**

12.2.2 Applying a Single Filter

A single filter is applied by:

- Checking the **Select** check box beside one filter, and
- Clicking on the Apply button.
- Only activities that comply to the filter criteria will be displayed when the **Replace activities shown in the current layout button** is checked. These activities will be highlighted in the **Select Activity** color when the **Highlight activities in current layout which match criteria** button is checked.

12.2.3 Applying a Combination Filter

A combination filter has two or more filters selected and has two options under **Show activities that match**:

- **All selected filters** where an activity to be displayed or highlighted has to match the criteria of all the filters, or
- **Any selected filters** where an activity to be displayed or highlighted has to match the criteria of only one filter.

 In many places in the software there will be an option of either clicking on the OK button or the Apply button:

- The Apply button applies the format however leaves the form open.
- The OK button applies the format and closes the form.

12.3 Creating a New Filter

Filters may be created from the **Filters** form by:

- Clicking on the [New...] button to open the **Filter** form and creating a new filter, or

- Copying an existing filter using the [Copy] and [Paste] buttons and then editing the new filter.

New filters will be created in the **User-Defined** filter area at the bottom of the list.

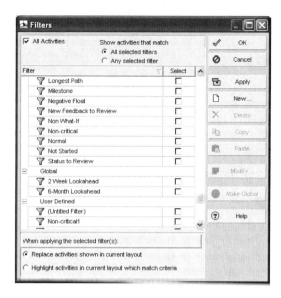

12.4 Modifying a Filter

There are a large number of options available to create a filter and from the following examples you should be able to experiment and add your own filters. To modify an existing filter, select it from the **Filters** form and click on the [Modify...] button.

12.4.1 One Parameter Filter

The example below is a filter to display incomplete activities:

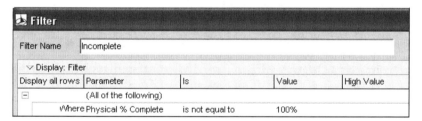

- **Parameter** is used to select any of the available database fields,

- Select one of the options from the **Is** drop down box:

- The parameter selected in the **Is** box determines if it is required to use only the **Value** (which is the same as the **Low Value** in P3 and SureTrak), or **Value** and **High Value**. **Value** and **High Value** are used with only the **is within range of** and **is not within range of** options.

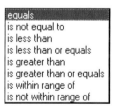

The example below is a filter to display in-progress activities using the **is within range of** and **Value** and **High Value** options:

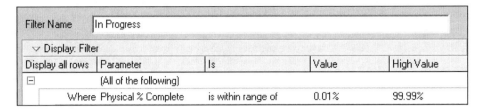

12.4.2 Two Parameter Filter

The example below is a filter to display incomplete activities on the critical path:

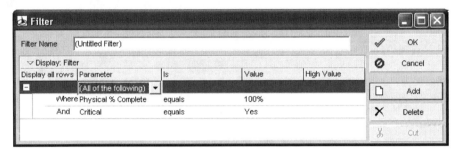

- The drop down box under **Parameter** has two options:
  - ➢ **(All of the following).** This is used when an activity must meet all of the parameters selected below.
  - ➢ **(Any of the following).** This is used when an activity must meet any of the parameters selected below.

  In the case of a filter that is to display the **Incomplete Critical Activities** it must be set to **All** and not **Any**, otherwise all of the **Incomplete** and all of the **Critical** activities will be displayed.

- The **Value** options on the second line are now **Yes** or **No**. The options for **Value** change with the data selected in the **Parameter** box.

12.4.3 Multiple Parameter Filter

The example below is a filter to display incomplete activities on the critical path with resources PEH and SEH:

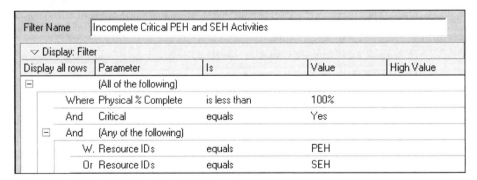

- In this example, **(Any of the following)** was selected from the **Parameters** drop down box which allows a nesting effect of filter parameters.

12.4.4   Editing and Organizing Filter Parameters

Lines in a filter are added, copied, pasted and deleted using the appropriate buttons in the **Filters** form.

The arrows allow the filter lines to be moved up and down and indented to the left and outdented to the right in a similar way to indenting and outdenting tasks in Microsoft Project.

A filter may be reorganized to delete the redundant filter lines using the **Optimize** command:

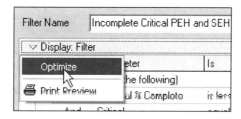

WORKSHOP 10

Filters

Background

Management has asked for reports on activities to suit their requirements.

Assignment
You will require the **OzBuild Bid** project to complete this exercise.

1. They would like to see all the critical activities
   - ➢ Ensure a column showing the **Total Float** is displayed, and
   - ➢ Apply the **Critical** activities filter.
   You will see only activities that are on the critical path and their associated summary activities.

2. They would like to see all the activities with float less than 5 days:
   - ➢ Create a new filter titled: **Float Less Than 5 Days**, and
   - ➢ Add the condition to display a total float of less than 5 days.
   - ➢ You should find that one extra activity **Proposal Draft Bid Document Revised** is now shown.

3. They would like to see all the activities that are critical and contain the word "Bid."
   - ➢ Copy the **Critical** filter,
   - ➢ Edit the filter title to read: **Critical or Contains "Bid,"**
   - ➢ Add the condition: **Or** Name (Activity Name) contains **Bid,** and
   - ➢ Apply the filter.
   There will be additional activities shown.

4. Now apply the **All Activities** filter.

ANSWERS TO WORKSHOP 10

After applying the **Critical** filter:

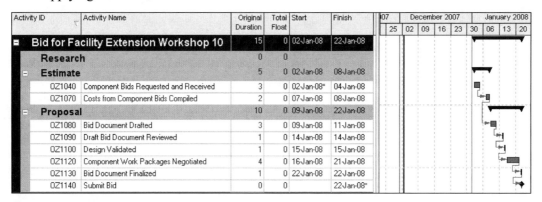

Creating the **Float Less Than 5 Days** filter:

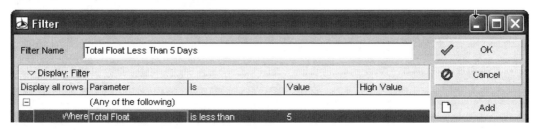

After applying the **Critical or Contains "Bid"** filter:

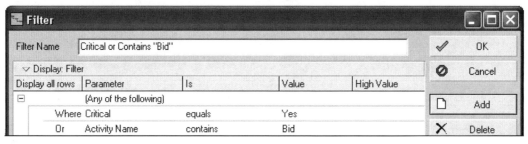

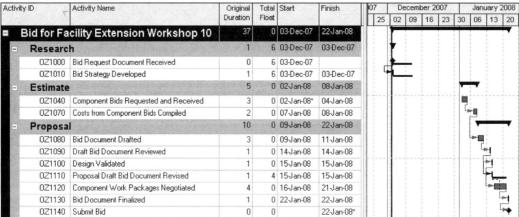

13 GROUP, SORT AND LAYOUTS

Group & Sort allows activities to be sorted and organized under other parameters such as **Dates** and **Resources** or user-defined **Activity Codes**. This function is similar to **Organize** in P3 and SureTrak and **Grouping** in Microsoft Project.

Layouts is a function in which the formatting of parameters such as the **Group & Sort**, **Columns** and **Bars** is saved and is similar to **Layouts** in P3 and SureTrak or **Views** in Microsoft Project. A **Layout** may be edited, saved or reapplied at a later date and may have a **Filter** associated with it.

This chapter will cover the following topics:

Topic	Notes on the Function
• Reformat the Grouping and Sorting of activities by opening the **Group and Sort** form:	• Click on the ⬚ button, or • Select **View, Group and Sort….**
• Group and Sort Projects at Enterprise Level	Projects may be Grouped and Sorted at Enterprise level in a similar method to activities in a project.
• Create or edit a Layout	Select either: • From the menu **View, Layout, Save As…,** or • From the Layout bar **Layout, Save As….**

The **Layout** bar location is indicated in the picture below:

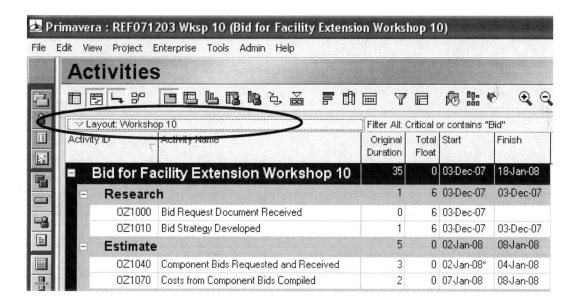

13.1 Group and Sort Activities

The **Group & Sort** function has been used in this book to group activities under WBS bands.

To reformat the Grouping and Sorting of activities the **Group and Sort** form is opened by:

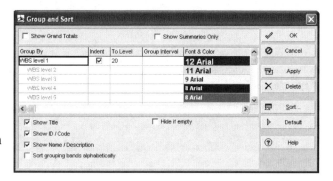

- Clicking on the ▤ button, or
- Selecting **View**, **Group and Sort…**.

There are a number of options in this form:

13.1.1 Show Grand Totals

This is the same as inserting a Project band in P3 or SureTrak with Organize or displaying a **Project summary task** in Microsoft Project.

This displays a Summary band for the project and adds up all the costs and hours for a project, displays the earliest and latest dates and a summary duration for the whole project. This feature is very useful when the project is not organized by WBS and there is therefore no project total line.

Activity ID	Activity Name	Original Duration	Actual Labor Cost	Remaining Labor Cost	Start	Finish
■ **Total**		37	$3,220	$45,920	03-Dec-07 A	22-Jan-08
0Z1000	Bid Request Document Received	0	$0	$0	03-Dec-07 A	
0Z1010	Bid Strategy Developed	1	$1,300	$0	03-Dec-07 A	03-Dec-07 A
0Z1150	New Activity	1	$0	$0	03-Dec-07 A	03-Dec-07 A
0Z1020	Technical Feasibility Study	8	$1,920	$4,800	04-Dec-07 A	17-Dec-07
0Z1030	Installation Requirements Documented	4	$0	$5,120	18-Dec-07	21-Dec-07
0Z1060	Technical Details Schedule Drafted	9	$0	$9,360	18-Dec-07	02-Jan-08
0Z1050	Project Schedule Developed	4	$0	$2,880	22-Dec-07	28-Dec-07
0Z1040	Component Bids Requested and Received	3	$0	$3,840	02-Jan-08*	04-Jan-08
0Z1070	Costs from Component Bids Compiled	2	$0	$1,280	07-Jan-08	08-Jan-08
0Z1080	Bid Document Drafted	3	$0	$6,720	09-Jan-08	11-Jan-08

13.1.2 Show Summaries Only

This option hides all the activities and displays only the WBS or Codes that have been used to summarize the activities:

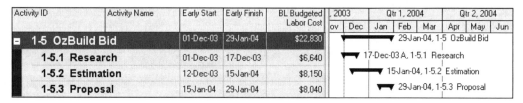

13.1.3 Group By Options

The Group By box has several options:

- **Group By and Indent**

When a hierarchical code such as a **WBS** and the **Indent** is selected, the subsequent bands are completed by the software and there are no other options available. The WBS is then displayed hierarchically:

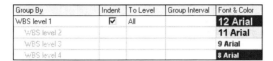 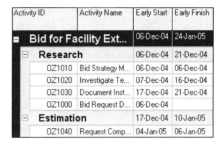

When a hierarchical code such as a **WBS** is selected and the **Indent** is **NOT** selected on a line then the subsequent bands are **NOT** completed by the software and other bands may be selected. The WBS is not displayed hierarchically:

 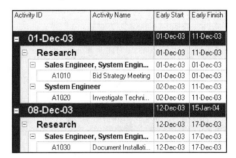

- **To Level**

The **To Level** option decides how many levels of the hierarchical code structure such as the WBS will be displayed. All activities are displayed under the lowest level of WBS, as chosen from the **To Level** drop down box.

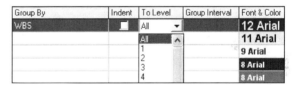

- **Group Interval**

This option is available with some fields such as **Total Float**, where the interval may be typed in, and **Date** fields, where a drop down box allows the selection of the time interval used to group activities:

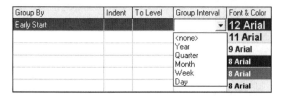 

- **Font and Color**

Double-click on these boxes to open the **Edit Font and Color** form to change the font and color of each band.

- **Show Title**, **Show ID / Code** and **Show Name / Description**

These options are set for each band. These options format the display of the band title. It is not possible to uncheck all the options as there then would not be a title in the band. The options change depending on the data displayed in the band:

> With all options checked

> With some options unchecked

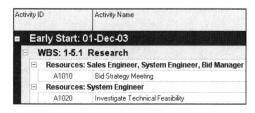 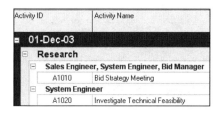

- **Sort Banding Alphabetically**

When a hierarchical code is selected, the bands are sorted by the **Code Value**. If this box is checked, the bands will be sorted alphabetically by the **Code Description**.

- **Hide if empty**

Check this box to hide bands that have not been assigned an activity.

13.1.4 Sorting

The [Sort...] button opens the **Sort** form where the order of the activities in each band may be specified. This order may be easily overridden by clicking on the column titles to reorder activities.

13.1.5   Reorganize Automatically

Primavera Version 4.1 introduced a function titled Reorganize Automatically, which is similar to the P3 and SureTrak function but applies to all Layouts, not just the selected Layout. Select **Edit, User Preferences…** to open the **User Preferences** form and click on the **Application** tab.

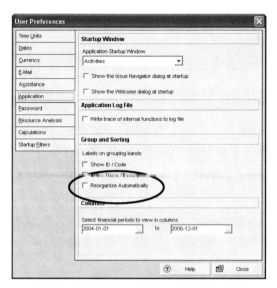

When the **Reorganize Automatically** box is checked, all views will reorganize automatically when data fields are changed that are used in the layout such as Grouping and Sorting.

It is often better to disable **Reorganize Automatically** when data is being edited that is used in the grouping of data in a Layout which will prevent the activities moving to their new position in the Layout until all data has been edited.

To reorganize a view, select **Tools**, **Reorganize Now** or **Shift+F2**.

The other Group and Sort options in the **Application** tab apply to views that do not have a Group and Sort form.

13.2 Group and Sort Projects at Enterprise Level

This topic is not covered in detail in this book; however, it functions in a similar way to the Grouping and Sorting of activities.

When a database is opened, the projects are by default displayed under the Enterprise Project Structure (EPS) in the Projects Workspace.

The projects may be Grouped and Sorted under a number of different headings by:

- Selecting **Layout: Projects**, **Group and Sort By**, or
- Right-clicking and selecting **Group and Sort ...**, or
- Selecting **View**, **Group and Sort By**.

Then selecting the option from the drop down list.

13.3 Understanding Layouts

There are several types of Layouts that may be displayed in either the top and/or bottom pane. Layouts are used to display alternate views of data and are similar to **Screens** in Microsoft Project. P3 and SureTrak have two types of layouts, Gantt and PERT.

A standard load of Primavera Version 5.0 is supplied with a number of predefined Layouts which are defined by default **Global Layouts** and any user on the system may apply these. These layouts may be copied and shared with other users or be available only to the current user in a similar way as filters.

Layouts are not exported with an XER file.

13.4 Applying an Existing Layout

Layouts may be applied from the **Open Layout** form by:

- Selecting the **Open** option from the **Layout Options** bar:

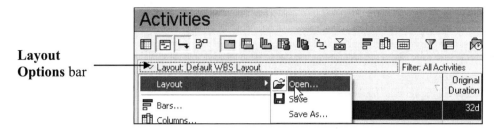

- Or, by selecting **View, Layout, Open…**.

When a Layout has been edited by changing any parameter, such as column formatting, a form will be displayed allowing the confirmation of the changes that have been made to the layout.

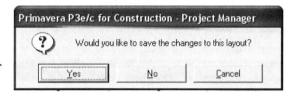

The **Open Layout** form will be displayed and an alternative layout may be selected from the list:

➢ Click on the ⌗ Apply button to apply the layout. This will leave the form open but allow the effect to be viewed, or

➢ Click on the 🖾 Open button to apply the layout and close the form:

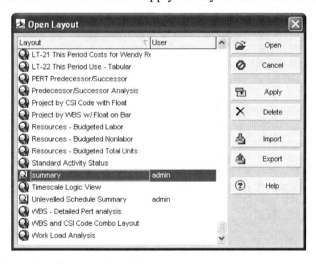

Clicking on the column headers reorders the Layouts.

13.5 Creating a New Layout

A new layout may be created by saving an existing layout with a new name and editing it. To create a new Layout:

- Apply the layout that closely matches the requirements of the new layout and apply.
- Select either:
  - ➤ From the menu **View**, **Layout**, **Save As…**, or
  - ➤ From the Layout Options bar **Layout**, **Save As…**:

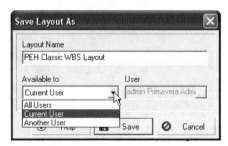

- Type in a new **Layout Name** and select who you wish the layout to be available to.
- Click on the ⟦🖫 Save⟧ button.

This layout may now be edited and the edits saved by selecting:
- ➤ From the menu **View**, **Layout**, **Save**, or
- ➤ From the Layout bar **Layout**, **Save**.

13.6 Editing a Layout

13.6.1 Layout Types

A layout is comprised of a **Top Pane** and a **Bottom Pane**. Each **Pane** may be assigned a **Layout Type**. The following is a list of the **Layout Types** and the panes they may be applied to:

Layout Name	Available in Top Pane	Available in Bottom Pane
• Gantt Chart	Yes	Yes
• Activity Details		Yes
• Activity Table	Yes	Yes
• Activity Network	Yes	
• Trace Logic		Yes
• Activity Usage Profile		Yes
• Resource Usage Spreadsheet		Yes
• Resource Usage Profile		Yes
• Activity Usage Spreadsheet	Yes	Yes

It is important to note that the available layouts vary depending on the Workspace open.

The **Activity Usage Profile**, **Resource Usage Spreadsheet**, **Resource Usage Profile**, **Activity Usage Spreadsheet** views display resource information.

13.6.2 Changing Layout Types in Panes

To change a **Layout Type** in a pane select from the menu:

- **View**, **Show on Top**, or

- **View**, **Show on Bottom**.

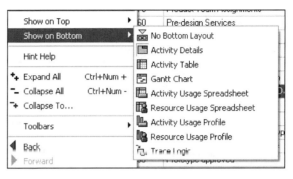

Then select the Layout Type required from the list.

13.7 Layout Types

Each Layout Type has a number of options and the formatting of these has been discussed in earlier chapters.

13.7.1 Gantt Chart

The Gantt Chart has two sides:

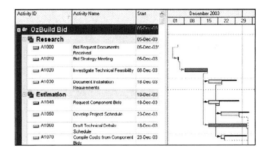

- The left hand side where the columns are displayed may be formatted with the **Columns**, **Sorting** and **Grouping** functions.

- The right hand side may be formatted using the **Timescale**, **Bars** and **Gridlines** functions.

13.7.2 Activity Details

These may be displayed at any time in the Bottom Pane with any of the tabs hidden or displayed.

13.7.3 Activity Table

This layout is the same as the left hand side of the Gantt Chart and has no Bars and Timescale on the right hand side.

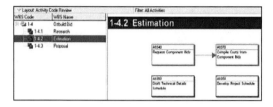

13.7.4 Activity Network

Like the Gantt Chart it has two panes:

- The **left hand** pane displays the WBS:
  - ➢ This side may not be formatted except by adjusting the width of the columns.
  - ➢ The selection of a WBS Node acts like a filter and will only display activities that are associated with the selected WBS Node and lower level member WBS Nodes. This allows the relationships between activities within one WBS Node to be checked.
- The **right hand** pane displays the activity data in boxes and is organized under headings:
  - ➢ The Activity Boxes may be formatted as described in the **NETWORK VIEW** chapter.
  - ➢ The activities may be Grouped which is covered in the **Grouping** section of this chapter.

13.7.5 Trace Logic

The Trace Logic options allow the selection of the number of predecessor and successor levels.

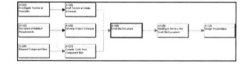

This is achieved by displaying the **Activity Table** in the top view and selecting **View**, **Show on Bottom**, **Trace Logic**.

To select the number of levels of predecessors to be displayed you are required to open the **Trace Logic Options** form. The form is then opened by either:

- Right-clicking in the lower pane and selecting **Trace Logic Options....** or
- Selecting View, Bottom Layout Options….

13.7.6 Copying a Layout To and From Another Database

A layout may be copied to another database by using the Import and Export function from the **Open Layout** form. The layout is saved in a **Primavera Layout File *.PLF** format as a stand alone file and is then imported into another database.

WORKSHOP 11

Organizing Your Data

Background

Having completed the schedule, you may report the information with different Layouts.

Assignment

Display your project in the following formats, noting the different ways you may represent the same data.

1. Ensure you have applied the all Activity Filter, use the ⧩ button to open the **Filter** form.
2. Hide and display the relationships, use the ⬎ button.
3. Display the **Activity Network**, use the button.
4. Zoom in, out and best fit using the buttons.
5. Scroll up and down or click on the **WBS** Nodes on the left hand side of the screen. You will notice that only the Activities associated with the highlighted WBS are displayed.
6. Display the **Activity Table** by clicking on the button.
7. Hide and display the **Bottom** pane by clicking on the button.
8. With the bottom pane displayed click on the to show the **Trace Logic** form; experiment with the form.
9. Right-click in the **Trace Logic** form, select **Trace Logic Options...** and change the number of Predecessor and Successor Levels displaying 1, 2 and 3 levels and note the change in the layout. Click on the predecessors and successors in each option.
10. Click on the button to display the **Activity Details** form.

(Continued)

11. Create a new layout titled **OzBuild Workshop 11 - With Float**, make it available to only yourself, displaying the columns and formatting the bars as below:

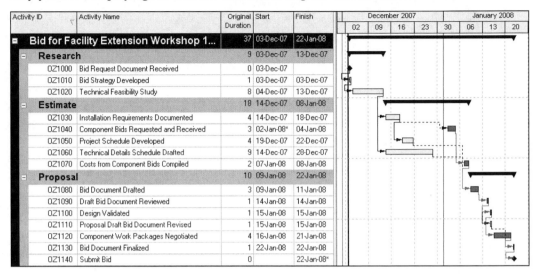

12. Save this layout and then make a copy of it titled **OzBuild Workshop 11 - Without Float**, make it available to only yourself, displaying the columns and formatting the bars as below:

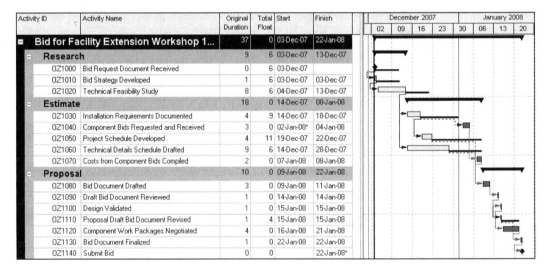

14 PRINTING

This is the stage at which the schedule is printed so people may review and comment on it. This chapter will examine some of the options for printing your project schedule.

There are two tools available to output your schedule to a printer:

- The **Printing** function prints the data displayed in the current Layout.

- The **Reporting** function prints reports, which are independent of the current Layout. Primavera Version 5.0 supplies a number of predefined reports that may be tailored to suit your own requirements. Reports will not be covered in this book.

 It is recommended that you consider using a product such as Adobe Acrobat to output your schedule in pdf format. You then will be able to e-mail high quality outputs that recipients may print or review on screen without needing a copy of Primavera Version 5.0.

14.1 Printing

When a Layout is split, the lower pane may also be printed unless it is a Details pane. This is similar to P3 and SureTrak, but different from Microsoft Project where only the active View may be printed.

Print settings are applied to the individual Layouts and the settings are saved with that Layout.

There are three commands used when printing:

- **File**, **Page Setup...**
- **File**, **Print Preview**
- **File**, **Print...** or **Ctrl+P**

Each of these functions will be discussed only for printing the Gantt Chart. Printing all other Layouts is a similar process. Some Layouts will have different options due to the nature of the data being displayed. These other options should be easily mastered once the basics covered in this chapter are understood.

 Each time you report to the client or management, it is recommended that you save a copy of your printout or report. A pdf is an excellent method of saving this data. This allows you to reproduce these reports at any time in the future and keep an electronic copy available for dispute resolution purposes.

It is good practice to keep a copy of the project after each update, especially if litigation is a possibility. A project may be copied either by creating a Baseline, by exporting the project as an XER file or by using the project copy function, then making the **Status** inactive in the **General** tab of the **Projects Workspace**. It is important to note that although the project may be marked as inactive it may still be opened and modified.

14.2 Print Preview

To preview the printout, use Primavera Version 5.0's **Print Preview** option. Select **File**, **Print Preview**:

The following paragraphs describe the functions of the icons at the top of the Print Preview screen from left to right:

- The ⊞ button opens the **Page Setup** form to be covered in the next paragraph.

- The ▣ opens the **Print Setup** form where the printer and paper size etc may be selected.

- The 🖨 button opens the **Print** form where the printer, the pages to be printed, and the number of copies to be printed may be selected.

- The ⟨ℚ⟩ button opens the **Publish to HTML** form and saves the view in HTML format where both the tables and bar charts are converted.

- The first six icons on the left, ⏮ ◀ ▶ ▲ ▼ ⏭, allow scrolling when a printout has more than one page.

- The magnifying glass ⊕ ⊖ buttons zoom in and out. You may also click in the Preview screen to zoom in.

- The ⊠ button closes the preview screen.

14.3 Page Setup

To open the **Page Setup…** form:

- Click the ⊞ button on the **Print Preview** toolbar, or

- Select **File**, **Page Setup…** to display the **Page Setup** form:

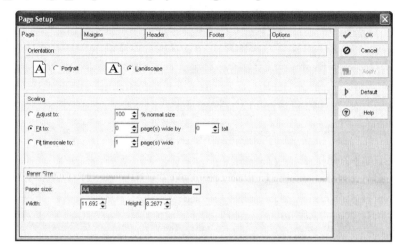

The **Page Setup** form contains the following tabs:

- Page
- Margins
- Header
- Footer
- Options

When changes are made to a header or footer then the buttons on the right hand side may be used:

- [Apply] – Applies the changes so they are visible without closing the form.
- [Default] – Resets the Page Setup settings to default.
- [OK] – Accepts the changes and closes the form.
- [Cancel] – Cancels the changes and closes the form.

14.3.1 Page Tab

The Primavera Version 5.0 options in the **Page** tab are:

- **Orientation** allows the selection of **Portrait** or **Landscape** printing.

- **Scaling** allows you to adjust the number of pages the printout will fit onto:

  ➢ **Adjust to:** – allows you to choose the scale of the printout that both the bars and column text are scaled to. Primavera Version 5.0 will calculate the number of pages across and down for the printout.

  ➢ **Fit to:** – allows you to choose the number of pages across and down and Primavera Version 5.0 will scale the printout to fit.

  ➢ **Fit timescale to:** – allows the user to select the number of pages the Gantt chart is scaled over but leaves the font of the columns un-scaled. This will often be the best setting with 1 page(s) wide selected. This functions in a similar way as P3 and SureTrak functions.

- Pages are numbered across first and then down, and does not follow the P3 and SureTrak convention of numbers down and letters across or the Microsoft Project convention of numbering pages down and then across.

14.3.2 Margins Tab

With this option, you may choose the margins around the edge of the printout.

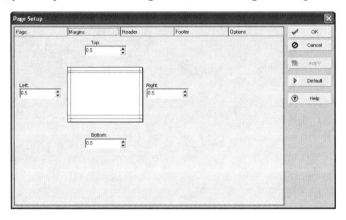

Type in the margin size around the page. It is best to allow a wider margin for an edge that is to be bound or hole punched. 1" or 2.5cm is usually sufficient.

14.3.3 Header and Footer Tabs

Headers appear at the top of the screen above all schedule information and footers are located at the bottom. Both the headers and footers are formatted in the same way. We will discuss the setting-up of footers in this chapter.

Click on the **Footer** tab from the **Page Setup** form. This will display the settings of the default footers and headers. You should modify the output to suit your requirements.

Slide for manually sizing the sections

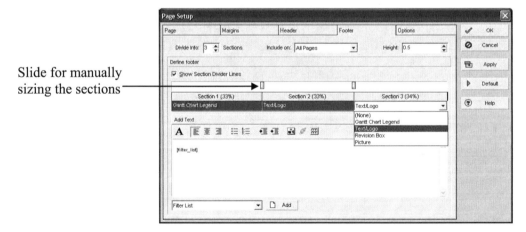

- **Divide Into:** – determines the number of sections the Header/Footer is divided into.
- **Include on:** – determines on which pages the Header/Footer is to appear: First Page, Last Page, All Pages or No Pages.
- **Height:** – enables the user to select the height of the Header/Footer.

- **Define Footer**
  - ➢ **Show Section Divider Lines** – check box, hides or displays the divider lines between the sections.
  - ➢ The sections may be sized by manually moving the divider lines with the mouse and the slide underneath the **Show Section Divider Lines**.

- **Section Content**

  The Section content may be selected by clicking on the ▾ button under the **Section** title, a subject type to be displayed may be selected.

  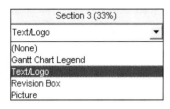

  - ➢ **(None)** – leaves the section blank.
  - ➢ **Gantt Chart Legend** – displays all the bars checked in the display column of the **Bars** form and only the fonts may be edited by clicking on the little font button at the bottom of the form.
  - ➢ **Text/Logo** – allows many types of data to be displayed including text, a data item selected from the drop down box, the fonts may be formatted by clicking on the formatting buttons ⎡A ≡ ≡ ≡ ≔ ≔ ⇥ ⇤⎤, a Logo inserted by clicking on the 🖼 button, tables added by clicking on the ⊞ button, and a Hyperlink added by clicking on the link button 🖉 which opens the Hyperlink form.
  - ➢ **Revision Box** has a **Revision Box Title:** – the following information may be entered manually Date, Revision, Checked, Approved.
  - ➢ **Picture** – allows a picture to be placed in the footer, its size can be manually adjusted of to fit the space or automatically adjusted by checking the **Resize picture to fit the selection** box.

14.4 Options Tab

The Options tab has three sections:

- **Timescale Start:** and **Timescale Finish:**

  These options allows the start and finish point of the timescale to be set.

  Click on the button and select a date from the drop down list. A **Custom Date...** may be selected from the menu and a calendar is opened to select the date.

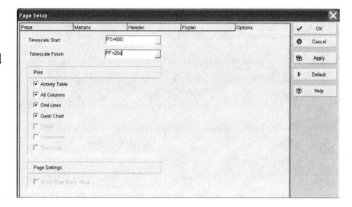

A lag from the nominated dates may be specified, see the picture to the above. This function work in a similar way to P3 and SureTrak

- The **Print** options alter depending on the Layout. The checkboxes allow a selection of the data to be printed.

- The **Break Page Every Group** puts a page break at each change of heading in the first group in the **Group and Sort** form.

14.5 Print Form

The **Print** form is be opened by:

- Selecting **File**, **Print...**, or

- Executing the keystrokes **Ctrl+P**, or

- Clicking on the print icon in the **Print Preview** screen.

14.6 Print Setup Form

The **Print Setup** form is be opened by:

- Selecting **File**, **Print Setup...**, or

- Clicking on the print icon in the **Print Preview** screen.

WORKSHOP 12

Printing

Background

We want to issue a report for comment by management.

Assignment

Open your **OzBuild Bid** project from the previous workshop to complete the following steps:

1. Apply the OzBuild Workshop 11 - With Float layout.
2. Select **File**, **Print Preview** and click on the ⊞ icon to open the **Page Setup** form.
3. In the **Page** tab select the printout to fit on one page by one page in landscape and your paper size; A4 or Letter.
4. In the **Margins** tab set all the settings to 0.5" or 12mm, except for the **Top:** settings which should to be set to 0.75" or 19mm to allow space for binding.
5. In the **Header** tab:
   ➢ **Divide Into:** 1 **Sections**
   ➢ Select **Text/Logo** under Section 1, insert the **[project_name]** Project Name from the drop down box at the bottom left hand side of the form, click on the ▭ Add button and align in center in Arial 12 Bold.
6. In the **Footer** tab:
   ➢ **Divide Into:** 3 **Sections**
   ➢ Section 1 – Text/Logo – Date aligned to the left **[date]** in Arial 10.
   ➢ Section 2 – Text/Logo Page Number **[page_number]**, Total Pages **[total_pages]** align in center in Arial 10.
   ➢ Section 3 – Gantt Chart Legend.
   ➢ Adjust the **Height:** of the footer as necessary.
7. In the **Options** tab set the **Timescale Start:** from the Project Start minus 5 days and **Timescale Finish:** be Project Finish plus 5 days, see the Options tab picture on the previous page. Show the Activity Table, All Columns, Grid Line and Gantt Chart.
8. Compare your result with the picture on the next page.

ANSWERS TO WORKSHOP 12

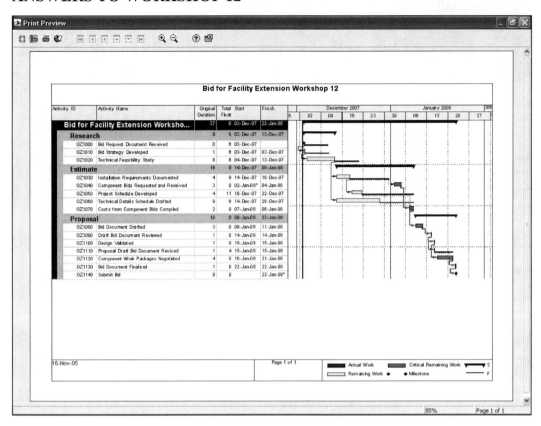

15 TRACKING PROGRESS

The process of Tracking Progress is used once you have completed the plan, or have completed sufficient iterations to reach an acceptable plan, and the project is progressing. Now the important phase of regular monitoring begins. Monitoring is important to help catch problems as early as possible, and thus minimize their impact on the successful completion of the project.

The main steps for monitoring progress are:

- Saving a **Baseline** schedule, also known as **Target**. This schedule holds the dates against which progress is compared. An existing project may be used or an existing project may be copied and used as a baseline.
- Recording or marking-up progress as of a specific date, often titled the **Data Date**, **Status Date**, **Current Date** and **As-Of-Date**.
- **Updating** or **Statusing** the schedule with **Actual Start** and **Actual Finish** dates where applicable, and adjusting the activity durations and percent complete.
- Comparing and Reporting actual progress against planned progress and revising the schedule, if required.

Comparing the status of an activity against more than one Baseline is useful, for example:

- The original plan, which could be Baseline 1, to see the slippage against the original plan.
- Last Period, which could be Baseline 2, to see the changes since the last update.

By the time you get to this phase you should have a schedule that compares your original plan with the current plan, showing where the project is ahead or behind. If you are behind, you should be able to use this schedule to plan appropriate remedial measures to bring the project back on target.

This chapter will cover the following topics:

Topic	Menu Command
• Saving and Deleting and Setting a **Baseline**	To save a Baseline, select **Project**, **Maintain Baselines...** to display the **Maintain Baselines** form
• Assigning a Baseline project	The baselines are assigned from the **Project**, **Assign Baselines...** form
• Recording Progress	Guidelines on how to record progress.
• **Retained Logic** and **Progress Override**	Open the **Advanced Schedule Options** form by selecting **Tools, Schedule...** and clicking on the ▷ Advanced... button.
• Setting the **Current Data Date** and **Scheduling** the project	Open the **Schedule** form by: • Selecting **Tools, Schedule...**, or • Pressing the **F9** key, or • Clicking on the 🖼 button.

15.1 Setting the Baseline

Setting the Baseline makes a complete copy of a project, including relationships, notebook entries and codes. Up to 50 baselines per project may be saved in a database.

- The number of baselines that may be saved is set up in the **Admin Preferences** form by selecting **Admin**, **Admin Preferences…**, **Data Limits** and setting the number in the **Maximum baselines per project** box.

- Up to three baselines may be compared at one time to the current project. Therefore, up to three baseline bars and three sets of baseline dates may be displayed and printed.

- A baseline project may be restored back into a database as a normal project. It may be edited and resaved as a baseline project.

Once the Baseline is set, it is possible to compare the progress with the original plan. You will be able to see if you are ahead or behind schedule and by how much. The Baseline schedule should be established before you status the schedule for the first time.

15.1.1   Saving a Baseline

To save a Baseline, select **Project**, **Maintain Baselines…** to display the **Maintain Baselines** form:

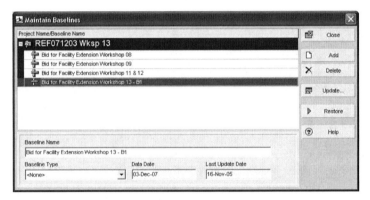

- To create a new baseline click on the [Add] button to open the **Add New Baseline** form:

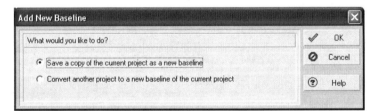

- Select either of the two options in the form:
  - ➢ **Save a copy of the current project as a new baseline** will make a copy of the currently open project, adds a - B1 after the name and return you to the **Baselines** form, or
  - ➢ **Convert another project to a new baseline of the current project** will open the **Select Project** form where another project may be selected to be a baseline. This project will then move from the current projects window into the **Maintain Baselines** form.

- Assign a **Baseline Type** from the drop down box. Baseline Types are defined in the **Admin**, **Admin Categories** form, **Baseline Type** tab.

15.1.2   Deleting a Baseline

To delete a project baseline from the database:

- Open the **Baselines** form by selecting **Project**, **Maintain Baselines…**,
- Select the baseline project to be deleted, and
- Click on the ⌷✕ Delete⌷ button.

15.1.3   Restoring a Baseline to the Database as an Active Project

To restore a project back to the database so it may be edited or used as a current project:

- Open the **Maintain Baselines** form by selecting **Project**, **Maintain Baselines…**,
- Ensure the baseline is not assigned as a project baseline in the **Baselines** form,
- Select the baseline project to be restored, and
- Click on the ⌷▷ Restore⌷ button.

15.1.4   Setting the Baseline Project

The baselines are assigned from the **Project**, **Assign Baselines…** form:

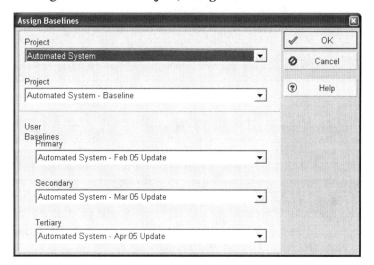

- Select from the dropdown box under **Project** which of the open projects is to have a baseline set.
- Select which from the drop down boxes under **User Baselines** which are to be the **Primary**, **Secondary** and **Tertiary** Baseline.
- The **Project Baseline** may be used for calculating **Earned Value**. See **Admin**, **Admin Preferences…**, **Earned Value** tab for other Earned Value options.
- Earned Value calculations may be performed using either the **Primary Baseline** values or the **Baseline** values, the values from the current project. Select the **Settings** tab in the **Projects** workspace. This is similar to the P3 option **Tools**, **Options**, **Earned Value**.

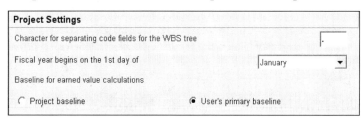

NOTE: When no Baseline is set the project will assume the current schedule calculated dates as the Baseline dates.

15.1.5 Update Baselines

The new Primavera Version 5.0 **Update Baseline** function is similar to the P3 function and allows the Baseline schedule to be updated with data from the current schedule or activities deleting that are no longer in the current schedule without restoring the Baseline schedule:

- Select **Project, Maintain Baselines…**and select the [Update…] button to open the **Update Baseline** form:

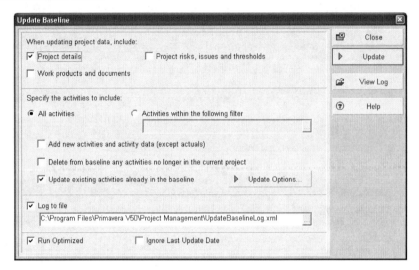

- When **Run Optimized** is not checked then an error log is kept during the updating process.
- **Ignore Last Update Date** may be used when a project has project is updated at different times and the last Baseline Update may not be valid for the current schedule although the Baseline has been updated with more recent data..
- Select [▷ Update Options…] to open the **Update Baseline Options** form to select which data items are updated.

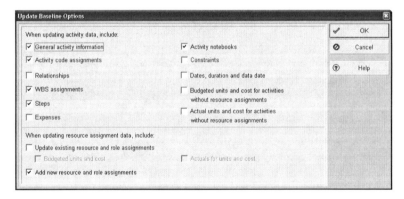

There is a new project privilege allowing a user to run Update Project Baselines.

15.1.6 Displaying the Baseline Data

The Baseline Dates may be displayed by:

- Displaying the **Baseline** columns:

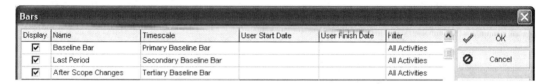

- Showing a baseline bar on the Bar Chart by selecting the appropriate bars in the **Bars** form:

Display	Name	Timescale	User Start Date	User Finish Date	Filter		
✓	Baseline Bar	Primary Baseline Bar			All Activities	✓	OK
✓	Last Period	Secondary Baseline Bar			All Activities	⊘	Cancel
✓	After Scope Changes	Tertiary Baseline Bar			All Activities		

15.2 Practical Methods of Recording Progress

Normally a project is statused once a week, bi-weekly, or monthly. Very short projects could be statused daily or even by the shift or hour. As a guide, a project would typically be statused between 12 and 20 times in its lifetime. A high risk project should be statused more often than a low risk project. Progress is recorded on or just after the **Data Date** and the scheduler updates the schedule upon the receipt of the information.

The following information is typically recorded for each activity when statusing a project:

- The activity start date and time if required,
- The number of days/hours the activity has remaining or when the activity is expected to finish,
- The percentage complete, and
- If complete, the activity finish date and time, if required.

A marked-up copy recording the progress of the current schedule is often produced prior to updating the project. Ideally, the mark-up should be prepared by a physical inspection of the work or by a person who intimately knows the work, although that is not always possible. It is good practice to keep this marked-up record for your own reference. Ensure that you note the date of the mark-up (i.e., the data date) and, if relevant, the time.

Often a Statusing Report or mark-up sheet, such as the illustration below, is distributed to the people responsible for marking up the project progress. The marked-up sheets are returned to the scheduler for data entry into the software.

The Layout, such as the one below which has a 4-week look ahead filter applied, is circulated for marking up. In this case, only activities in-progress or due to start in the next four weeks are displayed. A manual page break could be placed at each responsible person's band, and when the schedule is printed each person could have a personal listing of activities that are either in progress or due to commence. This is particularly useful for large projects.

Activity ID	Activity Name	Original Duration	Start	Actual Start	Activity % Complete	Remaining Duration	Finish	Actual Finish	Early Start
Estimation		21d	12-Dec-03 A	12-Dec-03		6d	09-Jan-04		02-Jan-04
A1040	Request Component Bids	3d	05-Jan-04*		0%	3d	07-Jan-04		05-Jan-04
A1060	Draft Technical Details S...	11d	12-Dec-03 A	12-Dec-03	70%	3d	07-Jan-04		02-Jan-04
A1070	Compile Costs from Com...	2d	08-Jan-04		0%	2d	09-Jan-04		08-Jan-04
Proposal		9d	12-Jan-04			9d	23-Jan-04		12-Jan-04
A1080	Draft Bid Document	3d	12-Jan-04		0%	3d	14-Jan-04		12-Jan-04
A1090	Meeting to Review the D...	1d	15-Jan-04		0%	1d	15-Jan-04		15-Jan-04
A1100	Design Presentation	1d	16-Jan-04		0%	1d	16-Jan-04		16-Jan-04
A1110	Edit Proposal Draft Bid D...	1d	19-Jan-04		0%	1d	19-Jan-04		19-Jan-04
A1120	Negotiate Component W...	3d	19-Jan-04		0%	3d	21-Jan-04		19-Jan-04
A1130	Final Review of Bid Doc...	1d	22-Jan-04		0%	1d	22-Jan-04		22-Jan-04

Other electronic methods, discussed next, may be employed to collect the data. Irrespective of the method used, the same data needs to be collected.

There are several methods of collecting data for the project status:

- By sending a printed sheet to each responsible person to mark up by hand and return to the scheduler.

- By cutting and pasting the data from Primavera Version 5.0 into another document, such as Excel, and e-mailing the document to them as an attachment.

- By giving the responsible party direct access to the schedule software to update it. This approach is not recommended, unless the project is broken into subprojects. By using the subproject method, only one person updates each part of the schedule.

- When the Primavera timesheets have been implemented this process may be used to update the activities.

Some projects involve a number of people. In such cases, it is important that procedures be written to ensure that the status information is collected:

- In a timely manner,
- Consistently,
- Complete, and
- In a usable format.

 It is important for a scheduler to be aware that some people have great difficulty in comprehending a schedule. When there are a number of people with different skill levels in an organization, it is necessary to provide more than one method of updating the data. You even may find that you have to sit down with some people to obtain the correct data, yet others are willing and comfortable to e-mail you the information.

15.3 Understanding the Concepts

There are some terms and concepts used in scheduling and some that are specific to Primavera Version 5.0 that must be understood before updating a project schedule:

15.3.1 Activity Lifecycle

There are three stages of an activities lifecycle:

- **Not Started** – The **Early Start** and **Early Finish** dates are calculated from the **Predecessors**, **Constraints** and **Activity Duration**.
- **In-Progress** – The activity has an **Actual Start** date but is not complete.
  - ➢ Assigning an **Actual Start** date overrides the **Start Constraints** and **Start Relationships** which are used to calculate the **Early Start**.
  - ➢ The end date may be calculated from the **Remaining Duration** or a **Finish Constraint** or a **Finish Relationship**.
- **Complete** – The activity is in the past, the **Actual Start** and **Actual Finish** dates have been entered into Primavera Version 5.0, and they override all logic and constraints.

15.3.2 Actual Start Date Assignment of an In-Progress Activity

This section will explain how Primavera Version 5.0 assigns the **Early Start** of an **In-Progress** activity. These activities have been started but not completed since the last update.

- When an **Actual Start** date is assigned in the **Actual Start** field by checking the **Started** check box, this date overrides the **Early Start date**.

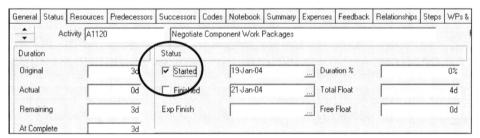

- The activity **Actual Start** date is set to equal the **Early Start** date when this box is checked.
- The **Actual Start** date calendar is opened by clicking on the ⬛ button to the right of the **Started** check box and a different start date may be assigned. This date should not be in the future of the project Data Date. It would not be logical to have an activity start in the future.

15.3.3 Calculation of Durations of an In-Progress Activity

The Primavera Version 5.0 has four Durations:

- An activity **Original Duration** is the duration from the **Early Start** to the **Early Finish** calculated over the **Activity Calendar** and is calculated when an activity has not yet started. When an **Actual Start** is entered, this duration is no longer recalculated or used for scheduling but may be edited.

- The **Actual Duration** is the worked duration of an activity and is either:
  - ➢ The duration from the **Actual Start** to the **Data Date** of an **In-progress** activity, or
  - ➢ The duration from the **Actual Start** to the **Actual Finish** of a **Completed** activity.

- The **Remaining Duration** is the unworked duration of an **In-progress** activity and is the duration from the **Data Date** to the **Early Finish** date of an activity.

- The **At Completion Duration** = **Actual Duration** + **Remaining Duration**. Before an activity has begun, the **Actual Duration** is zero and the **Remaining Duration** equals the **Original Duration**.

 The in-built proportional link between **Original Duration**, **Actual Duration**, **Remaining Duration** and **% Complete** that exists in Microsoft Project does not exist in Primavera Version 5.0.

15.3.4 Percent Complete

An activity percent complete may be assigned by the user or calculated by the software after an actual start has been assigned to an activity. There are three percent complete options; each new activity is assigned a project Default % Complete and then this may be edited for each activity as required.

Default % Complete

The **Default % Complete Type** for each new activity in each project is assigned in the **Defaults** tab of the **Details** form in the **Project Workspace**:

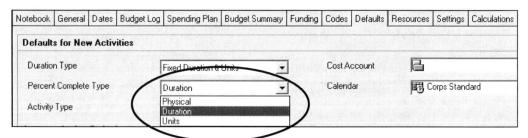

- The Percent Complete Type of a new activity will be set to the Default Percent Complete but may be changed at any time.

- **Duration % Complete** – This field is calculated from the proportion of the **Original Duration** and the **Remaining Duration**. When the **Remaining Duration** is greater that the **Original Duration** this percent complete is always zero. This is similar to the way P3 and SureTrak calculates the % Complete when the **Link Remaining Duration and Percent Complete** option is selected. In Primavera Version 5.0 this option may be applied to individual activities.

- **Physical % Complete** – This field allows the user to enter the percent complete of an activity and this value is independent of the activity durations. This is similar to the way P3 and SureTrak calculates the % Complete when the **Link Remaining Duration and Percent Complete** option is NOT selected. In Primavera Version 5.0 this option may be applied to individual activities.

- **Units % Complete** – This is where the percent complete is calculated from the resources units assigned to an activity and will be covered in the **UPDATING RESOURCES** chapter. This is similar to the Microsoft Project % Work Complete.

Activity % Complete

The percent complete that an activity utilizes is determined by the **% Complete Type** assigned to an activity in the **General** tab of the **Details** form in the **Activities Workspace** or from a column:

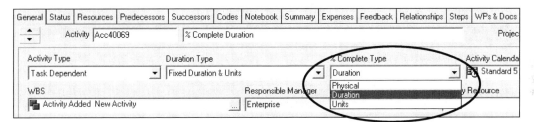

Primavera Version 5.0 also has a field titled **Activity % Complete**. This field adopts the value from the **% Complete Type** column, thus only one column needs to be displayed irrespective of the **% Complete Type**. See below:

Original Duration	Percent Complete Type	Activity % Complete	Physical % Complete	Duration % Complete	Units % Complete		September 2003			
							25	01	08	15
0d	Physical	30%	30%	0%	0%					
20d	Duration	50%	0%	50%	0%					
20d	Units	30%	0%	50%	30%					

15.3.5   Retained Logic and Progress Override

There are three options for calculating the finish date of the successor when the successor activity has started before the predecessor activity is finished. The selected option is applied to all activities in a schedule when it is calculated. Open the **Advanced Schedule Options** form by selecting **Tools**, **Schedule…** and clicking on the 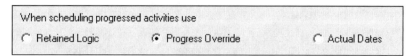 button:

When scheduling progressed activities use

   C Retained Logic   (•) Progress Override   C Actual Dates

- **Retained Logic**. In the example below, the relationship is maintained between the predecessor and successor for the unworked portion of the activity (the Remaining Duration) and continued after the predecessor has finished. In the example below the relationship forms part of the critical path and the predecessor has no float:

November 2003			December 2003		
09	16	23	30	07	14

- **Progress Override**. In the example below, the Finish-to-Start relationship between the predecessor and successor is disregarded, and the unworked portion of the activity (the Remaining Duration) continues before the predecessor has finished. The relationship is not a driving relationship and DOES NOT form part of the critical path. The predecessor in the example below has float:

November 2003			December 2003		
09	16	23	30	07	14

- **Actual Dates**. This function operates when there is an activity with Actual Start Dates in the future, which is not logical. With this option the remaining duration of an in-progress activity is calculated after the activity with actuals:

November 2003			December 2003		
09	16	23	30	07	14

When there are no Actual Dates in the future this option calculates as Retained Logic.

 Retained Logic and Progress Override are not terms used by Microsoft Project but are used in P3 and SureTrak and operate in the same way in Primavera Version 5.0. Retained Logic produces a more conservative schedule (a longer duration schedule) and is more likely to place an out of progress relationship on the critical path and adjustments may be made as required. If your schedule has Actual dates in the future of the Data Date (which may occur when the update information is collected at different times and the earlier date is used as the Data Date) then the use of Actual Dates would calculate the most conservative schedule.

15.3.6 Actual Finish Date

An **Actual Finish** date overrides an **Early Finish** date; finish date constraints and finish relationships are ignored.

15.3.7 Summary Bars Progress Calculation

Summary bars may not be statused, as in Microsoft Project, as they are virtual activities with their data created from summarizing the activities in the band.

15.3.8 Understanding the Current Data Date

The **Current Data Date** is also known as the **Data Date**, **Update Date**, **Status Date**, **Progress Date**, **As At Now Date** and the **Project Data Date**. Microsoft Project has several dates for the **Current Data Date** but Primavera Version 5.0 has one date, which is the same as for P3 and SureTrak.

The Primavera Version 5.0 **Current Data Date** is displayed as a vertical line on the schedule; this Data Date vertical line may now be formatted in Primavera Version 5.0 in the **Bars** form.

In scheduling software the function of the **Current Data Date** is to:

- Separate the completed parts of activities from incomplete parts of activities.
- Calculate or record all costs and hours to date before the data date, and to forecast costs and hours to go after the data date.
- Calculate the **Finish Date** of an in-progress activity from the **Current Data Date** plus the **Remaining Duration** over the **Activity Calendar**.

15.4 Updating the Schedule

The next stage is to update the schedule by entering the mark-up information against each activity.

When dealing with large schedules it is normal to develop a look-ahead schedule by creating a filter to display incomplete and un-started activities commencing in the near future only.

The schedule may be updated using the following methods:

- Using the fields in the **Status** tab of the **Details** form in the lower pane, or
- Displaying the appropriate tracking columns by:
  - ➤ Creating your own layout, or
  - ➤ Inserting the required columns in an existing layout.

15.4.1 Updating Activities Using the Status Tab of the Details Form

Open the **Status** tab:

General	Status	Resources	Predecessors	Successors	Codes	Notebook	Steps	Feedback	WPs & Docs	Expenses	Summary

Activity A1000 — First

Duration

			Status				
Original	20d	☑ Started	25-Aug-03	...	Physical %		30%
Actual	10d	☐ Finished	19-Sep-03	...	Total Float		0d
Remaining	10d	Exp Finish		...	Free Float		0d
At Complete	20d						

Constraints

Updating a **Complete** activity:

- Check the **Started** box and enter the actual **Start Date** if different from the displayed date.
- Check the **Finished** box and enter the actual **Finish Date** if different from the displayed date.

Updating an **In-progress** activity:

- Check the **Started** box and enter the actual **Start Date** if different from the displayed date.
- When the **Duration Type** is **% Duration** the **% Duration Complete** and **Remaining Duration** are linked, either:
  - ➢ The **Remaining Duration** is edited and the **% Complete** is calculated, or
  - ➢ The **% Complete** is entered and the software calculates the **Remaining Duration**, or
  - ➢ A **Remaining Duration** greater than the **Original Duration** may be entered and the **% Duration** will remain at zero, until the **Remaining Duration** is less than the **Original Duration**.

  Irrespective of the method used to calculate the **Remaining Duration**, after the schedule is recalculated the end date of the activity is calculated from the **Current Data Date** plus the **Remaining Duration** over the **Activity Calendar**.

Updating an activity that has not started:

- The **Original Duration**, **Relationships** and **Constraints** of an un-started activity should be reviewed.

15.4.2 Updating Activities Using Columns

An efficient method of updating activities is by displaying the data in columns. This may be achieved by:

- Inserting the required columns in an existing layout, or better
- Create a Layout with the required columns and update the schedule using these columns.

15.5 Progress Spotlight

Primavera Version 5.0 has a new function for highlighting the activities that should have progressed in the status period; then the user has the option of selecting some or all of the activities that should have progressed and statusing (updating) them as if they progressed exactly as they were scheduled.

It is often easier to **Autostatus** a project with functions like **Progress Spotlight** and then adjusting the Actuals as a second step in the statusing process.

This function is similar to the P3 Progress Spotlight function however does not have the additional SureTrak features of reversing progress and not updating the resources.

The Spotlight may be moved to reflect the new Data Date by either:

- Dragging the Data Date, or
- Using the Spotlight Icon -

15.5.1 Highlighting Activities for Updating by Dragging the Data Date

To highlight activities that should have been progressed in the last period by dragging the Data Date:

- Hold the mouse arrow on the Data Date line and display the double-headed arrow ↔ ,
- Press the left mouse button and drag the Data Date line to the required date.
- All the activities that should have been worked in the time period are highlighted.

15.5.2 Spotlighting Activities Using Spotlight Icon

The Spotlight facility highlights all activities that should have progressed in one minor time period of the timescale settings. To use **Progress Spotlight**:

- Set the Timescale to be the same as your Update Periods. If you are statusing weekly then set the time period to weeks in the **Timescale** form.
- Select **View**, **Progress**, **Spotlight** or click on the icon and the next period of time (one week if your scale is set to one week) will be highlighted.
- Click on the **Progress Spotlight** icon a second time to return the Spotlight back to the Data Date.

You are now ready to update progress.

15.5.3 Statusing Using Update Progress

To update a schedule using the **Update Progress** form select **Tools**, **Update Progress**.

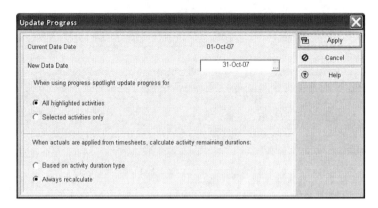

There are two options for setting the New Data Date:

- You may use the highlight facility before opening the Update Progress form and the New data date will be set to the highlighted Data Date; or
- You may select the New Data Date when opening the form.

Either all the activities that are Spotlighted may be updated or if some were selected before opening the form then just the selected ones may be updated.

- To update all the activities select **All highlighted activities** radio button, or
- To status selected activities highlight the activities (hold the Ctrl key and click on the ones you wish to status) before selecting **Tools**, **Update Progress…** and the click on the **Selected activities only** radio button.

The option **When actuals are applied from timesheets, calculate activity remaining durations:** decides how the Remaining Duration is calculated:

- **Based on the activity duration type** will take into account activity type and hours to date and reschedule the Remaining Duration in accordance with the activity Duration Type, or
- **Always recalculate** will override the activity Duration Type and calculate the activity Remaining Durations and Hours as if the activity was a Fixed Units and Fixed Units/Time activity.
- Click on [Apply] and the schedule will be statused as if all activities were completed according to the schedule.

15.6 Suspend and Resume

The new Primavera Version 5.0 Suspend and Resume function allows the work to be suspended and the activity resumed at a later date. Open the **Activity Details** form **Status Details** tab and enter the **Suspend** and **Resume** dates. This function works in a similar way to the P3 and SureTrak function and allows only one break in an activity.

The example below shows an activity suspended from 30 Apr 05 to the 10 May 05.

- This feature works when a task has commenced and normally the Suspend date is in the past and the Resume date in the future.
- The activity must have an actual start date before you can record a suspend date.
- Only Resource Dependent and Task Dependent activities may be Suspended and resumed.
- The suspend and resume time are at the start of a work period.
- The suspended period is not calculated as part of the task duration and resources are not scheduled in this period.

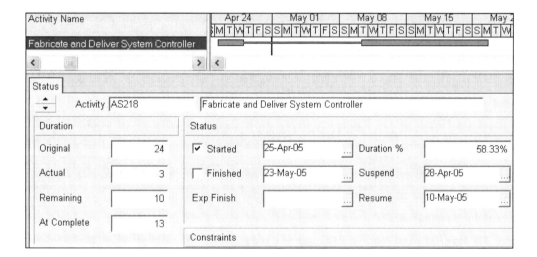

15.7 Scheduling the Project

At any time, but usually after all the activities have been updated, the project is scheduled :

- Open the **Schedule** form:
  - ➢ Select **Tools**, **Schedule…**, or
  - ➢ Press the **F9** key, or
  - ➢ Click on the 🔯 button.

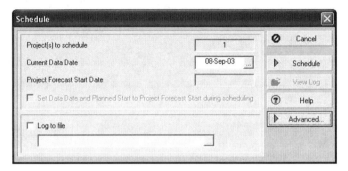

- Select the revised **Current Data Date** from the box and click on the [▷ Schedule] button.
- The software will recalculate all the early finish dates from the remaining durations and the new **Current Data Date**, taking into account the relationships and the **Retained Logic/Progress Override Options**.

15.8 Comparing Progress with Baseline

There will normally be changes to the schedule dates and more often than not there are delays. The full extent of the change is not apparent without having a Baseline bar to compare with the statused schedule.

To display one or more of the three **Baseline Bars** in the **Bar Chart** you must open the **Bars** form and check the **Display** box of one or more baseline bar.

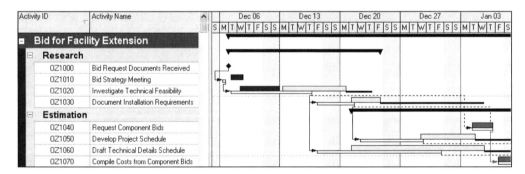

If you want to see the Start and Finish Date variances, they are available by displaying the **Variance - Start Date** and **Variance - Finish Date** columns. These variance columns use the **Primary Baseline** data.

15.9 Corrective Action

Date slippage occurs when an activity is rescheduled to finish later then originally planned. There are two courses of action available:

- The first is to accept the slippage. This is rarely acceptable, but it is the easiest answer.

- The second is to examine the schedule and evaluate how you could improve the end date.

Solutions to return the project to its original completion date must be cleared with the person responsible for the project, since he or she may have the most impact on the work.

Suggested solutions to bring the project back on track include:

- Reducing the durations of activities on, or near the critical path. When activities have applied resources, this may include increasing the number of resources working on the activities. Changing longer activities is often more achievable than changing the length of short duration activities.

- Changing calendars, say from a five-day to a six-day calendar, so that activities are being worked on for more days per week.

- Reducing the project scope and deleting activities.

- Changing activity relationships so activities take place concurrently. This may be achieved by introducing negative lags to Finish-to-Start relationships, which maintain a Closed Network. A negative lag will allow the successor activity to start before the predecessor is complete, which is often what happens in reality.

- Replacing Finish-to-Start relationships with Start-to-Start relationships. Activities are now progressing in parallel and therefore at the same time. This has the potential of creating an open network as the predecessor activity may no longer have a finish date successor and an extension in the duration of this activity may not affect the critical path. Should maintaining the critical path be important then this option should be avoided or a successor added to complete a closed network.

- Changing the logic or sequencing of activities to reduce the overall length of the critical path.

WORKSHOP 13

Progressing and Baseline Comparison

Background

At the end of the first week you have to update the schedule and report progress and slippage.

Assignment

Open your **OzBuild Bid** project file and complete the following steps:

1. Select **Project, Maintain Baselines...** and save a copy of the current project as a Baseline and title it **OzBuild End Workshop 11 Baseline**.
2. Select **Project, Assign Baselines...** and make this your Project Baseline and Primary Baseline and close the **Assign Baselines** form.
3. Apply the **OzBuild 11 – With Float** layout and save this as a new layout titled **OzBuild Workshop 13 – Baseline**.
4. Create and display the Primary Baseline Bar, in yellow and in row 2.
5. Show the following columns:
   - ➢ Activity ID
   - ➢ Activity Name
   - ➢ Activity % Complete
   - ➢ Original Duration
   - ➢ Remaining Duration
   - ➢ Start
   - ➢ Finish
   - ➢ Total Float
   - ➢ Variance BL1 – Finish Date
6. Make sure the Timescale is Weekly, click on the Progress Spotlight icon to move the Progress Spotlight to 10 Dec 07.
7. Select **Tools, Update Progress...** and progress the schedule so all Highlighted activities are updated.
8. Update the project activities with the following information:

Activity ID	Activity Name	Activity % Complete	Remaining Duration	Actual Start	Actual Finish
Bid for Facility Extension Workshop 13			32	03-Dec-07	
Research			6	03-Dec-07	
OZ1000	Bid Request Document Received	100%	0	03-Dec-07	
OZ1010	Bid Strategy Developed	100%	0	03-Dec-07	05-Dec-07
OZ1020	Technical Feasibility Study	60%	6	03-Dec-07	

9. Reschedule the project by pressing **F9** to open the **Schedule** form:
   - ➢ Check the data date to 10 Dec 07,
   - ➢ Open the **Schedule Options** form by clicking on the ⧁ Options… button and ensure **Retained Logic** is selected.
   - ➢ Click on the ⧁ Schedule to reschedule.
   - ➢ Check the answer below.

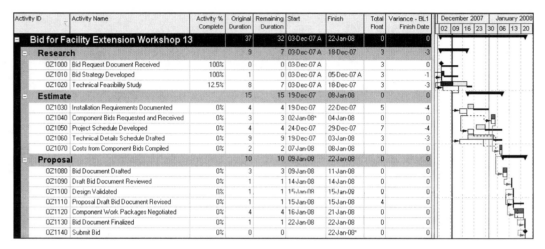

The lower bar is the Baseline and the delay to some activities is clear in the picture above created by the late scheduling on the Technical Feasibility Study activity.

10. Open the **General tab** of the Technical Feasibility Study activity and change the % Complete Type to **Duration**, reschedule and the **Percent Complete** will change to 25%. You will find that a link between the % Complete and Remaining Duration is established and the % Complete and Remaining Duration may not be entered independently. Try entering both a different % Complete or Remaining Duration, like the examples below:

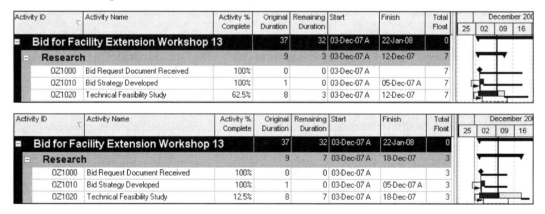

16 USER AND ADMINISTRATION PREFERENCES AND ADVANCED SCHEDULING OPTIONS

This chapter will look at the following topics:

- User Preferences,
- The Admin menu items,
- Admin Preferences, a multi tab form under the Admin menu, and
- Advanced Scheduling Options.

16.1 User Preferences

Select **Edit**, **User Preferences...** to open the **User Preferences** form. This form is used to set up a number of user-defined parameters, which will determine how data is displayed.

The **User Preferences** form may also be opened by right clicking in the right hand side of the bottom views when the **Resource Usage Spread Sheet** or **Resource Usage Profile** are being displayed.

16.1.1 Time Units Tab

The **Units Format** section of the tab is used to define the format of the **Unit of Time** that resource assignments are displayed with, e.g. days or hours.

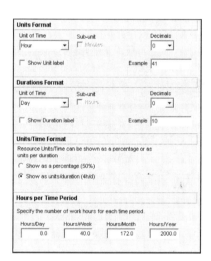

The **Durations Format** section of the tab is used to define the format of the **Unit of Time** that activity durations are displayed with, e.g. days or hours.

The **Units/Time Format** section of the form allows for the Microsoft Project-type formatting options of **Resource/Time Format** to show Resource utilization as a percentage (50%) or as units per duration (4h/d).

The **Hours per Time Period** is an option new to Primavera Version 5.0 and allows the user when assigned the rights to specify how summary durations are calculated. The default setting and the option to allow users to set their own **Hours per Time Period** are set in the **Admin**, **Admin Preferences...**, **Time Periods** form.

16.1.2 Dates Tab

The **Dates** tab is self-explanatory and is used to format the display of dates and time.

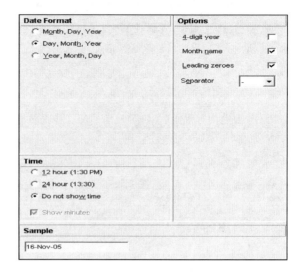

16.1.3 Currency Tab

The **Currency Options** tab selects the currency symbol used to display costs.

The **Currencies** form, available from the **Admin** menu item, is used to define the Base Currency. All costs are stored in the **Base Currency** and all other **Currencies** are calculated values using the **Base Currency** value and conversion rate.

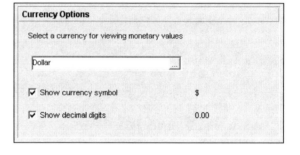

16.1.4 E-Mail Tab

The **E-Mail Protocol** tab sets up the current user's e-mail system.

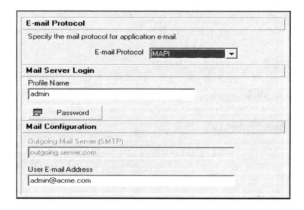

16.1.5   Assistance Tab

The **Assistance** tab specifies which
Wizards are run when creating
Resources and **Activities**.

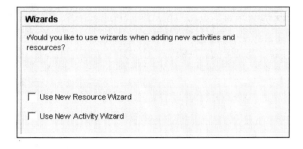

16.1.6   Application Tab

The **Application** tab specifies:

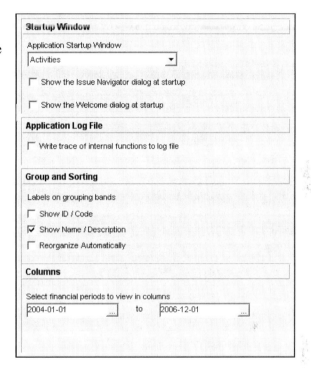

- **Startup Window** specifies which
  dialog boxes are displayed when the
  software is started.
- **Application Log File** creates a log
  of all data entries titled ERRORS
  LOG. This would be used by
  support staff.
- **Group and Sorting** specifies what
  information is displayed in the
  bands; one or both options of
  Description or Code may be
  selected. This setting is effective in
  situations where a Group and Sort
  form is not available.
- Primavera Version 5.0 introduced a
  function titled **Reorganize
  Automatically**, when the
  Reorganize Automatically box is
  checked, all views will reorganize
  automatically when data fields are
  changed that are used in the layout
  such as Grouping and Sorting. To
  reorganize a view when unchecked,
  select **Tools**, **Reorganize Now** or
  Shift+F2.
- Primavera Version 5.0 introduced
  Financial Periods and this is where
  the periods that may be displayed in
  columns is specified.

16.1.7 Resource Analysis Tab

The **Resource Analysis** tab has two sections:

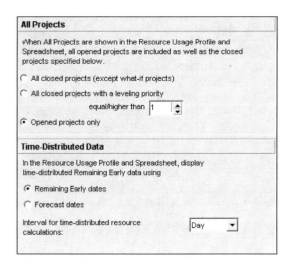

- The **All Projects** option specifies which projects are used to calculate the Resources Remaining Values in **Resource Usage Profiles**.

- **Time-Distributed Data**.

  ➤ It is possible to drag a project forward or backwards in time in the **Tracking Workspace** or **Portfolio Analysis**. This action creates a new set of dates titled **Forecast** dates. The **Resource Usage Profile** and **Resource Usage Spreadsheet** may be calculated using either the Current Schedule by checking **Remaining Early Dates** or the revised **Forecast Dates**.

  ➤ Interval for time-distributed calculations: This option determines the time increment for displaying the Resource Usage Profile and Resource Usage Spreadsheet data.

 The **Interval for time-distributed calculations:** must be equal to or smaller than the timescale or the resource data will be displayed in the first time increment of the timescale and not distributed over the whole time period.

16.1.8 Password Tab

The **User Password** tab is used to change the user password.

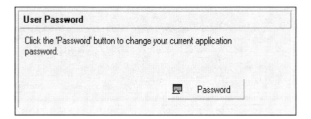

16.1.9 Calculations Tab

IT IS IMPORTANT TO UNDERSTAND THIS OPTION.

The **Calculations** tab has two options:

- **Preserve the Units, Duration, and Units/Time for existing assignments**. With this option, as Resources are added or deleted the total number of hours assigned to an Activity increases or decreases. The hours assigned for each resource are calculated independently.

- **Recalculate the Units, Duration, and Units/Time for existing assignments based on the activity Duration Type**. The total number of hours assigned to an activity will stay constant as second and subsequent resources are added or removed from an Activity, except when the Activity Type is **Fixed Duration and Units/Time**. This is similar to making an activity Effort Driven in Microsoft Project. There is no similar function in P3 and SureTrak.

```
┌─────────────────────────────────────────────────┐
│ Resource Assignments                            │
│                                                 │
│ When adding or removing multiple resource       │
│ assignments on activities                       │
│                                                 │
│ ⦿ Preserve the Units, Duration, and Units/Time  │
│   for existing assignments                      │
│                                                 │
│ ○ Recalculate the Units, Duration, and          │
│   Units/Time for existing assignments based on  │
│   the activity Duration Type                    │
├─────────────────────────────────────────────────┤
│ Assignment Staffing                             │
│                                                 │
│ When assigning a resource to an existing        │
│ activity assignment:                            │
│ ○ Always use the new resource's Units per Time  │
│   and Overtime factor                           │
│ ○ Always use current assignment's Units per     │
│   Time and Overtime factor                      │
│ ⦿ Ask me to select each time I assign           │
│                                                 │
│ When a resource and role share an activity      │
│ assignment:                                     │
│                                                 │
│ ○ Always use resource's Price per Unit          │
│ ⦿ Always use role's Price per Unit              │
│ ○ Ask me to select each time I assign           │
└─────────────────────────────────────────────────┘
```

- **Assignment Staffing** are new functions to Primavera Version 5.0 options available on the **Calculations** tab of the **User Options** form allowing the user to set the defaults for:

  ➢ Selecting the Units per Time when assigning a substitute resource to an existing resource assignment.

  ➢ Selecting the Price per Unit for a resource which is being assigned to a Role.

  The options are to select the existing resource, the new resource or to be prompted each time a resource/role is substituted.

16.1.10 Setup Filters Tab

The **Setup Filters** option allows the selection of filters for Resources, Roles, OBS, Activity Codes and Cost Accounts, which may be applied to the current project or to all data.

```
┌─────────────────────────────────────────────────┐
│ Startup Filters                                 │
│                                                 │
│ Choose the default filters to start the         │
│ application. If you choose to view all data the │
│ application may take longer to start. These     │
│ filters can be modified in the individual views.│
│                                                 │
│                    Current project   View all   │
│                     data only        data       │
│                                      (No Filter) │
│                                                 │
│  ▽ Resources          ○              ⦿          │
│  ▽ Roles              ○              ⦿          │
│  ▽ OBS                ○              ⦿          │
│  ▽ Activity Codes     ○              ⦿          │
│  ▽ Cost Accounts      ○              ⦿          │
└─────────────────────────────────────────────────┘
```

16.2 Admin Menu

The **Admin** command opens the **Admin** form.

Depending on how Primavera Version 5.0 has been installed and your access rights set, you may or may not have access to all these menus.

16.2.1 Users

The **Users** form is used to add and delete system users. The following information may be recorded:

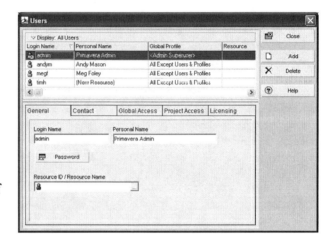

- **General** tab: The Personal Name (the person's name), Login Name, Password and Resource ID in the Resources Workspace.

- **Contact** tab: The person's telephone number and e-mail.

- **Global Access** tab: The type of information a person may change is specified here. This is achieved by assigning a

Global Profile to a person, which is created in the **Admin**, **Security Profiles...** form.

- **Project Access** tab: This is where the **User** is assigned to one or more OBS Nodes and may only access information associated with those OBS Nodes.

- **Licensing** tab: This is where a person is assigned a license.

The User should also be assigned to an OBS Node in the **Organizational Breakdown Structure** form which is covered in the **Organizational Breakdown Structure – OBS** section of this book.

16.2.2 Security

The **Security Profiles** form is used to set up security.

- **Global Profile** and **Project Profiles** may be established in this form.

- A **Global Profile** may be created or edited. Access to specific Enterprise functions may be assigned to the **Profile**.

- A **Global Profile** may then be assigned to a person.

- A **Project Profile** may be created and edited to allow access to specific Project functions.

- A **Project Profile** is assigned to a person after he or she has been assigned to a project from the **Organization Breakdown Structure** form.

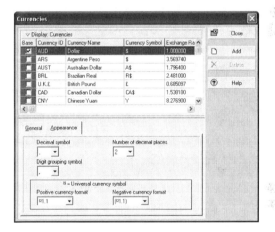

16.2.3 Currencies

The **Currencies** form is used to define system currencies. Currency fields are:

- **Currency ID**
- **Currency Name**
- **Currency Symbol**
- **Exchange Rate**

The **Base Currency** is assigned in this form and is used to store the data in the database.

16.2.4 Financial Periods

This is where the Financial Periods associated with Storing Period Performance are created.

For details on this function see the section on Store Period Performance in the **STATUSING A RESOURCED SCHEDULE** chapter.

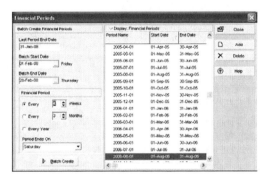

16.2.5   Purge Deletes

This function removes all deleted data from the database.

16.2.6   Timesheet Dates

The **Timesheet Periods** are chosen in the **Timesheet Dates Administration** form.

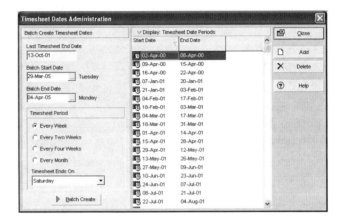

16.3 Miscellaneous Defaults

16.3.1   Default Project

Select **Set Default Project…** from the **Project** menu to open the **Set Default Project** form. When multiple projects are opened the default project's settings are used to:

- Schedule and level all open projects.

- New data items, such as issues, are assigned to the default project when they are added to the database.

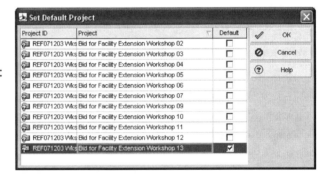

16.3.2   Set Language

Select **Tools**, **Set Language…** to open the **Set Language** form and select the language that the column headers and menu items are displayed in.

16.4 Admin Preferences

This form sets the default preferences for Primavera Version 5.0.

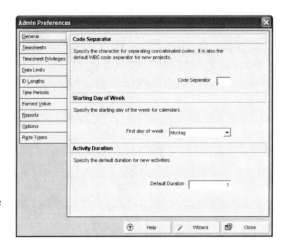

The **Admin Preferences** form has a number of tabs, which will be covered in more detail in the next section of this chapter.

If you do not have access to the **Admin Preferences**, then these options would have been set up by the system administrator for your organization.

Some preferences may only be changed in this form. Items described as **defaults** may be changed in other Workspaces.

Select **Admin**, **Admin Preferences...** to open the **Admin Preferences** form.

Click on the [✎ Wizard] button to run the **Admin Preferences Wizard**, which will assist in the setting up of the essential Administrators preferences.

16.4.1 General Tab

- **Code Separator** sets the default separator for new project WBS Codes and other codes such as Cost Accounts.
- **Starting Day of the Week** sets the day of the week that is shown on the timescale and the left hand column of calendars.
- **Activity Duration** sets the default duration for new activities.

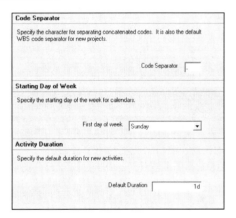

16.4.2 Timesheets Tab

The **Timesheets** tab allows specification of the default setup options when **Timesheets** are being used and is beyond the scope of this book. There are two tabs:

- **Entering Timesheets**
- **Timesheet Approval Level**

16.4.3 Timesheet Privileges Tab

The **Timesheet Privileges** tab is beyond the scope of this book. It has two sections:

- **Default time window to access activities**
- **Privileges for logging hours on timesheets**

16.4.4 Data Limits Tab

The **Data Limits** tab specifies:

- The maximum number of levels allowed in all hierarchical code structures,
- The maximum number of Activity Codes per project, and
- The maximum number of Baselines per project.

16.4.5 ID Lengths Tab

The **ID Lengths** tab specifies the maximum number of characters in the Code ID fields, not the Code Description.

16.4.6 Time Periods Tab

- **Hours per Time Period** values are used to convert from one time period Unit to another, for example, from days to hours. Therefore, a 5-day activity would be calculated as 40 hours with the setting displayed in the picture.

  IT IS IMPORTANT THAT THESE CONVERSIONS ARE UNDERSTOOD.

- **Time Period Abbreviations** are used to indicate the display durations.

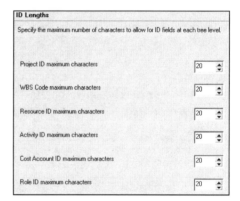

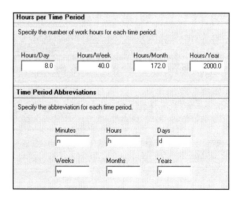

16.4.7 Earned Value Tab

This tab sets the defaults for calculating Earned Value and may be changed for each WBS.

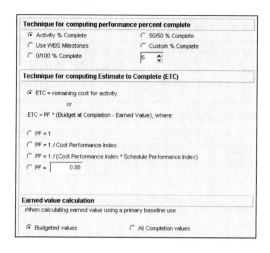

- The **Technique for computing performance percent complete** selects the formula for calculating the Earned Value.

- The **Technique for computing Estimate to Complete (ETC)** selects the formula for calculating the ETC. The ETC is a calculated field and is independent of the **At Completion Fields** but may contain the same value.

- **Earned Value Calculations** selects the value type (Budgeted or At Completion), that is to be used when calculating the earned value using a primary base line.

16.4.8 Reports Tab

The **Report Headers and Footers** form sets the default labels for reports.

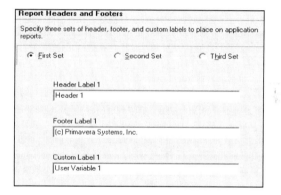

16.4.9 Options Tab

- The **Specify the interval to summarize and store resource spreads** tab sets the time period, such as week or month, for storing summarized activity data at WBS and Resource/Role Assignment Levels.

- The **Project Architect** check box allows the use of Project Architect to import methodologies.

- **Purge Deletes** removes data from the database that the **Undo** function could restore when exiting the system.

- **myPrimavera Server URL** is required to access collaboration documents.

- **Link to Contract Management Module** enable linking to this module when installed.

16.4.10 Rate Types Tab

Primavera Version 5.0 allows five resource rates types and the **Resource Rate Types** form allows you to rename the titles of the rates. You may have, for example, rates for:

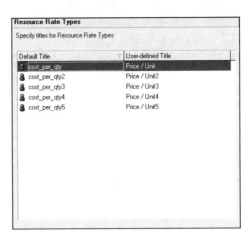

- Internal consulting,
- External consulting,
- Preparing evidence, and
- Giving evidence.

16.5 Scheduling Options

When a project is rescheduled there are some options available in the **Schedule Options** form which is opened by selecting **Tools, Schedule...**, ▷ Options... :

16.5.1 General Tab

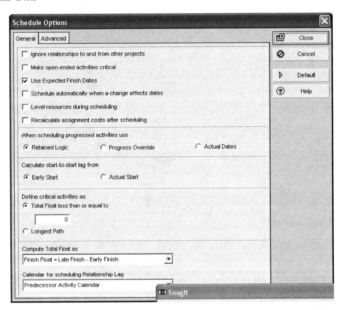

- **Ignore relationships to and from other projects** – Check this to ignore relationships/logic links with other projects. These relationships may be created when two projects are opened together.
- **Make open-ended activities critical** – An open-ended activity is an activity without a successor and which has float to the end of the project. Checking the box makes these activities critical with zero total float.
- **Use Expected Finish Dates** – Expected finish dates may be chosen in the Timesheets; check this box to use this date to calculate the activity finish date. This is always checked by default.
- **Schedule automatically when a change affects dates** – This is similar to automatic recalculation in other products. It recalculates the schedule when data that affects the timing of the schedule is changed.

- **Level resources during scheduling** – This levels the project resources each time it is scheduled.
- **Recalculate resource costs after scheduling** – This option recalculates resource costs after scheduling. Use this option when resources are assigned with multiple rates.
- **When scheduling progressed activities use** – In P3 and SureTrak, Out of Sequence Progress decides how original logic applies to the remaining work of a partially completed activity with an incomplete predecessor. There are three options for calculating this relationship:
  - ➢ **Retained Logic**
  - ➢ **Progress Override**
  - ➢ **Actual Dates**

  Refer to the paragraph on **Retained Logic and Progress Override** for further details.

- **Calculate start-to-start lag from** – The successor of an activity with a Start-to-Start and positive lag would start after the lag has expired. When the predecessor commences out of sequence the lag may be calculated from the predecessor calculated Early Start or the Actual start.
  - ➢ The Actual Start gives a less conservative schedule:

Activity ID	Activity Name	9	Nov 16	Nov 23	Nov 30	Dec 07	Dec 14
		F S S M T W T F S	S M T W T F S	S M T W T F S	S M T W T F S	S M T W T F S	S M T W T F S
A1000	First Activity						
A1010	Second Activity						
A1020	Start to Start + 10D						

  - ➢ The Early Start gives a more conservative schedule:

Activity ID	Activity Name	9	Nov 16	Nov 23	Nov 30	Dec 07	Dec 14
		F S S M T W T F S	S M T W T F S	S M T W T F S	S M T W T F S	S M T W T F S	S M T W T F S
A1000	First Activity						
A1010	Second Activity						
A1020	Start to Start + 10D						

- **Define critical activities as**. Both these options are used for analyzing schedules that utilize multiple calendars which may result in activities on the critical path possessing float.
  - ➢ **Total Float less than or equal to** – Activities may be marked as critical and with a chosen float value. Sometimes a small positive value is used to isolate the near critical activities on schedules or displaying the full critical path on multiple calendar schedules.
  - ➢ **Longest Path** – This option isolates the longest chain of activities in a schedule.
- **Compute Total Float as** – There are three options for this calculation:
  - ➢ Start Float = Late Start – Early Start
  - ➢ Finish Float = Late Finish – Early Finish
  - ➢ Smallest of Start Float and Finish Float

  The computed value may be different with Level of Effort Activities, but Finish Float is normally used.

- **Calendar for scheduling Relationship Lag** – There are four calendar options for the calculation of the lag for all activities:
    1. **Successor Activity Calendar** is the default, or
    2. **Predecessor Activity** Calendar, or
    3. **24 Hour,** or
    4. **Project Default Calendar**.

 P3 and SureTrak use the predecessor calendar and Microsoft Project uses the Project Base calendar. Microsoft Project also has the option of an Elapsed lag duration.

- **Default** – Reapplies the Primavera Version 5.0 default settings.

16.5.2   Advanced Tab

This tab selects the options for calculating multiple critical paths and is covered in detail in the **UTILITIES** chapter.

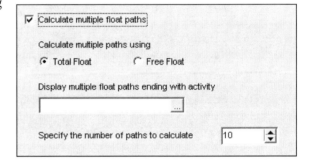

17 CREATING ROLES AND RESOURCES

Traditionally, planning and scheduling software defines a **Resource** as something or someone that is required to complete the activity and sometimes has limited availability. This includes people or groups of people, materials, equipment and money.

Primavera Version 5.0 is able to assign Costs, a Calendar, one or more Roles and some personal information to **Resources**.

Primavera Version 5.0 has a function titled **Roles**. A Role is normally used at the planning stage of a project and represents a skill or position. Later, and before the activity begins, a role would be filled by assigning a specific individual who would be defined as a resource. Roles may be assigned to both Resources and Activities. A search by Role may be conducted on all the Resources when it is required to replace an Activity Assigned Role with an individual from the Resource pool. Primavera Version 5.0 allows rates to be assigned to Roles.

There are a large number of resource functions available in Primavera Version 5.0. Without getting into too much detail, this book will outline the important resource-related functions that will enable you to create and assign Roles and Resources to your schedules.

This chapter will concentrate on:

Topic	Menu Command
Creating **Roles**	Select **Enterprise**, **Roles...** to open the **Roles** form.
Creating **Resources**	Open the **Resources Workspace**: • Select **Enterprise**, **Resources**, or • Click on the 🔒 button on the **Directory** toolbar, or • Select **Resources** from the **Home** Workspace.
Editing **Resource Calendars**	Select **Enterprise**, **Calendars...** to open the **Calendars** form.

The following steps should be followed to create and use resources in a Primavera Version 5.0 schedule:

- Create the resources in the **Resource Workspace**.
- Create the **Roles**, if required, in the **Roles** form.
- Assign Resources to Roles from either the **Resource Workspace** or the **Roles** form.
- Manipulate the Resource Calendars if resources have special timing requirements.
- Assign resources to Activities and review the resource loading.

17.1 Understanding Resources

There are typically two methods of using the Resource function for resource planning:

- Individual Resources, and
- Group Resources

17.1.1 Individual Resources

These resources are individual people who are often responsible for completing the activity or tasks associated with activities to which they have been assigned.

This is typically work undertaken in an office environment, such as an IT development project, where timesheets are often completed by the people undertaking the work and the timesheet system is directly linked to the scheduling system.

In this situation the updating of Activities that are in progress is completed by the person assigned as a Resource to an Activity, often via the timesheet system, and the scheduler has a review function in the project updating.

17.1.2 Group Resources

These resources represent groups of people, such as trades or disciplines on a construction site. On very large projects gangs or crews, which would be made up of equipment and a number of different trades, could also be considered. The person responsible for the work is not a resource assigned to an activity and individual people doing the work will not be assigning their timesheets directly to activities in the schedule.

Also, in this environment the scheduler normally updates the activities and the resources. In this situation it is recommended that a minimum number of resources be assigned to activities. This is because every resource added to the schedule will need to be statused and as more resources are added, the scheduler's workload will increase.

Resource minimization simplifies a schedule and makes it easier to manage large schedules. This is achieved by not cluttering the schedule with resources that are in plentiful supply or are of little importance, and by grouping trades or disciplines into crews and gangs on large projects.

When Group Resources are used the Role function tends to become redundant but could be used to plan the contractor type or the actual contractor that is planned to be used on the project.

17.1.3   Input and Output Resources

When you create your resources, you may also consider them within the context of the following headings:

- **Input Resources** – These resources are required to complete the work and represent the project costs:
  - ➢ Individual people by name.
  - ➢ Groups of people by trade, discipline or skill.
  - ➢ Individual equipment or machinery by name.
  - ➢ Groups of equipment or machinery by type.
  - ➢ Groups of resources such as Crews, Gangs or Teams made up of equipment and machinery.
  - ➢ Materials.
  - ➢ Money.
- **Output Resources** – These could be the project deliverables or outcomes and could have a direct relationship to the project income:
  - ➢ Specifications completed.
  - ➢ Bricks laid.
  - ➢ Tones of material loaded with an excavator.
  - ➢ Lines of code written.
  - ➢ Tests completed.

  This type of resource is often used in the mining environment where the output in tones/tonnes or volume is scheduled and/or leveled.

The analysis of and difference between the Input and the Output resources' value and timing may be used to represent the Cash Flow, Cash Position and Project Profit (or loss).

The type of contract that the work is being conducted under would often determine if the client is more interested in the Input or Output Resources.

17.2 Creating Roles

Roles are created, edited and deleted in a similar method as WBS's.

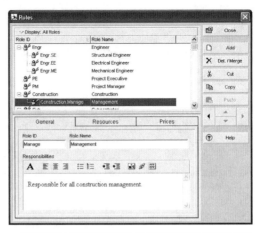

To create, edit or delete a **Role** select **Enterprise**, **Roles...** to open the **Roles** form:

The following formatting, filtering and sorting functions are available in the **Roles** form:

- Click on the **Role ID** title or the **Role Name** title to sort the Roles by **Role ID** or **Role Name.**

- Click on **Display: All Roles** and then the **Filter By** tab to open a menu where the roles can be filtered by **All Roles** or **Current Projects Roles**.

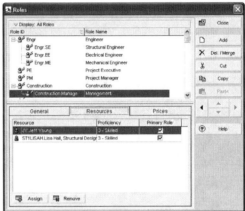

- **Roles** may also be displayed by the **Chart View**. The **Roles** form will have to be resized to use this function effectively.

- The **Find** function (or Ctrl+F) allows a Role name to be searched.

- The **Print** function opens the **Print Preview** form allowing the printing of the current list of Roles.

In the **General** tab each Role may be assigned:

- **Role ID**, a code used to assign the Role to an Activity.

- **Role Name**, the Name of the Skill or Trade.

- **Responsibilities**, where you may enter text, hyperlinks and pictures about the Role Responsibility.

In the **Resources** tab each Role may be assigned:

- To one or more Resources.

- The Resource is assigned by default a **Proficiency** of "3-Skilled" which may then be changed to any of the options shown in the list.

- The Resource may be assigned a **Primary Role**.

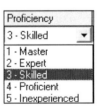

Primavera Version 5.0 supports **Rates for Roles**. Up to 5 rates (the same number of rates as resources) may be assigned to roles which may be used for estimating and cash flow forecasting of projects before the actual resource completing the work is assigned to the activity. Click on the **Prices** tab to edit the Role Price/Unit

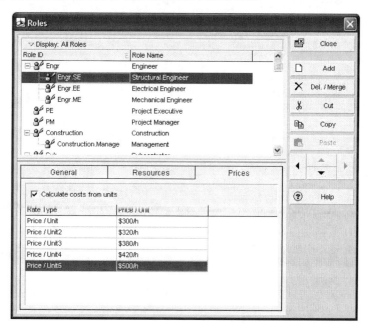

Different rates may be required for different clients such as an internal project rates and rates for different types of external clients.

All data columns may be sorted by clicking on the column titles.

17.3 Creating Resources and the Resources Workspace

To create, edit or delete resources open the **Resources** Workspace:

- Select **Enterprise**, **Resources…**, or
- Click on the ▣ button on the **Directory** toolbar, or
- Select **Resources** from the **Home** Workspace.

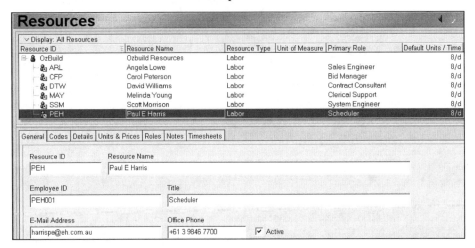

17.3.1 Resource Breakdown Structure - RBS

Resources may be added and organized hierarchically in a similar method to creating a WBS.

The OzBuild resources in the picture above are listed under a higher-level node titled **OzBuild Resources**. Primavera Systems calls this structure a **Resource Breakdown Structure** or **RBS**.

17.3.2 Formatting the Resources Workspace

The menu under the **Display: All Resources** has many functions that are similar to other forms:

- The **Details** check box displays or hides the **Details** form in the lower pane.
- **Chart View** displays the resources as a Chart. To use this format **Group and Sort By** must be set as **Default** or have the **Customize…** option grouped by Resources.
- **Columns**, **Table Font and Row…**, **Filter By** and **Group and Sort By** options work in a similar way to the formatting of the **Activities** Workspace. Click on the menus to see the options available with each.
- When the **Resources** are organized hierarchically, the **Expand All** and **Collapse All** options work in a similar way to other Workspaces and rolls up the Resources.

17.3.3   Adding Resources

New Resources are added and deleted in a similar method to adding Activities in the **Activity** Workspace. Use the **Insert** key, right-click and select **Add**, or use the **Command** toolbar by clicking on the ☐ Add button.

17.3.4   General Tab

The fields in this tab are self-explanatory:

- The **Resource ID** and **Resource Name** are mandatory,

- The **Employee ID**, **E-Mail Address**, **Title** and **Office Phone** are optional, and

- When the **Active** box is unchecked, the Resource is inactive and indicates that the resource is not available. When assigning Resources to Activities there is a filter to display only active Resources.

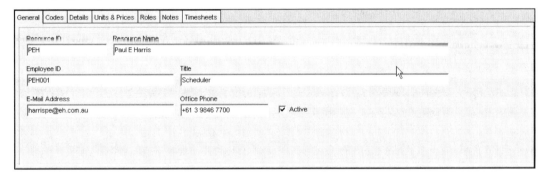

17.3.5   Codes Tab

Resource Codes are assigned to Resources allowing additional facilities to sort and report on them in the **Resource Usage Spreadsheet**:

- **Resource Codes** may be defined in the **Resource Code Definition** form, which is opened by selecting **Enterprise**, **Resource Codes…** and clicking on the ☐ Modify... button.

- Individual **Resource Code Values** may be added to a **Resource Code** in the **Resource Codes** form by selecting **Enterprise**, **Resource Codes…**.

- Resource Codes may then be selected in a layout to sort and group Resources.

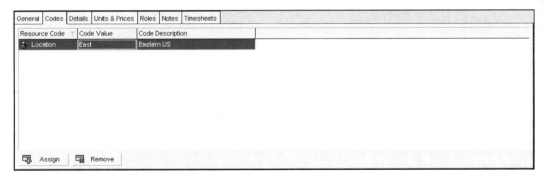

17.3.6   Details Tab

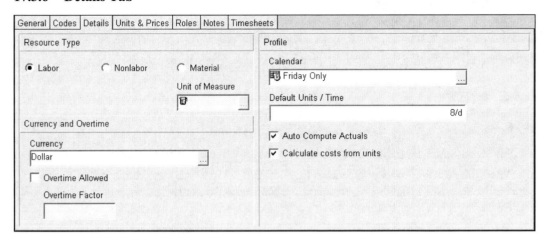

Resource Types

There are three types of Resource:

- **Labor**, this resource type is intended for people
- **Nonlabor**, this resource type is intended for equipment used to perform project work
- **Material**, and this resource type is intended for materials/supplies.

Material Resources may be leveled but have the following differences:

- They may be assigned a **Unit of Measure** which is created in the **Admin, Admin Categories…, Unit of Measure** tab. This is not available to Labor and Nonlabor resources.
- The may not be assigned a Role.
- They may not log Overtime.

Currency

An alternative **Currency** may be associated with a resource. This will not affect how the Resource Unit Rates costs are entered but provides a further tagging mechanism for sorting and reporting. The costs are stored in the default currency but are displayed using the conversion rate in the currency selected for the resource.

Overtime

A **Labor Resource** may be allowed to record O**vertime** in the **Primavera timesheet** system when the **Overtime** box is checked and the costs derived from the **Unit Rates** are multiplied by the **Overtime** Factor.

Calendar

The Resource is assigned a **Global** or **Resource Calendar** in this form. Unlike Microsoft Project, P3 and SureTrak each resource does not by default have its own calendar. A Resource Calendar may be created and assigned to more than one Resource. This topic will be covered in more detail in the next section of this chapter.

Default Units/Time

The **Default Units/Time** is the value that a resource adopts when it is first assigned to an activity. In a similar way to Microsoft Project, the **Units per Time Period** may be displayed as a **Percentage** or in **Units/Time**.

- Select **Edit**, **User Preferences**, **Time Units** tab and select the preferred display from the **Units/Time Format** section:

Units/Time Format
Resource Units/Time can be shown as a percentage or as units per duration
○ Show as a percentage (50%)
⊙ Show as units/duration (4h/d)

Default Units / Time
50%

Default Units / Time
4.00h/d

Resource and Activity Auto Compute Actuals

There are two places where the Resource **Auto Compute Actuals** field in Primavera Version 5.0 is displayed:

- Against each resource in the **Resources Workspace**, **Details** tab and displayed as a column in the **Resources Workspace**.
- Against each resource after it has been assigned to an activity and is displayed in the **Resources** tab of the bottom window in the **Activities Workspace**.

The option may only be switched on or off in the field in the **Resources Workspace**. When this option is checked Primavera Version 5.0 calculates the Actual Units and Remaining Units using the Budgeted Units and Activity % Complete. When unchecked the work for this resource may also be read from the Primavera Timesheet system.

The Activity **Auto Compute Actuals** field may be displayed as a column, when this option is checked all Resources Auto Compute Actuals irrespective of how they are checked in the **Resources Workspace**.

Calculate Costs from Units

With this option checked the costs for a resource are calculated from the **Resource Unit/Time** when a resource is assigned to an activity, when unchecked the costs remain at zero when a resource is assigned to an activity.

There is also a Resource Assignment field available after a resource has been assigned to an activity in the Resources tab of the Activities Workspace titled **Cost Units Linked**. This is checked to match the **Calculate Costs from Units** field in the Resources Workspace when a Resource is assigned to an Activity.

The **Activities Workspace** field titled **Cost Units Linked** is not linked to the **Calculate Costs from Units** field in the Resources Workspace and only adopts the setting when a resource is assigned to an Activity.

The picture below shows a resource with the **Cost Units Linked** field unchecked and therefore the costs are not being calculated from the **Resource Unit Rate**.

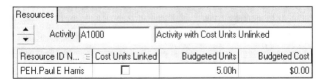

17.3.7 Units and Prices Tab
Effective Date and Rates

Each Resource may have up to five rates (Price/Unit) and these rates may be varied over time.

- To display the other rates their columns should be displayed.
- The Column Titles may have their description formatted to suit their intended purpose.
- When a rate is added the effective date is the date from which the rates is applied.

Shifts

Resource Shifts are used when Leveling and should not be assigned unless they are being used. **Resource Shifts** will not be covered in detail:

- **Resource Shifts** are created in the **Resource Shifts** form which is opened by selecting **Enterprise, Resource Shifts…**,
- The **Resource Shifts** and the number of shifts a resource works is assigned in the **Units and Prices** tab, **Shifts Calendar:**.

17.3.8 Roles Tab

- Λ Resource may be assigned more than one role, and their **Proficiency** for the Role, in this tab.
- When multiple Roles are assigned, one is assigned as the **Primary Role**.

Role ID	Role Name	Proficiency	Primary Role
Oz.BM	Bid Manager	3 - Skilled	☑
Oz.SC	Scheduler	4 - Proficient	☐

17.3.9 Notes Tab

Notes may be added here in the similar way as with Activities but there are no Notebook topics available.

17.3.10 Timesheets Tab

Originally called **Progress Reporter Tab,** when Timesheets are implemented, the user must be added as a system user in **Admin, Users…, Users** form where he or she is also assigned to a Resource, thus providing the link from the timesheet user to the Primavera Version 5.0 resource. This was covered in the **Admin Menu, Users** section.

For timesheets to operate, the **Uses Timesheets** box in the **Progress Details Tab** must also be checked and the **Timesheet Approval Manager** selected.

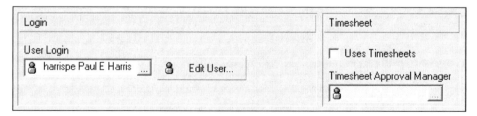

17.4 Editing Resource Calendars

Each resource may be assigned a **Resource Calendar**. The resource calendar is acknowledged when the **Activity Type** is set to **Resource Dependent** in the **Activities Workspace**, **General** tab.

Select **Enterprise**, **Calendars…** to open the Calendar form.

- **Resource Calendars** are edited in exactly the same way as other calendars.

- A **Resource Calendar** may be assigned to more than one resource or a resource may have a calendar of its own by assigning one calendar to a resource.

- It is important to create a coding system for Resource Calendars to ensure that shared and individual Resource Calendars are easily identified. This will guarantee that the edits to calendars may be made with confidence and the edits will affect the intended resources.

WORKSHOP 14

Adding Roles and Resources to the Database

Background

The Roles and Resources must now be added to the database.

Assignment

1. We have statused our project, but we need an unstatused project for this next task. Therefore, we will have to restore a copy of the Baseline schedule saved prior to statusing the current schedule (OzBuild End Workshop 11 Baseline) to provide and unrepressed schedule for this exercise. Select **Project**, **Assign Baselines…**and remove the project as a Baseline and then restore the project using **Project**, **Maintain Baselines…** .
2. Locate the restored schedule in the **Projects Workspace** and open it.
3. Open the **Roles** form and add the Roles in the picture below:

Role ID	Role Name
⊟ Oz	OzBuild Roles
Oz.BM	Bid Manager
Oz.SLS	Sales Engineer
Oz.SC	Scheduler
Oz.SE	System Engineer
Oz.CS	Clerical Support
Oz.CC	Contract Consultant

4. Now open the **Resource Workspace**.
5. Format the columns as in the picture below.
6. Add the resources as in the picture below:

Resource ID	Resource Name	Roles	Price / Unit
⊟ Oz	OzBuild Resources		$0/h
ARL	Angelo Lowe	Sales Engineer	$80/h
CFP	Carol Peterson	Bid Manager, Scheduler	$100/h
DTW	David Williams	Contract Consultant	$100/h
MAY	Melinda Young	Clerical Support	$50/h
SSM	Scott Morrison	Sales Engineer, System Engineer	$80/h
PEH	Paul E Harris	Scheduler	$90/h

7. Set the **Default Units/Time** to 8 hours per day for all the resources.
8. Make the **Proficiencies** to be **3-Skilled**.
9. Check **Calculate Costs from units** and **Auto compute actuals** for each resource.

18 ASSIGNING ROLES, RESOURCES AND EXPENSES

During the planning stage, **Roles** may be assigned to Activities to gain an understanding of the resources requirements at an early stage of a project and replaced by a **Resource** when it is known who will be undertaking the work. A Resource may be assigned:

- Directly to an Activity, or
- To a Role which has been assigned to an Activity.

There are three types of resources, **Labor**, **Nonlabor** and **Material**, and as discussed in the previous chapter, a Labor Resource has additional functionality including Overtime, Resource Calendars and user-defined Autocost rules. The **Labor** and **Nonlabor** resources are similar to the Microsoft Project **Work Resources**. A **Material** resource is similar to Microsoft Project **Material Resources**.

Primavera Version 5.0 also has a function titled **Expenses**, where costs may be assigned to activities without resources. This is similar to the **Costs** function in Microsoft Project but with far more functionality.

This chapter will cover the following topics:

- Understanding Resource Calculations and Terminology
- Project and Activity Workspace Resource and Role Preferences
- Details Status Form
- Activity Types and Duration Types
- Assigning and Removing Roles and Assigning Resources
- Resource and Activity Duration Calculation and Resource Lags
- Expenses
- Suggested Setup for Assigning Resources

Topic	Menu Commands
• Set **Units/Time Format** and **Resource Assignments**	Select **Edit, User Preferences…** to open the **User Preferences** form and select the **Time Units** tab and **Calculations** tab.
• Set **Default Duration Type** and **Default Activity Type**	Set these defaults in the **Defaults** tab in the **Projects Workspace**.
• Assign a **Role** to an Activity	Select the **Resources** tab in the **Activity Details** form and Click on the [⊞ Add Role] button to open the **Assign Roles** form.
• To assign a **Resource** to a **Role** that has been assigned to an activity	Select the Role to be assigned a Resource from the **Resources Details** tab and click on the [⊞ Assign by Role] button to open the **Assign Resources By Roles** form.
• To assign a **Resource** to an activity without a **Role**	Select the Activity to be assigned the Resource and click on the [⊞ Add Resource] to open the **Assign Resource** form.

18.1 Understanding Resource Calculations and Terminology

A Resource has two principal components after it has been assigned to an Activity:

- **Quantity**, in terms of **Work** in hours or **Material** quantities required to complete the activity, which are referred to as **Units** by Primavera Version 5.0, and

- **Cost**, which is calculated from the **Resource Unit Rate** x **Quantity**. The **Resource Unit Rate** is termed **Price/Unit** in Primavera Version 5.0.

Each Resource and Expense has the same four fields for **Costs** and **Units**: **Budget**, **Remaining**, **Actual** and **At Completion**. The relationship among these fields changes depending on whether the activity is Not Started, In-Progress or Complete.

- When an activity is Not Started and the % Complete is zero then:
  - ➢ **Budget** may be linked to **Remaining** and **At Completion** and therefore a change to one will change the other two and they will always be equal, and
  - ➢ **Actual** will be zero.

- When the activity is marked Started and would normally be In-Progress and the % Complete is between 1% and 99% then:
  - ➢ **Budget** becomes unlinked from **Remaining** and **At Completion**, thus allowing progress and the **At Completion** value to be compared to the **Budget**, and
  - ➢ **At Completion** = **Actual** + **Remaining** and have a link to **% Complete** and a change value to one will result in a change to other values.

- When the activity is Complete and the % Complete is 100% then:
  - ➢ **Remaining** is set to zero, and
  - ➢ **At Completion** = **Actual**.

In summary, the Budget values for Costs and Units are linked to the At Completion values until:

- An Activity has been marked as Started or has a % Complete, or

- The **Link Budget and At Completion for not started activities** in the **Project** workspace **Calculations** tab is unchecked, see below.

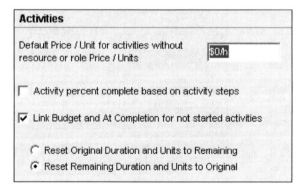

18.2 Project Workspace Resource Preferences

Preferences that affect how all resources in a project calculate are set in the **Project Workspace** and pertain to all activities and resources.

Preferences set in the **Activity Workspace** decide how each individual activity and resource calculate and are covered in the next section.

- The **Resources** tab in the Projects Workspace:

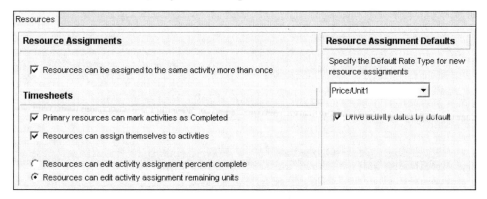

> **Resource Assignments**. Checking the **Resources can be assigned to the same activity more than once box** allows a resource to be assigned to an activity more than once. This is useful if it is required to assign a resource at the beginning of an activity and later at the end of an activity with a lag.

> **Drive activity dates by default**. A resource has the following fields that are linked and a change to one will make a change to another:
>   - **Original Lag**. The duration from the Activity Start Date to the Resource Start Date, which is the date the resource commences work.
>   - **Original Duration**. The duration that a resource is working.
>   - **Start**. The Resource Start Date =Activity Start Date + the Resource Original Lag.
>   - **Finish**. This date is calculated by the addition of the Activity Start Date + Original Lag + the Original Duration.

With this option checked, a resource will be assigned to an activity with the **Drive Activity Dates** field checked and then Activity Finish date is calculated from the latest Resource Finish date that has the Driving Activity dates option checked.

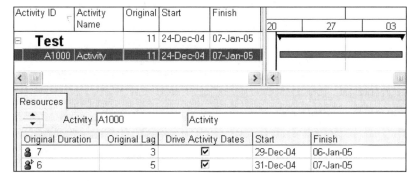

With this option unchecked, a resource will be assigned to an activity with the **Drive Activity Dates** field unchecked and the Activity Finish Date is therefore independent of the Resource Finish date. When one of the Resource fields listed on the previous page is edited the resource could be working outside the activity, as per the example below:

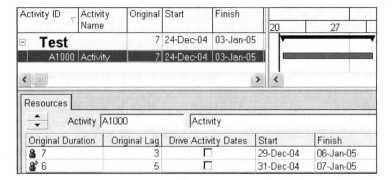

It is recommended that the **Drive activity dates by default** box is checked, thus Resources will be assigned as **Drive Activity Dates** and this ensures that all work is contained within the duration of an activity. This function works in a similar way in P3 and SureTrak when a Lag and/or Duration is assigned to a non driving resource but there is no equivalent in Microsoft Project

➢ **Timesheets**. This sets the defaults for the Timesheet, if it has been implemented.

➢ **Resource Assignment Defaults**. There are five Resource Rates available in Primavera Version 5.0; one rate may be set as a project default. After assignment to an activity, the Resource Rate may be changed using the **Rate Type** field in the Resources tab of the Activities Workspace.

- The **Calculations** tab in the **Projects Workspace**:

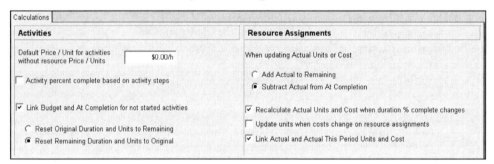

➢ **Activities – Default Price/Unit for activities without resource Price/Units**. When a resource does not have a rate, the default rate may be set in this tab.

➢ The other functions in this tab affect the statusing of resourced activities and are covered in the **STATUSING A RESOURCED SCHEDULE** chapter.

18.3 User Preferences Applicable to Assigning Resources

Select **Edit**, **User Preferences…** to open the **User Preferences** form:

18.3.1   Units/Time Format

Select the **Time Units** tab. The **Units/Time Format** allows Microsoft Project style formatting of **Resource/Time Format** showing Resource utilization as a percentage or as units per duration.

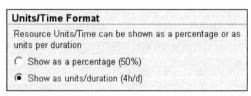

18.3.2 Resource Assignments

The **Calculations** tab has two **resource Assignment** options:

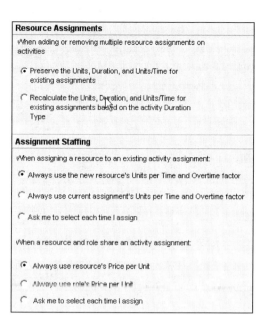

- **Preserve the Units, Duration, and Units/Time for existing assignments**. With this option as Resources are added or deleted the total number of hours assigned to an activity increases or decreases. Each Resource's hours are calculated independently.

- **Recalculate the Units, Duration, and Units/Time for existing assignments based on the activity Duration Type**. The total number of hours assigned to an activity will stay constant as second and subsequent resources are added or removed from an activity. **Note:** This function does not work when the Activity Type is **Fixed Duration and Units/Time**.

 This is similar to making a Task Effort Driven in Microsoft Project. There is no similar function in P3 and SureTrak.

The **Assignment Staffing** option needs to be considered carefully otherwise when assigning Resources to Roles and replacing resources the incorrect Unit Rate may be assigned.

18.4 Activity Workspace Resource Preferences and Defaults

18.4.1 Details Status Form

This form has a section titled **Labor Units** at the right hand side as seen in the picture below. The drop down menu allows you to select which data is to be displayed in this section of the form.

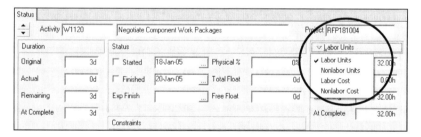

There is a link between the entries in this form and the values that are assigned to resources:

- The values in this form are the sum of the values assigned to Resources and Roles.

- When these values are edited, they will change the values assigned to Resources and Roles.

18.4.2   Activity Type

There are five **Activity Types** assigned in the **General tab** in the **Activities Workspace**:

Activity Type	Notes
Task Dependent	Activities assigned as Task Dependent acknowledge their **Activity Calendar** when scheduling and the Finish Date is calculated from the Activity Calendar.
Resource Dependent	Activities assigned as Resource Dependent acknowledge their **Resource Calendar** when being scheduled. This is similar to an Independent Activity Type in P3 and SureTrak. The Finish Date is calculated based on the longest Resource Duration.
Level of Effort (LOE)	This Activity Type spans other Activities. Therefore the Start Date, Finish Date and Durations may change as the start or finish date of activities that it is dependent on change during scheduling or updating. LOE Activity Type is similar to a Hammock in P3 and SureTrak, but more relationships may control the Start and Finish Dates. There is no equivalent in Microsoft Project. This type of activity does not create a critical path irrespective of the float calculations that are displayed. The Start Date is controlled by the following relationships: • Finish-to-**Start** predecessors • Start-to-**Start** predecessors • **Start**-to-Finish successors • **Start**-to-Start Successors The Finish Date is controlled by the following relationships: • Finish-to-**Finish** predecessors • Start-to-**Finish** predecessors • **Finish**-to-Start successors • **Finish**-to-Finish successors Resources assigned to a Level of Effort activity are not considered in calculations when a schedule is **Leveled**. Level of Effort activities may not be assigned a **Constraint**.
Start Milestone	This Activity Type is used to indicate the commencement of Phase, Stage or a major event in a project. It has only a Start Date and no Duration or Finish Date. It may only have **Start Constraints** assigned. It may not have time dependent resources assigned but may have a **Primary Resource** assigned to indicate who is responsible for the activity.

Activity Type	Notes
Finish Milestone	This Activity Type is used to indicate the completion of Phase, Stage or a major event in a project. It has only a Finish Date and no Duration or Start Date. It may only have **Finish Constraints** assigned. It may not have time dependent resources assigned but may have a **Primary Resource** assigned to indicate who is responsible for the activity.
WBS Summary Activity	The new Primavera Version5.0 **WBS Summary Activity** is an activity that spans the duration of all activities which are assigned exactly the same WBS Code and unlike a Level of Effort Activity it does not have any predecessors or successors. 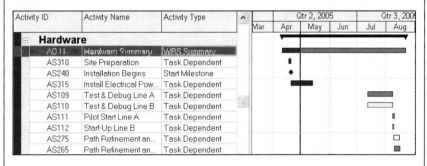 Therefore a WBS activity will change duration when either the earliest start or latest finish of activities that it spans is changed. This may happen as the project progresses and activities do not meet their original scheduled dates, or the duration of an activity is changed, or logic is changed, or the schedule is leveled. This function calculates the WBS Activity Duration in the same way as WBS activities in P3 or SureTrak, Topic activities in SureTrak. It is similar to the way Summary activity durations are calculated in Microsoft Project, except the activities do not need to be demoted below the detailed activities in as in Microsoft Project. WBS activities may be used for: • Reporting at summary level by filtering on WBS activities, • Entering estimated costs at summary level for producing cash flow tables while the detailed activities are used for calculating the overall duration for the WBS and day to day management of the project and • Recording costs and hours at summary level when is it not desirable or practicable to record at activity level, especially when the detailed activities are liable to change.

18.4.3   Duration Type

The Duration Type becomes effective after a resource has been assigned to an activity.

The **Duration Type** is set in the **Defaults** tab in the **Projects Workspace** and all new activities are assigned this Duration Type.

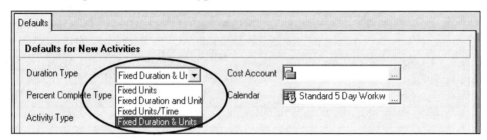

The **Duration Type** for each new activity may be changed in the **General** tab in the **Activities Workspace** or by displaying the **Duration Type** column:

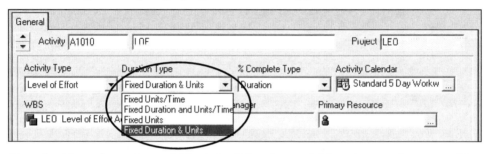

The Duration Type determines which of the following variables change when one of the others is changed in the equation:

- Resource Units = Resource Units per Time Period x Duration

For example, a 40-hour activity with 2 people working 8 hours per day will take 20 hours or 2.5 days:

- 40 hours of work = 2 people per hour x 20 hours

When an activity is in progress this equation is modified to:

- Remaining Resource Units = Resource Units per Time period x Remaining Duration

Primavera Version 5.0 has four options for Duration Type, Microsoft Project has three options, and P3 and SureTrak have two options (which are a lot easier to understand).

The Primavera Version 5.0 terminology that describes the way the software treats the relationship between Durations, Resource Units and Resource Units/Time Period is different from Microsoft Project, P3 and SureTrak. Primavera Version 5.0 has more options than all the other products and this gives the product more flexibility. The following table should clarify these options.

Purposes of the Duration Types

Duration Type	Purpose
• **Fixed Units/Time**	This option is used when the same number of people are required to complete an activity irrespective of the activity duration. For example, if a machine requires two people to operate and therefore a Resource is assigned to the Activity at 200%, changing either the Units or the Duration will not change the Units/Time and there will always be two people operating the machine.
• **Fixed Duration & Units/Time**	This **Duration Type** disables the **User Preferences**, **Calculations** tab option **Recalculate the Units, Duration, and Units/Time for existing assignments based on the activity Duration Type.** **Option 1** This option is used when the Duration of an activity should not change when Resources are added or removed or Units/Time changed. For example, when the time to complete an activity is fixed, the resources may be manipulated until a satisfactory resource loading is established without the activity duration changing. **Option 2** A change in the Duration will change the Units; however, the Units/Time will remain constant. For example, when there are two people assigned to an activity and the activity is increased in duration, there will still be two people working but for a longer period of time.
• **Fixed Units**	This option is used when the amount of work required to finish an activity is constant. For example, if there are 8,000 bricks to be laid and a bricklayer is able to lay 100 bricks per hour, there is 80 hours of work for one bricklayer, 40 hours for 2 bricklayers and 20 hours for 4 bricklayers. Changing the Duration or the Units/Time will not change the number of hours required to complete the activity.
• **Fixed Duration & Units**	**Option 1** This option is used when the Duration of an activity should not change when Resources are added or removed or Units/Time changed. For example, when the time to complete an activity is fixed, the resources may be manipulated until a satisfactory resource loading is established without the activity duration changing. **Option 2** A change to the Duration will change the Units; however, the Units/Time will remain constant. It one person is assigned to an activity for 8 hours per day and the activity is doubled in duration, the will be now be one person working on the activity for 4 hours per day and the activity will require the same number of hours to complete.

The table below displays what happens to the relationship in each of the four options when one variable is changed and

- The **User Preferences**, **Calculations** tab option **Recalculate the Units, Duration, and Units/Time for existing assignments based on the activity Duration Type** is selected:

Duration Type	Labor Units Change in Status Tab	Activity Duration Change	Resource Units Change	Units/Time Period Change	Add or Remove Resources
Fixed Units/Time	Duration Change	Units Change	Duration Change	Duration Change	Activity Units Change, Resource Units Constant, Duration Constant
Fixed Duration & Units/Time	Units/Time Change	Units Change	Units/Time Change	Units Change	Activity Units Change, Resource Units Constant, Duration Constant
Fixed Units	Duration Change	Units/Time Change	Duration Change	Duration Change	Activity Units Change, Resource Units Constant, Duration Constant
Fixed Duration & Units	Units/Time Change	Units/Time Change	Units/Time Change	Units Change	Activity Units Change, Resource Units Constant, Duration Constant

The table below displays what happens to the relationship in each of the four options when one variable is changed and

- The **User Preferences**, **Calculations** tab option **Preserve the Units, Duration, and Units/Time for existing assignments** is selected:

Duration Type	Labor Units Change in Status Tab	Activity Duration Change	Resource Units Change	Units/Time Period Change	Add or Remove Resources
Fixed Units/Time	Duration Change	Units Change	Duration Change	Duration Change	**Activity Units Constant, Resource Units Change, Duration Change**
Fixed Duration & Units/Time	Units/Time Change	Units Change	Units/Time Change	Units Change	Activity Units Change, Resource Units Constant, Duration Constant
Fixed Units	Duration Change	Units/Time Change	Duration Change	Duration Change	**Activity Units Constant, Resource Units Change, Duration Change**
Fixed Duration & Units	Units/Time Change	Units/Time Change	Units/Time Change	Units Change	**Activity Units Constant, Resource Units Change**, Duration Constant

- Bold descriptions in the right hand column on the table above indicate the differences with the table above.

- The **User Preferences**, **Calculations** tab option **Preserve the Units, Duration, and Units/Time for existing assignments** will not freeze the Activity Units when the **Duration Type** of **Fixed Units** is selected.

18.5 Assigning and Removing Roles

To assign a Role to an activity:

- Select the activity to be assigned the Role,
- Select the **Resources** tab in the **Activity Details** form,
- Click on the [Add Role] button to open the **Assign Roles** form,
- Use the **Display:**, **Filter By** menu to select either:
  - ➢ **All Roles**, which will display all Roles in the database,
  - ➢ **Current Project's Roles**. This option will only display Roles that have been assigned to this project, or
  - ➢ **Customize**, which opens a **Filter** form enabling the user to limit the number of displayed Roles by creating a filter.

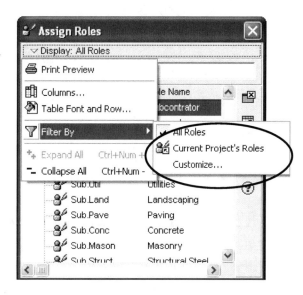

- Select one or more Roles to be assigned to an activity using the Ctrl-click function,
- Then to assign a Role:
  - ➢ Click on the [🞥] button, or
  - ➢ Double-click on one of the Roles.

To achieve the picture below you may need to format the columns in the **Resources Details** form.

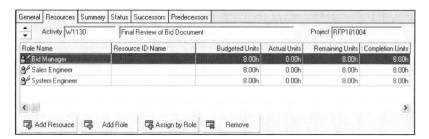

At this point, the Roles hours and costs may be edited as required.

Costs may be assigned to Roles but these costs are not calculated, as a Role Rate is not available from the database.

To remove a Role:

- Select the Role, and
- Click on the [Remove] button.

18.6 Assigning and Removing Resources

Resources may be assigned directly to:

- An activity that has an Assigned Role, or
- An Activity without a Role.

18.6.1 Assigning a Resource to an Assigned Role

To assign a Resource to a Role assigned to an activity:

- Select the activity to be assigned a Resource,
- Select the Role to be assigned a Resources from the **Resources Details** tab,
- Click on the [Assign by Role] button to open the **Assign Resources By Roles** form,
- Click on the **Display:** menu and select **Filter By** to open the **Filter By** form,
- Select which Resources you wish to have displayed in the **Assign Roles** form from the **Filter By** form,
- Select [Apply] to return to the **Assign Resources By Role** form,
- From the **Assign Resources By Role** form click on the Resource you wish to assign,
- To assign the Resource either:
  - ➢ Double-click on the Resource, or
  - ➢ Click on the [▦] button.

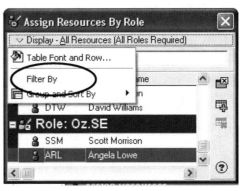

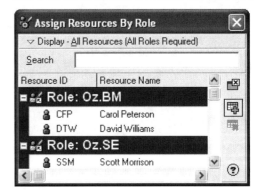

18.6.2　Assigning a Resource to an Activity Without a Role

To assign a Resource to an activity:

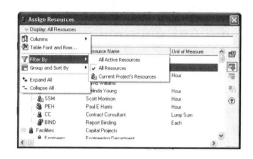

- Select the activity to be assigned the Resource,

- Click on the [Add Resource] button to open the **Assign Resource** form,

- Click on the **Display:** menu and select **Filter By** and then select from the three options which resources you wish to display in the **Assign Resources** form,

- To assign the Resource either:

  ➢ Double-click on the Resource, or

  ➢ Click on the 🔲 button.

You may now edit the hours or Units/Time Period for each resource.

18.6.3　Removing a Resource

Before you remove a Resource from an activity that has more than one resource assigned to it, you must be aware of your **Resource Assignment** preferences. These preferences determine if the total number of Units assigned to the activity (or work) will be reduced or remain constant.

To remove a resource, select the Resource in the Bottom Pane Resource tab and either:

- Strike the **Del** key, or

- Click on the [Remove] button.

18.6.4　Assigning a Resource to an Activity More Than Once

The option in the **Projects Workspace Resources** tab under the **Resources Assignments** heading allows a resource to be assigned more than once to an activity. A resource could be assigned to work at the start of an activity and then in conjunction with **Resource Lag** work again at the end of an activity.

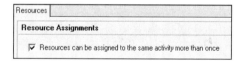

18.6.5   Resource and Activity Duration Calculation & Resource Lags

18.6.6   Activity Duration

An Activity Duration (or Activity Remaining Duration of an In-Progress Activity) is adopted from the longest Resource Duration (or Resource Remaining Duration of an In-Progress Activity) when more than one resource has been assigned to an activity.

In a situation where more than one Resource has been assigned to an activity with different Units and/or Units/Time, the Resources many have different durations.

In the example below the Activity Duration is 10 days, which is calculated from David William's **Resource Original Duration** of 10 days:

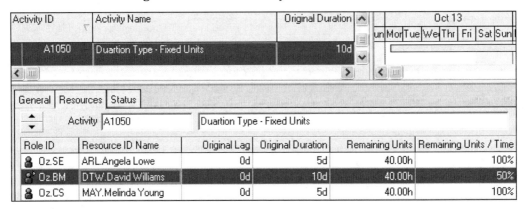

This is calculated in a similar way to P3 and SureTrak when all Resources are set to Driving.

18.6.7   Resource Lag

A Resource may be assigned a Lag, the duration from the start of the activity to the point at which the Resource commences work.

In the example below the Activity Duration is 12 days, which is calculated from Angela Lowe's **Resource Original Lag** of 7 days and **Resource Original Duration** of 5 days:

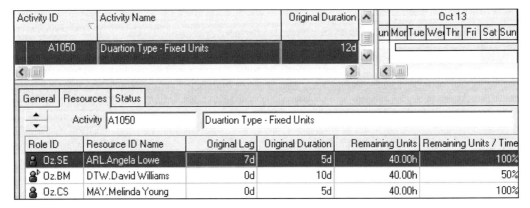

18.7 Expenses

Expenses are intended to be used for one off non-resource type costs and could include:

- Purchase of office equipment to set up a project office,
- Travel costs,
- Payment for a consultant's report,
- Insurance costs, and
- Training courses.

Expenses may be created using the:

- **Expenses Workspace** and assigned to an activity, or
- Created in the **Expenses** tab of an activity.

18.7.1 Expenses Workspace

The **Expenses Workspace** is opened by:

- Clicking in the 🖼 button on the **Directory** bar, or
- Selecting **Project**, **Expenses**.

Creating a new **Expense** is similar to creating a new activity:

- Select **Edit**, **Add**, or
- Strike the **Ins** key.
- The **Select Activity** form will then be displayed and the activity the expense is to be associated with is selected.

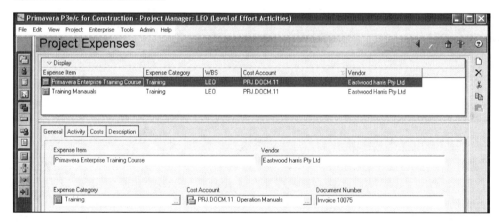

Enter the following Information in the tabs in the bottom window:

- **General Tab**
  - ➢ **Expense Item** – A free form field to enter the description of the Expense.
  - ➢ **Vendor** – A free form field to enter the vendor or supplier name.
  - ➢ **Expense Category** – Select the Expense Category, these are created in the **Admin Categories** form.

- ➢ **Cost Account** – Select a Cost Account should you wish to see or report the costs against a Cost Account. Costs accounts are created in a similar method to other hierarchical structures in Primavera Version 5.0, such as the WBS, by selecting **Enterprise, Cost Accounts…**.
- ➢ **Document Number** – A free form field to enter the document number that could represent the Purchase Order, Contract or Invoice Number.
- **Activity Tab** displays information mainly adopted from an activity, the Accrual Type, is editable:
  - ➢ **Accrual Type** – this allows you to select if the costs are accrued or cash flowed at the beginning, end, or uniformly over the duration of the activity.

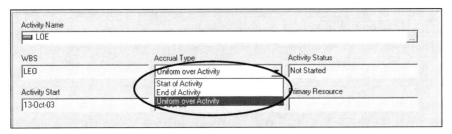

- **Costs Tab** is mainly self-explanatory. The following information is entered:
  - ➢ **Budgeted Units** – the quantity of the Expense item,
  - ➢ **Price/Unit** – the cost per Expense item,
  - ➢ **Unit of Measure** – the units of the Expense; for example, each, foot, meter, etc.
  - ➢ Check **Auto Compute Actuals** to allow the software to calculate the Actual and Remaining Costs and Units (quantities) based on the **Activity % Complete**,
  - ➢ The remainder of the fields are used when the activity is progressed.

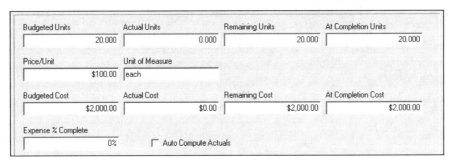

- **Description Tab** is where you enter an extended description of the Expense item.

18.7.2 Expenses Tab in the Activities Workspace

This tab may have all the columns of data available in the **Expenses Workspace** displayed. All the fields may be edited from this Tab:

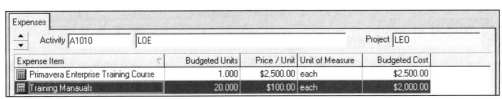

18.8 Suggested Setup for Creating a Resourced Schedule

The order that topics are introduced in this chapter is also a satisfactory order of actions that should be considered when preparing to assign resources to activities.

The simplest calculation options should be used as a default, and more complex options considered only when there is a specific scheduling requirement.

The table below lists process and suggested options that could be considered when creating a resourced schedule. It is important to set all the parameters before the activities are added otherwise a lot of time is wasted changing parameters on a number of activities. These are not intended to suit every project but are a starting point for less experienced users.

Step	Suggested Settings
• Set the **Units/Time** format by selecting **Edit, User Preferences...** to open the **User Preferences** form and select the **Time Units** tab.	There is a choice of **percentage (50%)** or **units/duration (4h/d)**. This should be set on personal preference.
• Set the **Resource Assignments** option by selecting **Edit, User Preferences...** to open the **User Preferences** form and select the **Calculations** tab.	It is suggested that the **Preserve the Units, Duration, and Units/Time for existing assignments** is selected. With this option as Resources are added or deleted the total number of hours assigned to an Activity increases or decreases. Each Resource's hours are calculated independently. The options under **Assignment Staffing** need to be carefully considered and understood so that when Resources are assigned to Roles and resource assignments are changed that the user understands which Unit Rate and which Unit Cost will remain against the activity.
• In the **Project Workspace**, **Defaults** tab set the default **Activity Type**.	It is suggested that **Task Dependent** is used as with this option Resource calendars are not used.
• In the **Project Workspace**, **Defaults** tab set the default **Duration Type**.	It is suggested that **Fixed Duration & Units** is used. With this option the Activity Duration does not change when resource assignments are altered, and when an Activity Duration is changed the Units do not change, so your estimate of hours and costs will not change.
• In the **Project Workspace**, **Defaults** tab set the default **Percent Complete Type**.	The author prefers to use **Physical** as this allows the Activity Percent Complete to be independent of the Activity Durations.
• In the **Project Workspace**, **Resource** tab set the default **Resource Assignment Defaults**.	Unless multiple Rates are being used then **Price / Unit** should be selected. Check **Drive activity dates by default**.

18.9 Reviewing Resources

There are a number of facilities for reviewing the resource, these are typically displaying a Layout or running a report. Reports are not in the scope of this book but the following layouts may be displayed in the Activities Workspace. Formatting of these Layouts is achieved by using the menus and right clicking. The displays are affected by the Timescale interval and these Layouts will not be covered in detail as they are self-explanatory.

18.9.1 Activity Usage Profile

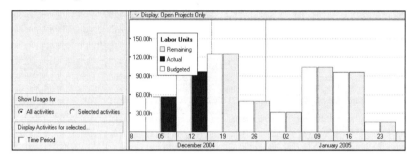

18.9.2 Resource Usage Spreadsheet

18.9.3 Resource Usage Profile

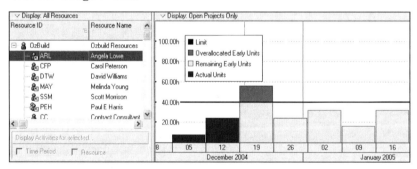

18.9.4 Activity Usage Spreadsheet

WORKSHOP 15

Assigning Roles and Resources to Activities

Background
The Resources and roles must now be assigned to their specific activities.

Assignment
Open the OzBuild with Resources project non-statused and complete the following steps.

1. In the **Activities Workspace** display the **Gantt Chart** in the top view and **Resources** tab of the **Activities Details** form in the bottom view.
2. Open the **User Preferences** form:
   - Select the **Calculations** tab and set the **Resource Assignments** option to **Preserve the Units, Duration, and Units/Time for existing assignments**.
   - Select the **Time Units** tab and set the **Units/Time** format to **units/duration (4h/d)** and the **Units Format**, **Units of Time** to **Hours** with **0 Decimal Places**.
   - Select the **Calculations** tab and select:
     - ➢ **Always use the new resources Units per Time and Overtime factor** and
     - ➢ **Always use resource's Price per Unit.**
3. Copy the **OzBuild Workshop 11 – Without Float** layout as **OzBuild Workshop 15 – Assigning Roles** layout.
4. Format the Resources tab with the columns shown below and assign the following Roles to the Activities using the [Add Role] button:

Activity	OZ1010	Bid Strategy Developed			
Role	Resource ID Name		Remaining Units / Time	Price / Unit	At Completion Units
Bid Manager			8/d	$0/h^	8
Sales Engineer			8/d	$0/h^	8
System Engineer			8/d	$0/h^	8

Activity	OZ1020	Technical Feasibility Study			
Role	Resource ID Name		Remaining Units / Time	Price / Unit	At Completion Units
System Engineer			8/d	$0/h^	64

Activity	OZ1030	Installation Requirements Documented			
Role	Resource ID Name		Remaining Units / Time	Price / Unit	At Completion Units
Sales Engineer			8/d	$0/h^	32
System Engineer			8/d	$0/h^	32

5. Reformat the Activity table columns as below the following values should be shown:

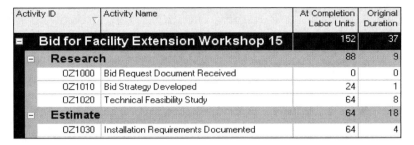

Activity ID	Activity Name	At Completion Labor Units	Original Duration
Bid for Facility Extension Workshop 15		152	37
Research		88	9
OZ1000	Bid Request Document Received	0	0
OZ1010	Bid Strategy Developed	24	1
OZ1020	Technical Feasibility Study	64	8
Estimate		64	18
OZ1030	Installation Requirements Documented	64	4

6. Assign the following Resources to the Roles using the Assign by Role button:

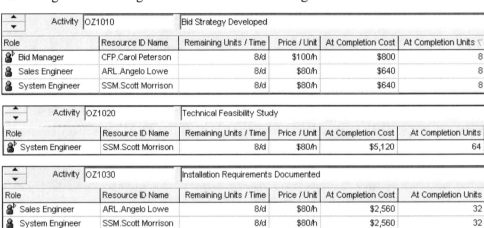

Activity OZ1010 — Bid Strategy Developed

Role	Resource ID Name	Remaining Units / Time	Price / Unit	At Completion Cost	At Completion Units
Bid Manager	CFP.Carol Peterson	8/d	$100/h	$800	8
Sales Engineer	ARL.Angelo Lowe	8/d	$80/h	$640	8
System Engineer	SSM.Scott Morrison	8/d	$80/h	$640	8

Activity OZ1020 — Technical Feasibility Study

Role	Resource ID Name	Remaining Units / Time	Price / Unit	At Completion Cost	At Completion Units
System Engineer	SSM.Scott Morrison	8/d	$80/h	$5,120	64

Activity OZ1030 — Installation Requirements Documented

Role	Resource ID Name	Remaining Units / Time	Price / Unit	At Completion Cost	At Completion Units
Sales Engineer	ARL.Angelo Lowe	8/d	$80/h	$2,560	32
System Engineer	SSM.Scott Morrison	8/d	$80/h	$2,560	32

7. Assign the remainder of the Resources to the Activities using the Add Resource button at 8 hours per day:

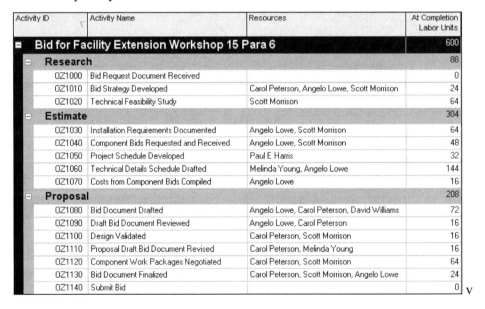

Activity ID	Activity Name	Resources	At Completion Labor Units
Bid for Facility Extension Workshop 15 Para 6			600
Research			88
OZ1000	Bid Request Document Received		0
OZ1010	Bid Strategy Developed	Carol Peterson, Angelo Lowe, Scott Morrison	24
OZ1020	Technical Feasibility Study	Scott Morrison	64
Estimate			304
OZ1030	Installation Requirements Documented	Angelo Lowe, Scott Morrison	64
OZ1040	Component Bids Requested and Received	Angelo Lowe, Scott Morrison	48
OZ1050	Project Schedule Developed	Paul E Harris	32
OZ1060	Technical Details Schedule Drafted	Melinda Young, Angelo Lowe	144
OZ1070	Costs from Component Bids Compiled	Angelo Lowe	16
Proposal			208
OZ1080	Bid Document Drafted	Angelo Lowe, Carol Peterson, David Williams	72
OZ1090	Draft Bid Document Reviewed	Angelo Lowe, Carol Peterson	16
OZ1100	Design Validated	Carol Peterson, Scott Morrison	16
OZ1110	Proposal Draft Bid Document Revised	Carol Peterson, Melinda Young	16
OZ1120	Component Work Packages Negotiated	Carol Peterson, Scott Morrison	64
OZ1130	Bid Document Finalized	Carol Peterson, Scott Morrison, Angelo Lowe	24
OZ1140	Submit Bid		0

8. Display the **Activity Usage Spreadsheet** by clicking on the 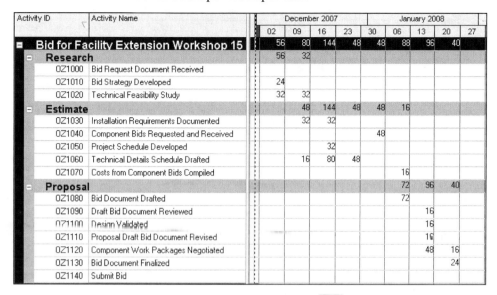 button, the picture below shows the number of hours per week per task:

9. Display the **Resource Usage Sheet** by clicking on the 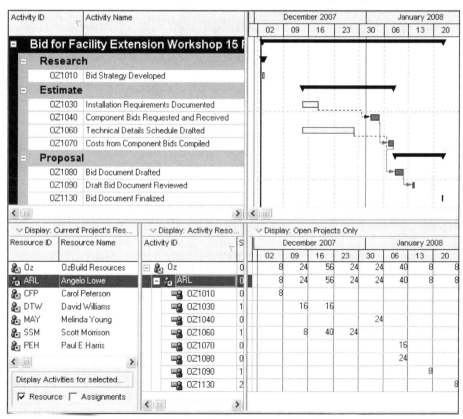 button, use the **Display** option to display the **Current Project's Resources** only, select **Angela Lowe** (in the bottom left hand window), select **Resource** for the option **Display Activities for selected…** (in the bottom left hand corner of the screen). It may be seen that Angela Low is overloaded and working 56 hours on the week beginning 16 Dec07.

10. Display the **Resource Usage Profile** by clicking on the 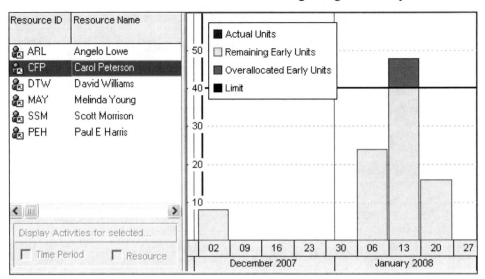 icon, you will also see that Carol Peterson is overloaded on the week beginning 13 January.

19 STATUSING A RESOURCED SCHEDULE

Statusing a project with resources employs a number of preferences and options, which are very interactive and will require a significant amount of practice by a user to understand and master them.

It is often considered best practice to update a project between 10 and 20 times in its lifecycle. Some companies update schedules to correspond with accounting periods, which are normally every month. This frequency is often too long for projects that are less than a year in duration, as too much change may happen in one month. Therefore more frequent updating may identify problems earlier.

After reading this chapter and before working on a live project, inexperienced users should gain confidence with the software by:

- Creating a new project and setting the **Defaults**, **Preferences** and **Options** to reflect the method you wish to enter information and how you want Primavera Version 5.0 to calculate the project data.
- Creating two or three activities and then assigning two or three resources to each activity.
- Update the Activities and Resources as if you were updating a schedule and observe the results.
- Alter the preferences and defaults if you are not receiving the result you require. Re-update and note the preferences and defaults for future reference.

Some of these settings may have been set by your organization and you may not be assigned access rights to change the settings. You should still go through the statusing process in a test project with dummy data similar to your real project data and be prepared to change those settings to which you do have access, as required.

Statusing a project with resources takes place in two distinct steps:

- The dates, durations and relationships are statused using the methods outlined in the **TRACKING PROGRESS** chapter, and
- The Resource, Expenses Units (hours and quantities) and Costs, both the Actual to Date and To Complete, are then updated. These values may be automatically updated by Primavera Version 5.0 from the % Complete or imported from accounting and timesheet systems or updated by the Primavera Timesheet system.

This chapter covers the following topics:

- Understanding **Budget** data and **Baseline Projects**
- Understanding the **Current Data Date** with respect to resources
- Information required to update a resourced schedule
- Project and Activity Workspace Defaults
- Updating Resources and Expenses
- Reviewing the statused schedule

19.1 Understanding Budget Values and Baseline Projects

19.1.1 Cost and Units Budget Values

The Budget Values in Primavera Version 5.0 are assigned to both Units and Costs for each Resource and Expense at the time the Resource or Expense is assigned to an Activity.

Budget Values reside in the current project and in all Baseline Projects.

The Budget values may be linked to the At Completion values until the activity is in progress by being marked as Started or having a % Complete.

 Should you wish to re-estimate the cost of a project and compare it to a previous value when activities have not started you should then create a Baseline Project before re-estimating the project and compare your revised costs to the Baseline.

19.1.2 Baseline Project and Values

A Baseline project is a complete copy of a project including the relationships, resource assignments and expenses.

The creation and assignment of a Baseline Project was covered in the **TRACKING PROGRESS** chapter.

- **Baseline Dates** are also known as Target Dates and are normally considered to be the approved Project Early Start and Early Finish dates, which are recorded by saving a Baseline project.

- **Baseline Duration** is the original planned duration of an activity, calculated from the Early Start to the Early Finish of an Activity.

- **Baseline Costs** are also known as Budgets (not to be confused with Primavera Version 5.0 Budget Costs) and represent the original project cost estimate. These are the figures against which the Actual Costs and Cost at Completion (or Estimate at Completion) may be compared.

- **Baseline Quantity** is also known as Budgeted Quantity and represents the original estimate of the project quantities. These are the quantities against which the consumption of resources may be compared.

The Baseline values are values against which project progress is measured. All these values may be read by and compared with the current project values and show variances from the original plan.

A Baseline would normally be created prior to statusing a project for the first time.

The Primavera Version 5.0 Variance columns use Baseline data from Baseline Projects to calculate variances.

19.2 Understanding the Current Data Date

The **Current Data Date** is a standard scheduling term. It is also known as the **Review Date**, **Status Date**, **As of Date** and **Update Date**.

- The **Current Data Date** is the date that divides the past from the future in the schedule. It is not normally in the future but is often in the recent past due to the time it may take to collect the information required to status the schedule.
- **Actual Costs** and **Quantities/Hours** or **Actual Work** occur before the data date.
- **Costs** and **Quantities/Hours to Complete** or **Work to Complete** are scheduled after the Data Date.
- **Actual Duration** is calculated from the **Actual Start** to the **Current Data Date**.
- **Remaining Duration** is the duration required to complete an activity. It is calculated forward from the **Current Data Date** and the Early Finish date or an in-progress activity is calculated from the **Current Data Date** using the:
  - ➤ **Activity Calendar** when the Activity Type is Task Dependent or is Resource Dependent but no Resources have been assigned, or
  - ➤ **Resource Calendar** when the Activity Type is Resource Dependent and uses the longest Resource Duration.

Primavera Version 5.0 has one Data Date, the **Current Data Date,** which operates in the same way as the P3 and SureTrak Data Date. Microsoft Project has four dates associated with updating a schedule. The Microsoft Project Status Date is similar in function to the Primavera Version 5.0 **Current Data Date.**

19.3 Information Required to Update a Resourced Schedule

A project schedule is usually updated at the end of a period, such as each day, week or month. One purpose of updating a schedule is to establish differences between the plan, which is usually saved as a Baseline, and the current schedule.

The following information is required to status a resourced schedule:

Activities completed in the update period:
- **Actual Start** date of the activity.
- **Actual Finish** date of the activity.
- **Actual Costs** and **Quantities** (Units) consumed or spent on **Labor Resources, Material Resources** and **Expense.**

Activities commenced in the update period:
- **Actual Start** date of the activity.
- **Remaining Duration** or **Expected Finish** date.
- **Actual Costs** and/or **Actual Quantities.**
- **Quantities to Complete** and **Costs to Complete.**

Activities Not Commenced:

- Changes in Logic or Constraints, or
- Changes in Duration, or
- Changes in estimated **Costs**, **Hours** or **Quantities**.

The schedule may be updated once this information is collected.

Primavera Version 5.0 may calculate Actual Costs and the Costs to Complete by turning on a relationship between the Units and Resource Units. When this relationship is turned off costs may be entered manually. If the Actual Costs are to be calculated by Primavera Version 5.0 then the Actual Costs do not need to be collected.

A marked-up copy of the schedule recording the progress of the current schedule is often produced prior to updating the data with Primavera Version 5.0. Ideally, the mark-up should be prepared by a physical inspection of the work or by a person who intimately knows the work, although that is not always possible. It is good practice to keep this marked-up record for your own reference. Ensure that you note the date of the mark-up (i.e., the data date) and, if relevant, the time.

Often a Statusing Report or mark-up sheet is distributed to the people responsible for marking up the project's progress. A page break could be placed at each responsible person's band, and when the schedule is printed, each person would have a personal listing of activities that are either in progress or due to commence. This is particularly useful for large projects. The marked-up sheets are then returned to the scheduler for data entry into the software system.

Other electronic methods, such as the Primavera Timesheet system or an e-mail based system with spreadsheet or pdf attachments, may be employed to collect the data. Irrespective of the method used, the same data needs to be collected.

It is recommended that only one person updates each schedule. There is a high probability for errors when more than one person updates a schedule.

19.4 Project Workspace Defaults for Statusing a Resourced Schedule

The Project Workspace settings affect all activities in a project that are being updated. When more that one project is open, the settings of the **Default Project** are used to calculate all open projects when they are scheduled or leveled. The Default Project is set in the **Set Default Project** form opened by selecting **Project**, **Set Default Project…**.

The **Calculations** tab in the **Projects Workspace** sets some important resource defaults:

Calculations

Activities	Resource Assignments
Default Price / Unit for activities without resource Price / Units $0.00/h	When updating Actual Units or Cost
☐ Activity percent complete based on activity steps	○ Add Actual to Remaining
	◉ Subtract Actual from At Completion
☑ Link Budget and At Completion for not started activities	☑ Recalculate Actual Units and Cost when duration % complete changes
○ Reset Original Duration and Units to Remaining	☐ Update units when costs change on resource assignments
◉ Reset Remaining Duration and Units to Original	☑ Link Actual and Actual This Period Units and Cost

- **Activities**
  - ➢ **Default Price/Unit for activities without resource Price/Units**. When a resource does not have a rate, the default rate may be set in this tab.
  - ➢ **Activity percent complete based on activity steps**. The Primavera Version 5.0 **Step** function allows activities to be broken down into elements called Steps. Each element earns a designated % Complete when the Step is marked as complete. Physical % Complete must be selected to use Steps.
  - ➢ Unchecking **Link Budget an At Completion for not started activities** allows the user to re-estimate the cost of unstarted activities while preserving the **Original Budget** of an activity. This is the same as the P3 Auto Cost Rule No 6 and was new to Primavera Version 4.1.
  - ➢ The next two options **Reset Original Durations and Units to Remaining** and **Reset Remaining Duration and Units to Original** determine how the Original Duration and Units are set when progress is removed from activities. This was new to Primavera Version 4.1.
- **Resource Assignments**
  - ➢ **When updating Actual Units or Costs**. There are two options, which is the same as the P3 Autocost Rule Number 3:
    - – **Add Actual to Remaining**. When Actual Costs are entered, the At Completion increases by the amount of the Actual Costs.
    - – **Subtract Actual from At Completion**. When Actual Costs are entered, the To Complete does not change and the To Complete is reduced by the value of the Actual. This is the author's preferred option as the At Completion does not change until the At Completion is exceeded by the Actual.
  - ➢ **Recalculate Actual Units and Cost when duration % complete changes**. This option links the % Complete of **Duration Type** activities to the Actual and To Complete, thus an increase in % Complete will increase the Actual and decrease the To Complete values.
  - ➢ **Update units when costs change on resource assignments**.
    - – With this option checked a change in Costs will recalculate the Units.
    - – With this option unchecked a change in costs may be made independently of units after units have been changed.

> ➤ **Link Actual and Actual This Period Units and Cost**. This is the same as the P3 Autocost Rule Number 6. With this option checked, when you enter an **Actual this period**, the **Actual to date** will be calculated by increasing the original value by the value of the **Actual this period**. Or, you may enter the **Actual to date** and Primavera Version 5.0 will calculate the **Actual this period**. When unchecked, the two fields are unlinked and you may enter any figure in each field. This option is grayed out if the project is not open.

19.5 Activity Workspace - Percent Complete Types

There are three **% Complete** types which may be assigned to each activity. The default is adopted from the setting in the **Defaults** tab in the **Projects Workspace**.

- **Physical**
- **Duration**
- **Units**

19.5.1 Assigning the Project Default Percent Complete Type

A project default **Percent Complete Type** is assigned in the **Defaults** tab of the Projects Workspace and is assigned to each new activity created in a project. This may be changed at any time and only affects new activities created from that time onward:

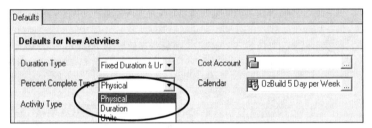

Once an activity has been created, the **Percent Complete Type** may be changed in the **General** tab of the **Activities Workspace**:

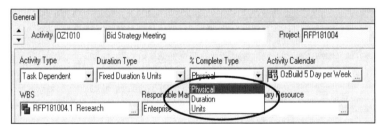

The Activity Percent Complete may be updated in the **Status** tab of the **Activities Workspace** where the **Percent Complete Type** is also displayed:

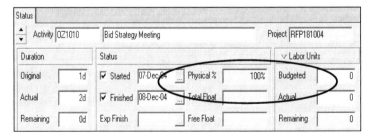

Each **Percent Complete Type** has its own data column. There is also an **Activity %**
Complete column which is linked to and displays the value from the **Percent Complete**
Type column that has been assigned to the activity. See the picture below:

Activity ID	Activity Name	Percent Complete Type	Activity % Complete	Physical % Complete	Duration % Complete	Units % Complete
AA1000	% Complete Physical	Physical	50% ⟷	50%	0%	0%
AA1010	% Complete Duration	Duration	50% ⟵	0% ⟶	50%	0%
AA1020	% Complete Type Units	Units	50% ⟵	0%	0% ⟶	50%

19.5.2 Physical Percent Complete Type

An activity assigned Physical Percent Complete Type may be entered in the **Physical %**
Complete or the **Activity % Complete**. This field has no impact and is not linked to either
the Resource Units or the Actual and Remaining Durations of the Activity.

Physical % Complete muct be used when Steps are being used to record progress.

The **Physical Percent Complete** type is used when the progress of an Activity is being
measured outside Primavera Version 5.0. For example, an activity representing the
installation cable that is measured by length of cable installed would have the percent
complete calculated by:

- % Complete = Qty. of Cable Installed / Total Qty. of Cable to be Installed

For example, the activity may only have the installation labor assigned to it, and therefore
the installation labor parameter may not be used for the measurement of the Activity %
Complete. Also because the percent complete of the activity is based on the length of cable
installed, the activity % Complete (the progress of the work) may be compared to the
resource **Units % Complete** (the amount of labor used) which is calculated from the
formula:

- Units % Complete = Actual Units / At Completion Units

This example is demonstrated in the picture below:

- The Activity Physical % Complete is set at 50%.
- The Activity Unit % Complete is calculated from the At Completion Units and not the
  Budget Units.

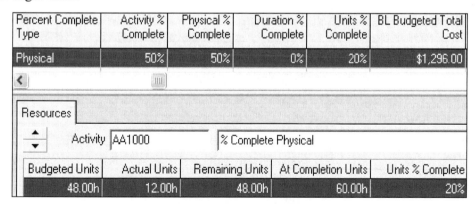

After a second resource is added, the Activity Units % Complete of 40% is calculated from the addition of the two resource Actual Units and At Completion Units:

- Activity Unit % Complete = Actual Labor Units / At Completion Labor Units
- Therefore, 40% = (12 + 36) / (60 + 60)

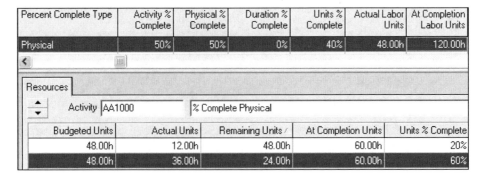

19.5.3 Duration Percent Complete Type

With Duration Percent Complete there is a link established between:

- **Duration % Complete**
- **Original Duration**
- **Remaining Duration**

A **Duration % Complete** may only be entered after an Actual Start Date has been assigned and should be in the past with respect to the Current Data Date.

A change in one parameter will change one other:

- A change in the **Duration % Complete** will change the **Remaining Duration,** and
- A change in the **Original Duration** or **Remaining Duration** will change the **Duration % Complete**:

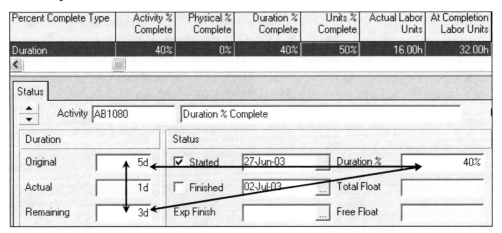

The **Actual Duration** is calculated from the duration of **Actual Start** to the **Current Data Date**.

The Activity **Units Percent Complete** is still calculated from the Resource Units.

19.5.4 Units Percent Complete Type

When **Units Percent Complete** type is selected:

- This option creates a link between the **Activity % Complete** and the activity **Units % Complete**, and

- The **Duration % Complete** is calculated from the relationship between the **Original Duration** and **Actual Duration**.

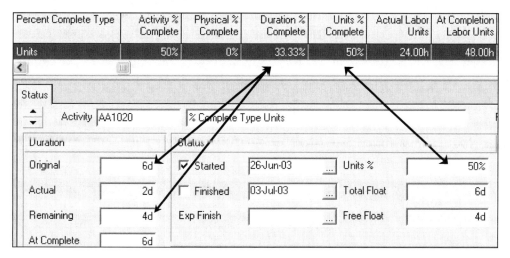

19.6 Using Steps to Calculate Activity Percent Complete

An activity percent complete may be defined by using steps. A Step is a measurable or identifiable task required to complete an activity. In summary to use steps:

- Check the **Activity percent complete based on steps** check box in the **Projects Workspace**, **Calculations** tab,

- Select the **Physical** in the **% Complete Type** for each activity that is to be measured by steps in the **General** tab of **Activity Workspace**,

- Select the **Steps** tab in the **Activity Workspace**,

- Format the columns you wish to display,

- Add the number of steps you require,

- Edit the descriptions,

- Edit the **Step Weight** so the **Step Weight Percent** reflects the desired value of the Step,

- Check the **Completed** check box as each step is complete.

Step Name	% Complete	Step Weight	Step Weight Percent	Completed
Specify Document Composition	100%	10.0	10.0	☑
Document First Draft	100%	40.0	40.0	☑
Final Draft and Internal Approval	0%	25.0	25.0	☐
Client Approval	0%	25.0	25.0	☐

19.7 Updating the Schedule

19.7.1 Preferences, Defaults and Options for Statusing a Project

The options to be considered and checked before statusing a schedule:

Function	Discussion
• **% Complete Type**	It is the author's preference to use **Physical % Complete** when the resources are **Input** resources, i.e. those doing the work. This allows the % of deliverables complete to be measured independently of the resource(s) doing the work, thus allowing a comparison of the deliverables completed against the resources consumed.
• **Activity Type**	Activities with known durations should be set as **Task Dependent** and will use the Activity calendar (not the Resource Calendar) for calculating the finish date of the activity. **Resource Dependent** activities should only be used if there are resource availability issues which may only be resolved by the use of **Resource Calendars**. **Level of Effort** and **WBS** activities are useful but should be avoided by the novice user as these add an additional level of complexity that is not required.
• **Project Workspace Calculations tab**	The **Calculations** tab in the **Projects Workspace** sets some important resource defaults that should be reviewed, understood and set so the schedule calculates the desired way. The **Link Actual and Actual This Period Units and Cost** option found in the **Calculations** tab of the **Project Workspace** should be checked it is intended to **Store Period Performance**.
• **Duration Type**	It is the author's preference to use **Fixed Duration and Units** because the estimate to complete is not altered by changing the Activity Duration or Units/Time.
• **Timesheets**	Timesheets may be used to update actuals for none, some, or all resources. Organizations using timesheets should have procedures managing their use. Timesheets are out of the scope of this book but if they are being used the actual values should be carefully checked before being applied to ensure they are logical.

• **Resources Cost Calculation**	Resource Costs may be calculated from the Resource Unit Rates for each individual resource assignment.
	Each resource assignment has a field titled **Cost Units Linked**. When this is checked the resource costs are calculated from the resource units.
	The **Calculate costs from units** check box in the **Resource Workspace**, **Details** tab sets the default value for **Cost Units Linked** for new resource assignments.
	The two fields are not linked and the resource assignment setting may be changed at any time.
• **Resource Workspace Details Tab**	• **Auto Compute Actuals**
	This field is linked to all resources assignments. When this option is checked for a resource, Primavera Version 5.0 calculates the Actual Units and Remaining Units using the Budgeted Units and Activity % Complete. This option may be overridden by applying the Activity **Auto Compute Actuals**.
	• **Calculate costs from units**
	There is a field available when a resource is assigned to an activity titled **Cost Units Linked.** With this option checked the costs for a resource are calculated from the **Resource Unit/Time** when a resource is added to an activity and whenever the Resource Units are changed.
• **Advanced Schedule Options**	One of the more important options to review is the Retained Logic and Progress Override options, as these affect how out of progress sequence is handled. These options should be reviewed to ensure that when the schedule is recalculated you will understand what is happening.
	The author prefers Retained Logic as this gives a more conservative schedule and those relationships that need editing may be edited to reflect retained logic as required.
• **Steps**	Should it be decided to use Steps to update a schedule the **Projects Workspace Calculations** tab should have the **Activity percent complete based on activity steps** option checked and the Activity must be assigned **Physical % Complete Type** in the **General tab** of the **Activity Workspace** for each activity.

19.7.2 Updating Dates and Percentage Complete

The schedule should be first updated as outlined in the **TRACKING PROGRESS** chapter. In summary, this is completed by entering:

- The **Actual Start** and **Actual Finish** dates of **Complete** activities.
- The **Actual Start**, **% Complete** and/or **Remaining Duration** of **In-Progress** activities.
- Adjust **Logic**, **Constraints** and **Durations** of **Unstarted** activities.

Before updating the **% Complete**, the **% Complete Type** should be checked to ensure that the Actual and Remaining Durations, Costs and Units calculate as required. This ideally should be done by setting the project defaults at the time the project is created and adjusting the settings as activities are added and resources assigned.

19.8 Updating Resources

There are many permutations available for calculating resource data. Due to the number of options available in Primavera Version 5.0, it is not feasible to document all the combinations available for resource calculation.

Resource units and costs may be updated by either:

- Estimating Progress Automatically, a process titled **Applying Actuals**, or
- Entering the data using the **Resource** tab in the **Activities Workspace**, or
- Entering the data using the right hand section of the **General** tab in the **Activities Workspace**.

19.8.1 Resource Tab

The **Resources** tab may be used to update the resource **Units** (and Costs if the Units and Costs have been unlinked with the **Cost Units Linked** filed). An updating layout could be created and the columns in the Resources tab formatted to your statusing method, see below:

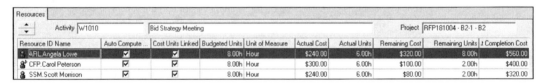

19.8.2 Status Tab

The right hand window may be used for statusing the resources.

- When there is one resource there will be a direct link between this form and the values assigned to the resource.
- When there is more than one resource there will be a proportional change to all the resource values when a change is made in this form.

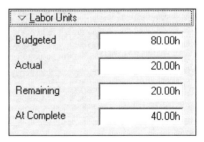

19.8.3   Applying Actuals

This function automatically:

- Statuses activities with resources as if it went according to plan and only updates activities in the period from the old to the New Data Date, or

- Apply actuals entered in the Primavera Timesheet system.

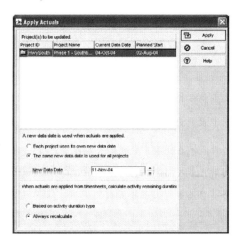

To Apply Actuals:

- Select **Tools**, **Apply Actuals…** to open the **Apply Actuals** form,

- Enter the **New Data Date** and click on ⌸ Apply button.

- If more than one project is open a different data date may be selected for each project.

- The Activity requires the Activity **Auto Compute Actuals** field checked for this function to apply to an Activity and all the Resources assigned to an activity.

- When the Resource **Auto Compute Actuals** field is not checked only the resources that have the Resource **Auto Compute Actuals** field checked in the **Resource Workspace** will be updated. If one resource is checked and one not, then the checked resource will be updated and the unchecked resource's update will be delayed until after the **Current Data Date**.

There are some important issues with using **Apply Actuals** that must be understood:

- Only activities with resources are updated, so activities without resources are not updated and would have to be updated manually.

- The Apply Actuals function does not work in the same way as the P3/SureTrak function "Update Progress" or the Microsoft Project function "Update Project" which both update all activities irrespective of resource assignment. The Apply Actuals function only updates resourced activities and unresourced activities such as milestones have to be updated manually.

- **IMPORTANT NOTE:** Therefore with the introduction of **Progress Spotlight** there is no need to use **Apply Actuals** to auto status a project and **Progress Spotlight** should be used.

19.9 Updating Expenses

Expenses are updated in a similar way to resources and will not be covered.

19.10 Store Period Performance

This new function to Primavera Version 5.0 allows:

- The creation of user definable financial periods, say monthly or weekly, and
- The ability to record the actual and earned costs and quantities for each period.

Therefore, actual costs and quantities which span over more than one past period will be accurately reflected per period in all reports. If **Store Period Performance** is not used then the actuals are spread equally over the actual duration of an activity, which may not accurately reflect when the work performed and what was achieved in each period. These Periods apply to all projects in the database.

This function is similar to the P3 **Store Period Performance** function but will not Store Period Performance on Microsoft Project managed projects

The steps required to store period performance are:

- Ensure that the user has the necessary global privileges to Edit Financial Period Dates, Store Period Performance and Edit Period Performance when past actuals need to be edited.

- Open the appropriate project and ensure **Link Actual and Actual This Period Units and Cost** is enabled, select the **Calculations** tab in the lower pane of the **Projects** window and click on the check box. This option is grayed out if the project is not open.

- Set the **Financial Periods** by selecting **Admin, Financial Periods....** Which will open the **Financial Periods** form:

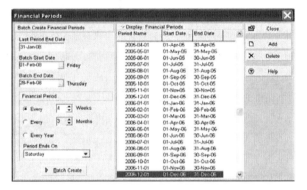

- To store the period performance select **Tools**, **Store Period Performance...** to open the **Store Period Performance** form, select the projects to have the period performance stored and click on the [Store Now] button.

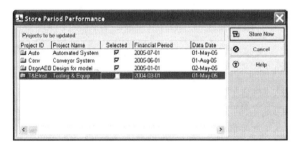

Finally these results may be viewed and edited in the Past Period Actuals columns of the Resources Assignments Window, Activity Details Resources tab and the Activity Table.

WORKSHOP 16

Statusing a Resourced Schedule

Background
We now need to status the activities and resources as at 10 Dec 07.

Assignment
1. Set a Primary Baseline for the project, select **Project**, **Maintain Baselines…** and save a copy of the current project as a Baseline and set it as the Primary Baseline using **Project**, **Assign Baselines…**.
2. In the **Project** workspace **Calculations** tab uncheck **Link Budget and At Completion for not started activities**.
3. Apply the **Workshop 11 – With Float** Layout, format the columns as below, the Primary Baseline bar and save the Layout as **Workshop 16**.
4. Status the project using **Progress Spotlight** by clicking on the ⬜ **Progress Spotlight** icon and moving the data date forward on week. Select **Tools**, **Update Progress…** and update the progress as at 10 Dec 07. The activities with resources have been updated as if they have progressed exactly according to plan. Should you wish dates and durations may be edited to suit the actual situation.
5. Display the columns shown in the Resources tab below, see how the resources have been statused:

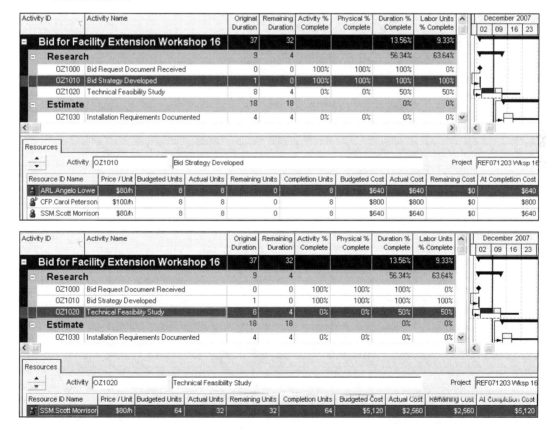

6. 60 % of the Technical Feasibility Study is complete so enter 60% against the **Physical % Complete** of **Technical Feasibility Study** and see the **Activity % Complete** change to 60%.

7. Select the **Bid Strategy Developed** activity, open the **Status tab** and change the **Actual Hours** from 24h to 15h. Now open the **Resources tab** and all three resources now show 5h remaining each and the Actual Costs and Remaining Costs should be recalculated if the **Cost Units Linked** boxes are checked.

Resource ID Name	Price / Unit	Budgeted Units	Actual Units	Remaining Units	Completion Units	Budgeted Cost	Actual Cost	Remaining Cost	At Completion Cost	Cost Units Linked
ARL.Angelo Lowe	$80/h	8	5	0	5	$640	$400	$0	$400	☑
CFP.Carol Peterson	$100/h	8	5	0	5	$800	$500	$0	$500	☑
SSM.Scott Morrison	$80/h	8	5	0	5	$640	$400	$0	$400	☑

(Activity OZ1010 — Bid Strategy Developed — Project REF071203 Wksp 16)

8. Change the **Remaining Duration** of **Technical Feasibility Study** to 6 days. Note the change in the Units and Costs.

9. Now edit the Actual Units to 24 hours and Remaining Units to 60, note how the costs and % Completes are recalculated.

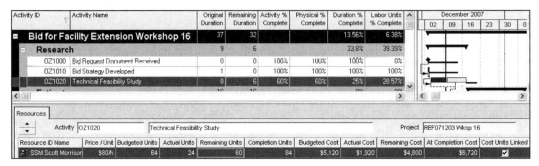

10. At this point you may experiment with this activity. Uncheck **Auto Compute Actuals** will allow you to change the Costs and they are not recalculated for the Resource Rate.

20 ACTIVITY, PROJECT & RESOURCE CODES

The **Enterprise Project Structure - EPS** and **Work Breakdown Structure - WBS** functions were discussed earlier as a method of organizing projects and activities under hierarchical structures. There are alternative features available in Primavera Version 5.0 for grouping, sorting and filtering activities, resources and project information:

- Activity Codes
- Project Codes
- Resource Codes
- Cost Accounts
- OBS
- EPS Level Activity Codes

These functions are addressed in this book but are not examined in detail.

20.1 Understanding Project Breakdown Structures

A Project Breakdown Structure represents a hierarchical breakdown of a project into logical functional elements. Some organizations have highly organized and disciplined structures with "rules" for creating and coding the elements of the structure. Some clients also impose a WBS code on a contractor for reporting and/or claiming payments. The following are examples of such structures:

- WBS **Work Breakdown Structure**, breaking down the project into the elements of work required to complete a project.

- COA **Code of Accounts** or also know as **Cost Breakdown Structure**. Often this includes costs that are not included in a schedule such as insurances and overheads. The WBS would in this situation represent part of the COA.

- OBS **Organization Breakdown Structure**, showing the hierarchical management structure of a project. Primavera Version 5.0 has a predefined field for this breakdown structure.

- CBS **Contract Breakdown Structure**, showing the breakdown of contracts into elements.

- SBS **System Breakdown Structure**, a **System Engineering** method of breaking down a complex system into elements.

- PBS **Product Breakdown Structure**, a **PRINCE2** term used for the breakdown of project deliverables under two headings of Project Management and Specialists products.

We will discuss the following functions available in Primavera Version 5.0 to represent these structures in your schedule.

20.2 Activity Codes

Activity Codes may be used to Group, Sort and Filter activities from one or more open projects.

- **Activity Codes**, such as Phases, Trades or Disciplines, are defined in the **Activity Codes Definition** form.

- **Activity Code Values** are defined in the **Activity Codes** form, such as:
    - ➢ Phases of Design, Procure, Install and Test,
    - ➢ Trades of Brickwork, Plumbing and Electrical, and
    - ➢ Disciplines of Concrete, Mechanical, Pipework.

- **Activity Codes** are assigned from the **Activities Workspace** using the **Codes** tab in the lower pane or displaying the Activity Code column.

P3 and SureTrak have one WBS Code Dictionary and a hierarchical structure of WBS Codes in the one Dictionary, effectively producing an unlimited number of WBS Codes with a maximum of 20 levels. Microsoft Project 2002 introduced Custom Outline Codes, which is a hierarchical coding structure that may be assigned to activities and allows the activities to be Grouped under these codes. There are 10 codes available with every project and which may be renamed to suit the project requirement. The Primavera Version 5.0 Activity Code function is similar in operation to both the P3 and SureTrak WBS Code function and the Microsoft Project Custom Outline Codes, but allows an unlimited number of Code Dictionaries and Values for each Code Dictionary.

20.2.1   Creating Activity Codes

There are two types of Activity Codes:

- **Project Activity Codes** that may only be created when a project is opened and applied only to the project they were created for. These may be made Global by clicking on the ⬢ Make Global button in the **Activity Codes Definition - Project** form.

- **Global Activity Codes** that may be created at any time and applied to any project.

Activity Codes may be added, deleted or modified:

- Select **Enterprise**, **Activity Codes...** to open the **Activity Codes** form,

- Select either the **Global** or **Project** depending on whether the codes are for a specific project or are to be available to all projects,

- Select from the dropdown box which code structure is to be operated on.

- The code structure is modified in a similar way to WBS codes.

- Each Activity Code has a Code and a Description. The length of the Code is defined when the code is created; see the next paragraph.

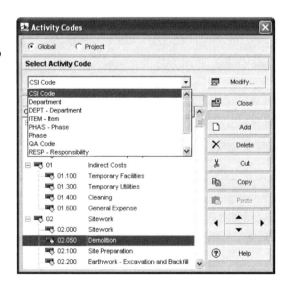

20.2.2 Defining an Activity Code

Defining an Activity Code is similar to creating a Code Dictionary in P3 and SureTrak or renaming a Microsoft Project Custom Outline Code:

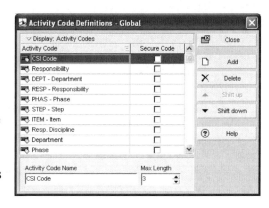

- From the **Activity Codes** form select **Project** or **Global**,

- Click on the [Modify...] button to open the **Activity Codes Definition** form,

- The Activity Codes may be created, deleted, made Global and reordered in this form.

- The **Maximum Length** is the maximum number of characters a code may be assigned when it is created in the **Activity Codes form**.

The **Activity Codes Definition - Project** form has an addition button [Make Global] that is used to make a Project Activity Code a Global Activity Code.

20.2.3 Assigning Activity Codes to Activities

Activity Codes may be assigned to an activity by:

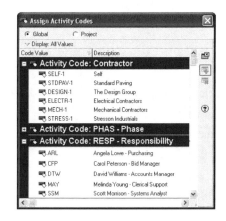

- Selecting the **Codes** tab in the lower pane by clicking on the [Assign] button to open the **Assign Activity Codes** form.

- Display the appropriate activity code column and either:
  - ➢ Typing in the code, or
  - ➢ Clicking twice on the Activity Code cell and opening the **Select "Code"** form.

- Right click in the top pane and select **Assign, Activity Codes…**.

20.2.4 Grouping, Sorting and Filtering with Activity Codes

When more than one project is open an Activity Code may be used to group activities from all the open projects under one code structure.

Activity Codes are Grouped and Filtered in the same way as WBS codes.

20.3 Project Codes

Project Codes in Primavera Version 5.0 work in a similar way to Project Codes in P3. The codes are assigned to projects and allow projects to be Grouped and Sorted under an alternative structure to the EPS.

For example, when an EPS represents the physical location of offices by country, state/county and city, the Project Codes function enables projects to be given tags such as Reason for the Project, Safety, Compliance, New Product, and Increase Production. The Projects may be grouped under these headings.

Therefore, project codes are used to Group and Sort Projects in a similar way that Activity Codes are used to Group and Sort Activities.

To create a Project Code:

- Select **Enterprise**, **Project Codes...** to open the **Project Codes** form.
- The Project Codes are created, edited and deleted in a similar way to Activity Codes.

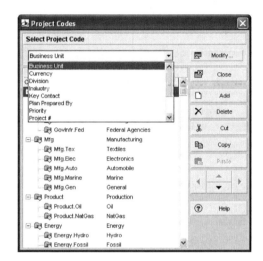

Project Codes may be Assigned to Projects in the Projects Workspace in a similar way as Activity Codes are assigned to activities by:

- Displaying the appropriate Code Column, or
- Opening the **Codes** tab in the Project Workspace.

Projects may be Grouped, Sorted and Filtered in the **Projects Workspace** using the Group and Sort and the Filter functions.

20.4 Project Phase or WBS Category

The **Project Phase** or **WBS Category** may be created, deleted and reordered in the **Project Phase** tab of the **Categories** form.

The **Project Phase** are assigned to **WBS Nodes** in the **WBS Workspace** and may be used to Group and Sort WBS Nodes under different a different set of heading in a similar way to Project Codes in P3.

This would enable say all design WBS Nodes that were distributed all through a project WBS to be grouped together under one heading without assigning an Activity Code to each activity.

20.5 Resource Codes

Resource Codes are to Resources as Activity Codes are to Activities and allow resources to be Grouped, Sorted and Filtered by these codes. Resources may have codes such as Office, Location or Employment Status assigned to them.

To create a Resource Code:

- Select **Enterprise**, **Resource Codes...** to open the **Resource Codes** form.

- The Resource Codes are created, edited and deleted in a similar way to Activity Codes.

Resource Codes may be Assigned to Resources in a similar way to Activity Codes by:

- Displaying the appropriate Code Column, or

- Opening the **Codes** tab in the **Resources Workspace**.

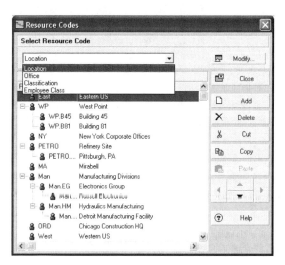

20.6 Cost Accounts

Cost Accounts are to Resources as Activity Codes are to activities and are intended to reflect the accounting code structure of a project. As in P3, a Cost Account in Primavera Version 5.0 is assigned to a resource.

Cost Accounts have additional functions that Activity Codes do not have:

- A default Cost Account for each new Resource or Expense may be specified in the **Projects Workspace**, **Defaults** tab. This is used for each new Resource or Expense and does not affect existing assignments. The **Project Default Cost Account** may be changed at any time:

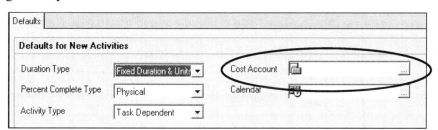

- Cost Accounts may be merged when a Cost Account is Deleted and a different account selected for all costs that have been assigned to the account selected for deletion.

- Cost Accounts may have a descriptive field when they are created.

Costs accounts are created in the **Cost Accounts** form by selecting **Enterprise, Cost Accounts...** and opening the **Cost Accounts** form.

Cost Accounts are assigned to Resources of Expenses by displaying the Cost Account column in the **Activities Workspace** lower pane **Resources** and **Expenses** Tab.

20.7 Organizational Breakdown Structure – OBS

The OBS is an Enterprise hierarchical structure that represents the Organization's hierarchy:

- People in the OBS may be assigned to projects or nodes in the EPS to represent the person responsible for that project or EPS node.

- A person assigned to an EPS is by default responsible for all projects associated with all elements of the EPS.

- The OBS may also be used to assign access by individual people to projects and WBS Nodes of a project.

20.7.1 Creating an OBS Structure

To create, edit or delete an OBS:

- Select **Enterprise**, **OBS…** to open the **Organizational Breakdown Structure** form.

- Add, delete and edit the OBS Nodes in a similar way to a WBS.

20.7.2 General Tab

The description of the OBS may be added in the **OBS General** tab.

20.7.3 Users Tab

The Login Name is assigned to the OBS in the OBS **Users** tab. Users should therefore be assigned:

- A resource for when they are assigned to work on an activity, and

- An OBS Node for the work they are responsible for or should have access to.

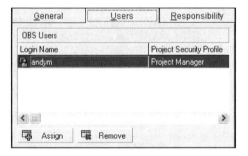

20.7.4 Responsibility Tab

The OBS **Responsibility** tab is used to indicate to which EPS or WBS Node a person has been assigned. The person is assigned to:

- A WBS in the **General** tab of the **WBS** Workspace.

- A Project in the **General** tab of the **Projects** Workspace.

- An EPS in the **General** tab of the **Projects** Workspace.

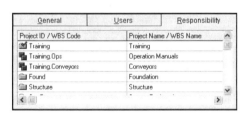

20.8 EPS Level Activity Codes

EPS Activity Codes may be created and assigned only to project activities that belong to EPS Node for which the EPS Activity Codes have been created. This enables the display of all project activities under one or more EPS Nodes utilizing dedicated alternative hierarchical structure. There are also specific privileges for the management of these codes.

20.8.1 Create an EPS Level Activity Code Dictionary

- Select **Enterprise, Activity Codes…** to open the **Activity Code** form and click on the **EPS** radio button,
- Select ☐ Modify... to open the **Activity Code Definition – EPS** form where the new code dictionary is created,
- Click on ☐ Add to open the **Select EPS** form and select an EPS Node that the New Code will be used with and click on ⊞ to select the node,
- Type in the EPS Activity Code Name and assign the Max length of the code

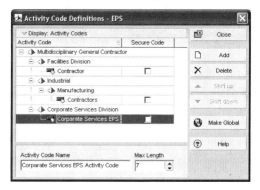

- The ☐ Make Global button converts the Activity Code to a Global Activity Code.
- The **Secure Code** box is used to hide the code from people without the required access privileges.
- Select ☐ Close to return to the **Activity Code Definition – EPS** form.

20.8.2 Create EPS Activity Codes

- Select the code dictionary to be modified from the drop down list under the heading **Select Activity Code** in the **Activity Codes** form, **EPS** tab.
- Click on ☐ Add to add a hierarchical set of codes in the same method as other codes.

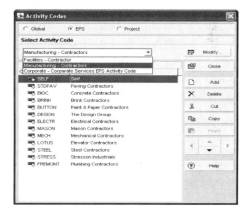

20.8.3 Assigning EPS Activity Codes to Activities

EPS Activity Codes may only be assigned to activities belonging to projects that are a member of the EPS Node and are assigned in the same way as Global and Project Activity Codes

---

21 UTILITIES

21.1 Advanced Scheduling Options

Primavera Version 5.0 has a new option that allows individual critical paths to be banded as per the picture below and is useful when analyzing larger projects that have more than one critical path:

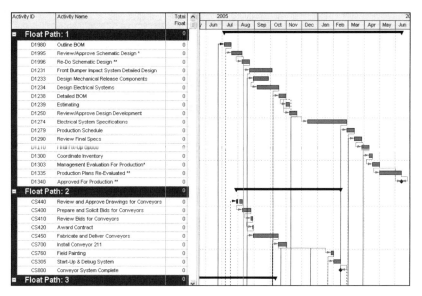

There are 2 steps involved, firstly calculating the multiple paths and secondly displaying the multiple paths:

21.1.1   Calculating Multiple Paths

To calculate multiple critical paths:

- Select **Tools**, **Schedule**, **Options**, **Advanced** tab,

- Click on **Calculate multiple float paths**,

- Select if your wish to the software to use the **Total Float** or **Free Float** to calculate the multiple paths.

- The **Display multiple float paths ending with activity** is used to select an activity that is in the middle of a schedule and the driving paths top this activity are calculated.

- Select the number of paths for the software to calculate in the **Specify the number of paths to calculate** box.

- Select [Close] and schedule the project.

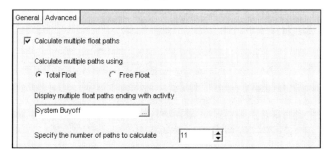

21.1.2 Displaying Multiple Paths

There are two fields that are populated in this process:

- **Float Path** and
- **Float Path Order**

Either select multiple path Layout or create a Layout that Groups by **Float Path** and Sorts by **Float Path Order** as per the examples below which show a before and after grouping:

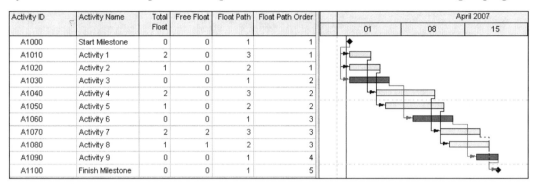

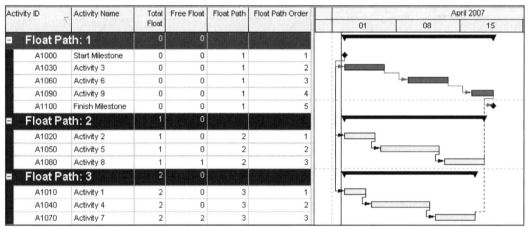

The reader may wish to read the help file or experiment with the software to see the results.

21.2 Audit Trail Columns

Primavera Version 5.0 introduced four basic audit trail columns that may be displayed in the Activities window which display the date user that added the activity when and by whom it was modified:

- Added By - the user that added the activity,
- Added Date - the date the activity was added,
- Modified By - the user that last modified the activity and
- Modified Date - the date the activity was last modified.

21.3 Excel Import and Export Tool

Primavera Version 5.0 has a built in tool for importing to and exporting from Excel the following data when the user is assigned a Superuser security profile:

- Activities
- Relationships
- Resources
- Resources Assignments and
- Expenses

To import or export data to Excel select **File**, **Import…** or **Export…** and follow the instructions in the Wizards. **Export Templates** may be created and re-used at a later date with this tool.

When attempting to import data using this type of tool there are some guidelines that apply to many applications, not just to this Primavera tool:

- Create a test project and experiment with this function before using I on a live project.
- Export some data first as this exports the correct column headings and sheet names.
- Change or add data to the exported spreadsheet and import new data into the test environment. Then check the data is importing correctly and that the schedule is calculating as expected.
- Back up or take a copy of your project before importing into a live project.
- Usually is better not to try and import calculated fields as these are normally re calculated after the data has been imported and the schedule recalculated.
- When only exporting some data on a one off basis then it may be easier just to copy and paste the data into a spreadsheet.

A few points to understand when using the Primavera Version 5.0 function:

- The following sheets are created on export and these sheet names must not be changed:
  - ➢ **TASK** containing Activity data
  - ➢ **TASKPRED** containing Activity Relationships data
  - ➢ **PROJCOST** containing Expenses data
  - ➢ **RSRC** containing Resources data
  - ➢ **TASKRSRC** containing Resource Assignments data
  - ➢ **USERDATA** containing user data that should not be changed.
- Do not change the language between importing and exporting.
- The first row of data in each sheet that is exported contains the database field name. The first row must not be changed otherwise the data will not be imported.
- The second row in the spreadsheet contains **Captions** that may be changed.
- Dictionary data that is being imported must exist before the data is imported.
- Only a maximum of 200 columns of data may be exported.
- **Sub-units** of time are not supported and the Sub-unit checkboxes in the **Edit, User Preferences, Time Units** tab and should be unchecked.
- **Percent Completes** must be must have a value of between 0 and 100.

There is substantially more information in the Help file under **Reference, Importing and Exporting**.

21.4 Project Import and Export

Projects may be imported and exported from and to the following formats:

- **XER**, which is a Primavera proprietary format, used to exchange projects between Primavera Version 5.0 databases regardless of the database type in which it was created.

- **Project (*.mpp)**. This is the default file format that Microsoft Project 2000 and 2002 uses to create and save files.

- **MPX (*.mpx)**. This is a text format data file created by Microsoft Project 98 and earlier versions. MPX is a format that may be imported and exported by many other project scheduling software packages.

- **Primavera Project Planner P3** and **SureTrak** files saved in **P3** format. A SureTrak project should be saved in Concentric (P3) format before importing.

- With Primavera Version 5.0 the importation of P3 files has been improved:
  - ➢ One or more individual subprojects may now be imported, and
  - ➢ The import EPS locations specified, which may be different for each subproject
  Select **File**, **Import…** or **Export…** to open the appropriate form.

- New to Version 4.1, Microsoft Project formats such as **Project Database (*.mpd)**, **Microsoft Access Database (*.mdb)** and **(*.mpt)** can be imported, however **Microsoft Project 98**, **2000** or **2002** is require to be installed on the computer.

- Primavera Version 5.0 projects that are open may be exported in XER format that may be imported into **Primavera Contractor 4.1**.
  - ➢ Select **File**, **Export…** to open the **Export** form.

 It is recommended that you read the notes carefully in the user manual before importing a schedule from a non- Primavera Version 5.0 format and even consider importing it into a blank database to clearly understand how the data is imported.

21.5 Check In & Check Out

Check In & Check Out function is similar to the P3 and SureTrak function of the same name, which enables a project to be copied from a database, worked on in a remote location, and then be checked in to the original database at a later date.

One or more projects may be checked out in XER format and may not be opened with Primavera Version 5.0 in this format. The project may be checked into another installation of Primavera Version 5.0 irrespective of the database format, edited, checked out and then checked back into its original database at a later date.

A checked out project retains the relationships that it had in the original project database.

22 WHAT IS NEW IN VERSION 5.0

22.1 MSDE Database for Standalone Installations

Primavera Version 5.0 now uses the Microsoft SQL Server Desktop Engine (MSDE) for standalone installations, Version 4.1 used Interbase.

22.2 Undo

Primavera Version 5.0 has a new multiple **Undo** function that operates on Resources, Resource Assignments, and Activities windows, but no **Redo** function.

There are many functions will erase the Undo memory such as scheduling, summarizing, importing, opening a project, opening Code forms, opening User and Admin Preferences and closing the application.

22.3 WBS Summary Activity

The new Primavera Version5.0 **WBS Summary Activity** is an activity that spans the duration of all activities which are assigned exactly the same WBS Code and unlike a Level of Effort Activity it does not have any predecessors or successors.

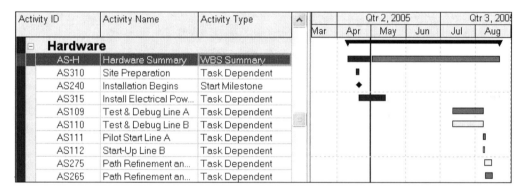

Therefore a WBS activity will change duration when either the earliest start or latest finish of activities that it spans is changed. This may happen as the project progresses and activities do not meet their original scheduled dates, or the duration of an activity is changed, or logic is changed, or the schedule is leveled.

This function calculates the WBS Activity Duration in the same way as WBS activities in P3 or SureTrak, Topic activities in SureTrak. It is similar to the way Summary activity durations are calculated in Microsoft Project, except the activities do not need to be demoted below the detailed activities in as in Microsoft Project.

WBS activities may be used for:

- Reporting at summary level by filtering on WBS activities,
- Entering estimated costs at summary level for producing cash flow tables while the detailed activities are used for calculating the overall duration for the WBS and day to day management of the project and
- Recording costs and hours at WBS level when is it not desirable or practicable to record at activity level, especially when the detailed activities are liable to change.

22.4 EPS Level Activity Codes

EPS Activity Codes may be created and assigned only to project activities that belong to EPS Node for which the EPS Activity Codes have been created. This enables the display all project activities under one or more EPS Node utilizing dedicated alternative hierarchical structure. There are also specific privileges for the management of these codes.

22.4.1 Create an EPS Level Activity Code Dictionary

- Select **Enterprise, Activity Codes…** to open the **Activity Code** form and click on the **EPS** radio button,
- Select [Modify…] to open the **Activity Code Definition – EPS** form where the new code dictionary is created,
- Click on [Add] to open the **Select EPS** form and select an EPS Node that the New Code will be used with and click on the icon to select the node,
- Type in the EPS Activity Code Name and assign the length of the code

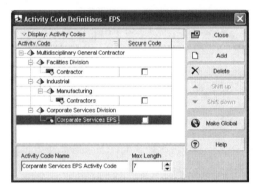

- The [Make Global] button converts the Activity Code to a Global Activity Code.
- The **Secure Code** box is used to hide the code from people without the required access privileges.
- Select [Close] to return to the **Activity Code Definition – EPS** form.

22.4.2 Create EPS Activity Codes

- Select the code dictionary to be modified from the drop down list under the heading **Select Activity Code** in the **Activity Codes** form, **EPS** tab.
- Click on the [Add] to add a hierarchical set of codes in the same method as other codes

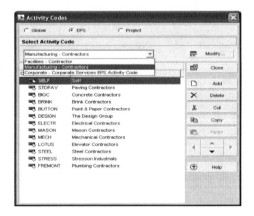

22.4.3 Assigning EPS Activity Codes to Activities

EPS Activity Codes may only be assigned to activities belonging to projects that are a member of the EPS Node and are assigned in the same way as Global and Project Activity Codes

---

22.5 Activity Step Templates

The new Primavera Version5.0 function allows Templates to be created for Steps and then the Steps assigned to other activities. Existing Steps may be also converted into Step Templates. Select **Enterprise**, **Activity Step Templates...**to open the **Activity Step Template** form:

- The Step Template name is added in the upper pane,
- The Steps are added in the lower left pane and
- Comments on the Step may be added in the bottom left hand pane.

Steps may be assigned to activities from the **Activities Details** form **Steps Details** tab by clicking on the [Add from Template] button and selecting the Step Template required:

Existing Steps may be converted to a Step Template by:

- Selecting the required Steps to be made into a Step Template, and
- Right Clicking and selecting **Create Template...**.

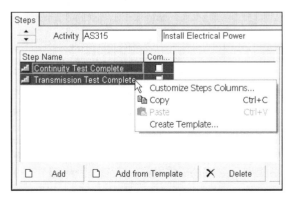

22.6 Assignment Staffing

There are new Version 5.0 options available on the **Calculations** tab of the **User Options** form allowing the user to set the defaults for:

- Selecting the Units per Time when assigning a substitute resource to an existing resource assignment.
- Selecting the Price per Unit for a resource which is being assigned to a Role.

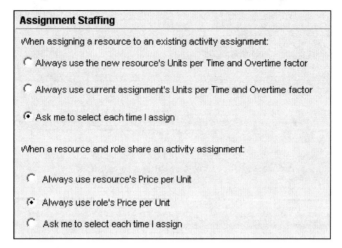

The options are to select the existing resource, the new resource or to be prompted each time a resource/role is substituted.

22.7 Resource Security

The Primavera Version5.0 **Resource Security** has the ability to restrict access to resources. The security may be established at a resource Node level allowing the user access to all the children of that Resource node.

- Select **Admin**, **Users**, **Global Access** tab to open the **Users** form,
- Uncheck the **All Resources Access** check box,
- Click on the right hand side of the **Resources Access** bar to open the **Select Resource Access** form and
- Select the resources from the list:

22.8 Baseline Functionality

22.8.1 Update Baselines

The new Primavera Version 5.0 **Update Baseline** function is similar to the P3 function and allows the Baseline schedule to be updated with data from the current schedule or activities deleting that are no longer in the current schedule without restoring the Baseline schedule:

- Select **Project, Maintain Baselines…** and select the [Update…] button to open the **Update Baseline** form:

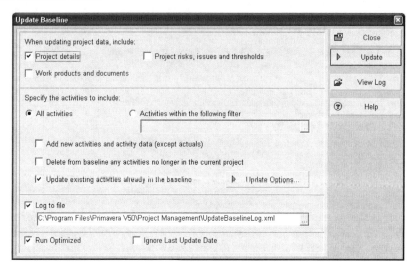

- When **Run Optimized** is not checked then an error log is kept during the updating process.

- **Ignore Last Update Date** may be used when a project has project is updated at different times and the last Baseline Update may not be valid for the current schedule although the Baseline has been updated with more recent data..

- Select [Update Options…] to open the **Update Baseline Options** form to select which data items are updated.

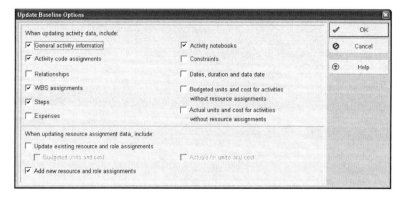

There is a new project privilege allowing a user to run Update Project Baselines.

22.8.2 Assign Baselines

The new Primavera Version 5.0 **Assign Baselines** form is used to assign up to three project baseline schedules: primary, secondary, and tertiary.

The **Project Baseline** may be used for calculating **Earned Value**. See the next para for more options. Also see **Admin**, **Admin Preferences…**, **Earned Value** tab for other Earned Value options.

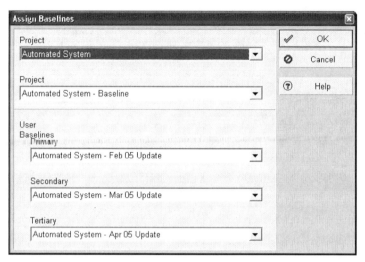

22.8.3 Baseline Used for Earned Value Calculations

Earned Value calculations may be performed using either the **Primary Baseline** values or the **Baseline** values, the values from the current project. Select the **Settings** tab in the **Projects** workspace. This is similar to the P3 option **Tools**, **Options**, **Earned Value**.

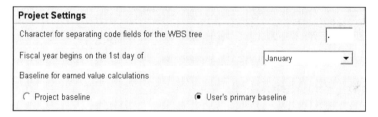

22.9 Progress Spotlight

Primavera Version 5.0 has a new function for highlighting the activities that should have progressed in the status period; then the user has the option of selecting some or all of the activities that should have progressed and statusing (updating) them as if they progressed exactly as they were scheduled.

It is often easier to **Autostatus** a project with functions like **Progress Spotlight** and then adjusting the Actuals as a second step in the statusing process.

This function is similar to the P3 Progress Spotlight function but does not have the additional SureTrak features of reversing progress and not updating the resources.

The Spotlight may be moved to reflect the new Data Date by either:

- Dragging the Data Date, or
- Using the Spotlight Icon - 🔦

22.9.1 Highlighting Activities for Updating by Dragging the Data Date

To highlight activities for that should have been progressed in the last period by dragging the Data Date:

- Hold the mouse arrow on the Data Date line and display the double-headed arrow ↔ ,
- Press the left mouse button and drag the Data Date line to the required date.
- All the activities that should have been worked in the time period are highlighted.

22.9.2 Spotlighting Activities Using Spotlight Icon

The Spotlight facility highlights all activities that should have progressed in one minor time period of the timescale settings. To use **Progress Spotlight**:

- Set the Timescale to be the same as your Update Periods. If you are statusing weekly then set the time period to weeks in the **Timescale** form.
- Select **View**, **Progress**, **Spotlight** or click on the 🔦 icon and the next period of time (one week if your scale is set to one week) will be highlighted.
- Click 🔦 icon a second time to return the Spotlight back to the Data Date.

You are now ready to update progress.

22.9.3 Statusing Using Update Progress

To update a schedule using the **Update Progress** form select **Tools**, **Update Progress**.

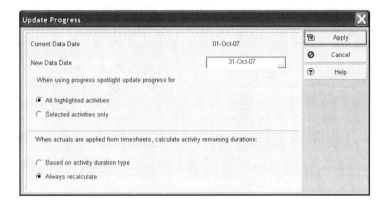

There are two options for setting the New Data Date:

- You may use the highlight facility before opening the Update Progress form and the New data date will be set to the highlighted Data Date; or
- You may select the New data date when opening the form.

Either all the activities that are Spotlighted may be updated or if some were selected before opening the form then just the selected ones may be updated.

- To update all the activities select **All highlighted activities** radio button, or
- To status selected activities highlight the activities (hold the Ctrl key and click on the ones you wish to status) before selecting **Tools**, **Update Progress…** and the click on the **Selected activities only** radio button.

The option **When actuals are applied from timesheets, calculate activity remaining durations:** decides how the Remaining Duration is calculated:

- **Based on the activity duration type** will take into account activity type and hours to date and reschedule the Remaining Duration in accordance with the activity Duration Type, or
- **Always recalculate** will override the activity Duration Type and calculate the activity Remaining Durations and Hours as if the activity was a Fixed Units and Fixed Units/Time activity.
- Click on ⌗ Apply and the schedule will be statused as if all activities were completed according to schedule.

22.10 Suspend and Resume

The new Primavera Version5.0 Suspend and Resume function allows the work to be suspended and the activity resumed at a later date. Open the **Activity Details** form **Status Details** tab and enter the **Suspend** and **Resume** dates. This function works in a similar way to the P3 and SureTrak function and allows only one break in an activity.

The example below shows an activity suspended from 30 Apr 05 to the 10 May 05.

- This feature works when a task has commenced and normally the Suspend date is in the past and the Resume date in the future.
- The activity must have an actual start date before you can record a suspend date.
- Only Resource Dependent and Task Dependent activities may be Suspended and resumed.
- The suspend and resume time are at the start of a work period.
- The suspended period is not calculated as part of the task duration and resources are not scheduled in this period.

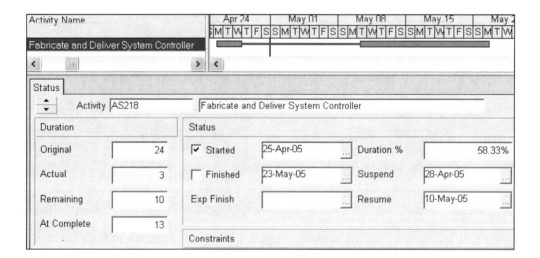

22.11 Store Period Performance

This new function to Primavera Version 5.0 allows:

- The creation of user definable financial periods, say monthly or weekly, and
- The ability to record the actual and earned costs and quantities for each period.

Therefore, actual costs and quantities which span over more than one past period will be accurately reflected per period in all reports. If **Store Period Performance** is not used then the actuals are spread equally over the actual duration of an activity, which may not accurately reflect when the work performed and what was achieved in each period. These Periods apply to all projects in the database.

This function is similar to the P3 **Store Period Performance** function but will not Store Period Performance on Microsoft Project managed projects

The steps required to store period performance are:

- Ensure that the user has the necessary global privileges to Edit Financial Period Dates, Store Period Performance and Edit Period Performance when past actuals need to be edited.
- Open the appropriate project and ensure **Link Actual and Actual This Period Units and Cost** is enabled, select the **Calculations** tab in the lower pane of the **Projects** window and click on the check box. This option is grayed out if the project is not open.
- Set the **Financial Periods** by selecting **A**dmin, **F**inancial Periods.... Which will open the **Financial Periods** form:

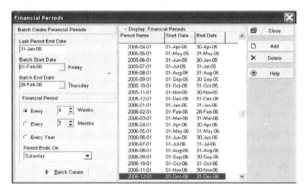

- To store the period performance select **T**ools, **Store Period Performance...** to open the **Store Period Performance** form, select the projects to have the period performance stored and click on the [Store Now] button.

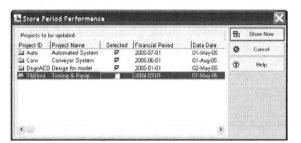

Finally these results may be viewed and edited in the Past Period Actuals columns of the Resources Assignments Window, Activity Details Resources tab and the Activity Table.

22.12 Advanced Scheduling Options

Primavera Version 5.0 has a new option that allows individual critical paths to be banded as per the picture below and is useful when analyzing larger projects that have more than one critical path:

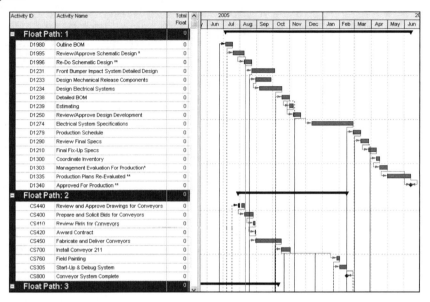

There are 2 steps involved, firstly calculating the multiple paths and secondly displaying the multiple paths:

Calculating Multiple Paths

- Select **Tools**, **Schedule**, **Options**, **Advanced** tab,

- Click on **Calculate multiple float paths**

- Select if your wish to the software to use the **Total Float** or **Free Float** to calculate the multiple paths.

- The **Display multiple float paths ending with activity** is used to select an activity that is in the middle of a schedule and the driving paths top this activity are calculated.

- Select the number of paths for the software to calculate in the **Specify the number of paths to calculate** box.

- Select [Close] and schedule the project.

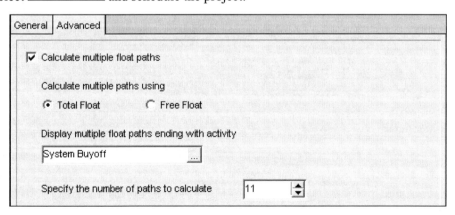

Displaying Multiple Paths

There are two fields that are populated in this process:

- **Float Path** and

- **Float Path Order**

Either select multiple path Layout or create a Layout that Groups by **Float Path** and Sorts by **Float Path Order** as per the examples below which show a before and after grouping:

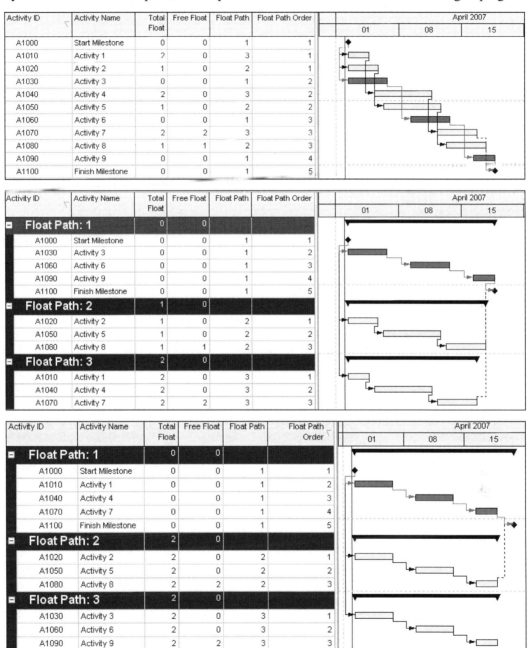

The reader may wish to read the help file or experiment with the software to see the results.

22.13 Rates for Roles

Primavera Version 5.0 supports rates with Roles. Up to 5 rates (the same number of rates as resources) may be assigned to roles which may be used for estimating and cash flow forecasting of projects before the actual resource completing the work is assigned to the activity. Select **Enterprise**, **Roles...** to open the **Roles** form:

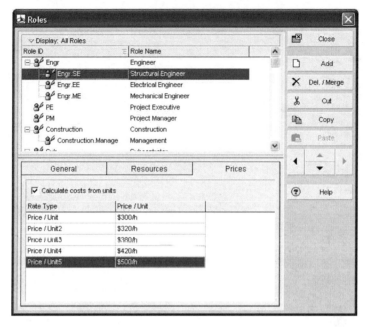

Different rates may be required for different clients such as an internal project rates and rates for different types of external clients.

22.14 Excel Import and Export Tool

Primavera Version 5.0 has a built in tool for importing to and exporting from Excel the following data when the user is assigned a Superuser security profile:

- Activities
- Relationships
- Resources
- Resources Assignments and
- Expenses

To import or export data to Excel select **File**, **Import…** or **Export…** and follow the instructions in the Wizards. **Export Templates** may be created and re-used at a later date with this tool.

When attempting to import data using this type of tool there are some guidelines that apply to many applications, not just to this Primavera tool:

- Create a test project and experiment with this function before using I on a live project.
- Export some data first as this exports the correct column headings and sheet names.
- Change or add data to the exported spreadsheet and import new data into the test environment. Then check the data is importing correctly and that the schedule is calculating as expected.
- Back up or take a copy of your project before importing into a live project.
- Usually is better not to try and import calculated fields as these are normally re calculated after the data has been imported and the schedule recalculated.
- When only exporting some data on a one off basis then it may be easier just to copy and paste the data into a spreadsheet.

A few points to understand when using the Primavera Version 5.0 function:

- The following sheets are created on export and these sheet names must not be changed:
  - ➢ **TASK** containing Activity data
  - ➢ **TASKPRED** containing Activity Relationships data
  - ➢ **PROJCOST** containing Expenses data
  - ➢ **RSRC** containing Resources data
  - ➢ **TASKRSRC** containing Resource Assignments data
  - ➢ **USERDATA** containing user data that should not be changed.
- Do not change the language between importing and exporting.
- The first row of data in each sheet that is exported contains the database field name. The first row must not be changed otherwise the data will not be imported.
- The second row in the spreadsheet contains **Captions** that may be changed.
- Dictionary data that is being imported must exist before the data is imported.
- Only a maximum of 200 columns of data may be exported.
- **Sub-units** of time are not supported and the Sub-unit checkboxes in the **Edit, User Preferences, Time Units** tab and should be unchecked.
- **Percent Completes** must be must have a value of between 0 and 100.

There is substantially more information in the Help file under **Reference, Importing and Exporting**.

22.15 P3 Subproject Import

With Primavera Version 5.0 the importation of P3 files has been improved:

- One or more individual subprojects may now be imported, and
- The import EPS locations specified, which may be different for each subproject

Select **File**, **Import…** or **Export…** to open the appropriate form.

22.16 Export to Primavera Contractor Version 4.1

Primavera Version 5.0 projects that are open may be exported in XER format that may be imported into Primavera Contractor 4.1.

Select **File**, **Export…** to open the **Export** form.

22.17 Audit Trail Columns

Primavera Version 5.0 introduced four basic audit trail columns that may be displayed in the Activities window which display the date user that added the activity when and by whom it was modified:

- Added By - the user that added the activity,
- Added Date - the date the activity was added,
- Modified By - the user that last modified the activity and
- Modified Date - the date the activity was last modified.

22.18 Enhanced or New Graphics Functions

The following are a list of the new graphics functions in Primavera Version 5.0:

22.18.1 Bar Label Placement

Primavera Version 5.0 introduced two more positions for bar labels titled Top and Bottom.

22.18.2 Three Timescale Units

Primavera Version 5.0 introduced the option of two or three timescale lines in the Gantt Chart Timescale and may be used to show ordinal and/or calendar dates.

Ordinal dates display the time scale by counting in the selected units starting from a user definable start date. This option works in a similar way to the P3 function where the Ordinal start date may be selected.

When 3 lines are displayed the ordinal dates and calendar dates may displayed

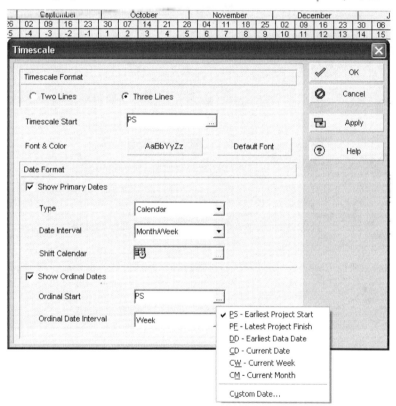

22.18.3 Vertical Sight Lines

Primavera Version 5.0 introduced a new **Bar Chart Options** form **Sight Lines** tab bar which now allows the specification of both vertical and horizontal Sight Lines, which brings the functionality up to match P3, SureTrak and Microsoft Project:

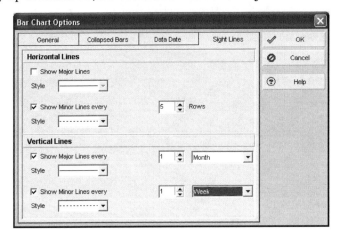

22.18.4 Reorganize Automatically

Primavera Version 5.0 introduced a function titled Reorganize Automatically, which is similar to the P3 and SureTrak function but applies to all Layouts, not just the selected Layout. Select **Edit, User Preferences...** to open the **User Preferences** form and click on the **Application** tab.

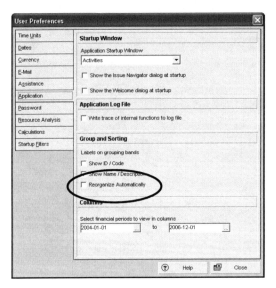

When the **Reorganize Automatically** box is checked, all views will reorganize automatically when data fields are changed that are used in the layout such as Grouping and Sorting.

It is often better to disable **Reorganize Automatically** when data is being edited that is used in the grouping of data in a Layout which will prevent the activities moving to their new position in the Layout until all data has been edited.

To reorganize a view, select **Tools**, **Reorganize Now** or **Shift+F2**.

22.18.5 Gantt Chart Curtains

Primavera Version 5.0 introduced a function allowing the placing of multiple curtains on the Gantt Chart which may be all hidden or displayed.

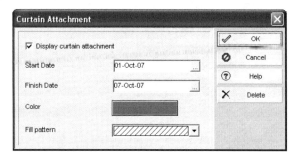

Select **View**, **Attachments** to display the **Curtain** menu:

- **Add Curtain** opens the **Curtain Attachment** form used to create a curtain:

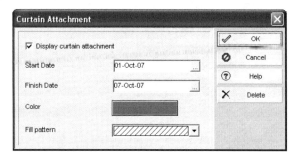

- **Show All** shows all the curtains,
- **Hide All** hides all the curtains and
- Clicking on a curtain in the Gantt Chart also opens the **Curtain Attachment** form where individual curtains may be deleted or hidden.

22.19 Improved Report Wizard Functionality

The Primavera Version5.0 **Report Wizard** has been enhanced with the following additional features:

- Enhanced column formatting and
- Multiple subject area selection.

23 WHAT IS NEW IN VERSION 4.1

The following features were introduced from Version 3.5:

23.1 Project Import & Export

Microsoft Project formats such as **Project Database (*.mpd)**, **Microsoft Access Database (*.mdb)** and **(*.mpt)** can be imported, however **Microsoft Project 98, 2000** or **2002** is require to be installed on the computer.

23.2 Format Gridlines

Gridlines are important to help divide the visual presentation with lines on the Bar Chart. The functions available for formatting the gridlines in Primavera Version 4.1 have improved and now allow the setting of colors and styles to the **Data Date** only.

- **Bar Chart Horizontal Gridlines** are formatted in the **Bar Chart Options** form. Select [Options...] from the **Bars** form to open the **Bar Chart Options** form, **General** tab:

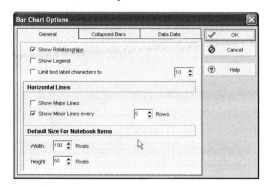

  - ➤ **Show Major Lines** places a black horizontal dotted line above each WBS band across the bar chart.
  - ➤ **Show Minor Lines** places a gray dotted line at the interval selected in the **Rows** box.

- **Bar Chart Vertical Gridlines** may not be formatted and are shown as solid black lines from the major timescale.

- Column Horizontal and Vertical Gridlines may not be formatted and are displayed in solid gray.

- The **Data Date** may have its thickness, color and pattern formatted in the **Data Date** tab of the **Bar Chart Options** form.

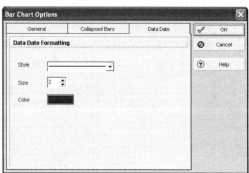

23.3 Format Bars

23.3.1   Bar Necking

Bar Necking Settings

Bar Necking displays a thinner bar during times of inactivity such as weekends and holidays and applies only to bars set as Current Bar in the **Timescale** column in the **Bars** form.

Un-necked bars   Necked bars

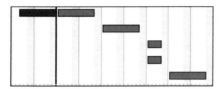   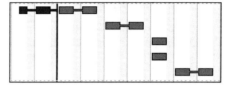

- **Calendar nonwork time** necks the bar based on the activity's calendar.
- **Activity nonwork intervals** necks the bar when Out of Sequence Progress options of Actual Dates or Retained Logic causes a break in the work. See the **Advanced Scheduling Options** paragraph.

23.3.2   User Defined Bars Based on User Defined Dates

User Defined Dates to be used for formatting a **User Defined Bars Style**, see the first line on the bars form below:

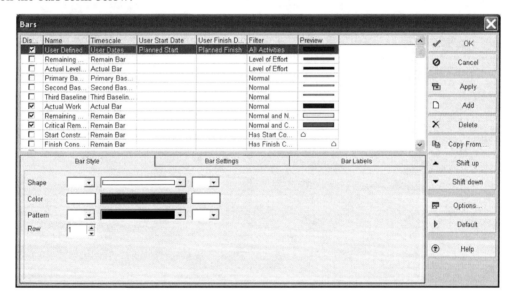

23.4 Material Resources

Material Resources are now available resulting in three types of Resources:

- **Labor**, this resource type is intended for people,
- **Nonlabor**, this resource type is intended for equipment, and
- **Materials**, this resource type is intended for materials/supplies.

Material Resources may be leveled but have the following differences:

- They may be assigned a **Unit of Measure** which is created in the **Admin**, **Admin Categories…**, <u>Unit</u> **of Measure** tab. This is not available to Labor and Nonlabor resources.
- The may not be assigned a Role.
- They may not log Overtime.

23.5 Close Out Period Actuals

This is a function similar to the P3 function of the same name, that was removed in Version 5.0 with the introduction of Store Period Performance. It allow the calculation of:

- The Actual Costs and/or Actual Units this Period when the total to date is entered, or
- The Actual Costs and/or Actual Units to date when the Actual Costs and/or Actual Units this period are entered.

The function operates in the following way.

- The picture shows a resource with 10 Units expended to date:

Planned Units	Actual This Period Units	Actual Units	At Completion Units
20	0	10	20

- Add 5 Units in the **Actual This Period Units** or enter 15 in the **Actual Units** and the result will be the same, as the **Actual This Period Units** and **Actual Units** fields are linked:

Planned Units	Actual This Period Units	Actual Units	At Completion Units
20	5	15	20

- Select **Tools**, **Period Closeout** to set Actual This Period Units to zero and this will leave the **At Completion Units** unchanged, ready for the next update. The result will be as follows:

Planned Units	Actual This Period Units	Actual Units	At Completion Units
20	0	15	20

23.6 Project Workspace Defaults for Statusing a Resourced Schedule

The following functions are new to the **Calculations** tab in the **Project Workspace**:

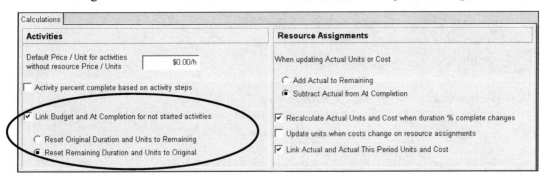

- Unchecking **Link Budget an At Completion for not started activities** allows the user to re-estimate the cost of unstarted activities while preserving the **Original Budget** of an activity. This is the same as the P3 Auto Cost Rule No 6.

- The next two options **Reset Original Durations and Units to Remaining** and **Reset Remaining Duration and Units to Original** determine how the Original Duration and Units are set when progress is removed from activities.

23.7 Printing

The **Printing** form **Header** and **Footer** tabs have been reformatted please see the Printing Chapter for details.

24 TOPICS NOT COVERED IN THIS BOOK

The following topics are not covered in this book:

- Project Manager SAM
- Budgets, including
  - ➢ Budget Summary
  - ➢ Budget Log
  - ➢ Funding
  - ➢ Spending Plan
- Work Products and Documents
- Thresholds
- Issues
- Risks and Risk Calculation
- Resources Shifts
- Top-Down Estimation
- Resource Curves
- Leveling Resources
- External Applications
- Timesheets
- Timesheet Date Administration
- Job Services to automatically run more than one function
- Summarize Projects
- Spelling
- Claim Digger

25 INDEX

DecisionEdge Suite for Primavera
Complete Set of Project Graphics and Reports for Better Business Decisions

The DecisionEdge Suite for Primavera gives project managers, schedulers, cost analysts and the entire project team the enhanced graphics and reports they need to better understand and communicate key project information. With seamless integration to Primavera scheduling tools, Primavera Expedition, and Primavera Cost Management, more than 120 new and improved graphics and reports are just a few clicks away.

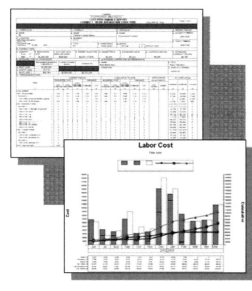

✓ **Understand** – Choose from over 120 new and improved charts and reports for Primavera Project Management, Expedition, and Cost Management

✓ **Communicate** – Share project snapshots with full support for common graphic file formats and a wide range of printers and plotters

✓ **Control** – Filter, scroll, and drill-down to see trends and make earlier decisions

✓ **Interact** – Not just pretty pictures, the DecisionEdge Suite is an interactive portal into live business data

✓ **Customize** – Change colors and styles to make graphics look just the way you want them

✓ **Create** – With *DecisionEdge Designer,* developers can create and share completely new charts and reports with all DecisionEdge users

The DecisionEdge Suite for Primavera includes both DecisionCharts and DecisionReports
It comes with more than 100 bundled charts (over 40 for Primavera schedules, 30 for Expedition, and 20 for Cost Management) and 20 bundled reports (including the CPR Format 1-5 and C/SSR reports for earned value compliance) that help managers better understand and publish key information about their tasks, resources, costs, and overall project performance. They can view and customize any of these charts and reports by filtering data, changing colors, adding and moving logos, and making other changes. They will also keep the whole team informed by sharing project snapshots in standard file formats such as bitmap (.BMP), JPEG (.JPG), Acrobat (.PDF)*, and TIFF, or by sending them directly to a printer or plotter.

Companies with specific visibility requirements will want *DecisionEdge Designer*. Developers and technical consultants can use this toolkit to create completely new Primavera charts and reports that can be shared with all DecisionEdge users. DecisionEdge Designer provides unlimited possibilities for showing and formatting data with different chart and report types, computed elements, and interactive dashboards.

The DecisionEdge Advantage:
- Get started quickly with new charts and reports designed specifically for Primavera
- Understand and communicate key information with interactive, real-time graphics and reports
- Keep the whole team informed of project status more effectively with pictures
- Generate the custom graphics and reports you need to run your business
- Stop using spreadsheets and other manual workarounds
- Deploy a complete business intelligence solution for better business decisions

*Adobe Acrobat or similar PDF writer required to generate PDF files.

DecisionCharts Graphic Types

Bar/Line Chart
Great for showing trends over time.

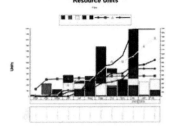

Dashboard Chart
This chart combines up to four different charts into one interactive portal, giving stakeholders the ability to understand key project information in just one glance.

Gantt Chart
Classic plot of time-based activities.

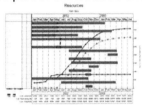

Pie Chart
Shows the percentage composition of a data element.

Bubble/Matrix Chart
Allows for comparison across data elements by adding the dimension of bubble size.

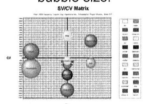

Map/Diagram Chart
This special custom chart helps managers better understand how data fits into the overall project.

DecisionReports Features

Add custom colors for greater impact →

Use *DecisionEdge Designer* to create custom reports for specific needs →

Show details about any project element →

← Create calculated fields with VBScript to show the right information

← Enhance understanding with numbers that change color based on custom limits

---

Requirements
Software: - O/S: Windows 2000 or Windows XP; *Primavera:* Primavera 3.0 or higher, Cost Management 3.5.1 or higher, and/or Expedition 8.0 or higher. Not designed for use with P3, SureTrak, or Contractor.
Hardware: 30MB hard drive for each client; at least 256MB RAM

DecisionEdge, Inc.
+1 (610) 665-400 2
+1 (610) 665-4003 (FAX)

www.decisionedge.com
www.eh.com.au

DECISIONEDGE™
SOFTWARE FOR BETTER BUSINESS DECISIONS

1293217